On Site

D1602049

On Site

Methods for Site-Specific Performance Creation

STEPHAN KOPLOWITZ

OXFORD
UNIVERSITY PRESS

Oxford University Press is a department of the University of Oxford. It furthers
the University's objective of excellence in research, scholarship, and education
by publishing worldwide. Oxford is a registered trade mark of Oxford University
Press in the UK and certain other countries.

Published in the United States of America by Oxford University Press
198 Madison Avenue, New York, NY 10016, United States of America.

© Oxford University Press 2022

All rights reserved. No part of this publication may be reproduced, stored in
a retrieval system, or transmitted, in any form or by any means, without the
prior permission in writing of Oxford University Press, or as expressly permitted
by law, by license, or under terms agreed with the appropriate reproduction
rights organization. Inquiries concerning reproduction outside the scope of the
above should be sent to the Rights Department, Oxford University Press, at the
address above.

You must not circulate this work in any other form
and you must impose this same condition on any acquirer.

Library of Congress Control Number: 2021057546
ISBN 978-0-19-751523-5 (hbk.)
ISBN 978-0-19-751524-2 (pbk.)

DOI: 10.1093/oso/9780197515235.001.0001

1 3 5 7 9 8 6 4 2

Paperback printed by Marquis, Canada
Hardback printed by Bridgeport National Bindery, Inc., United States of America

In loving memory of my parents, Bill and Maria
To Jane, my life partner
And Denny, treasured friend and critic
Your love, friendship, and perspective have carried me.

Contents

Preface

Photo Preface 1 The windows, Vanderbilt Avenue side, Grand Central Terminal, New York, NY. Photo © Stephan Koplowitz.

The place: Grand Central Terminal

The time: Afternoon in October 1987

The scene: Choreographer sitting on the terminal floor and looking up at four stories of 36 dancers performing on the catwalks inside the windows of the terminal. The stationmaster approaches the choreographer, says nothing, and looks up at the dancers.

CHOREOGRAPHER: (to stationmaster) So, what do you think of the dance?

STATIONMASTER: Well . . . I think the dancers could be more graceful.

CHOREOGRAPHER: (after several moments of silence) Umm, ok, we'll work on it.

I was that choreographer, and I didn't expect that comment. I thought the stationmaster would rave. How often does anyone see dancers high up in those catwalks? Never. It had never been done before, yet that didn't matter to the stationmaster.

My experience with *Fenestrations* in Grand Central Terminal, my first site-specific creation, informed much of what I know now about the nature of the work. Soon after that encounter, I realized something that mitigated the sting of the stationmaster's words. This was his turf, and he felt comfortable saying what he thought about an art form not normally seen in his workplace. Creating art on site (in this case, dance) made that art more accessible and participatory; it stimulated thought and invited honest reactions. By animating this site, I realized that my "esoteric-contemporary-art-of-dance" would reach hundreds, thousands of people who might otherwise never attend a dance performance.

I have been creating site-specific work for over 30 years, and a lot has changed. Site artists tend to embrace and find inspiration in change. We develop a flexible, open mind and an ability to remain calm that serve us well as we deal with everything from sudden weather events to a worldwide pandemic. In the 1980s, there was no internet. Digital technology did not exist. Projecting images outside of a theater onto surfaces other than screens was a costly and cumbersome process. The pace of technological innovation has had a profound effect on the arts and especially on site-specific performance. The portability and affordability of supportive production technology (lighting, sound, video, etc.) have helped spawn the popularity and ubiquity of site work. The internet alone has expanded its reach and helped attract larger audiences to alternative spaces and performances. Working remotely has enabled us to do some of our work more quickly, efficiently, and accurately. Research can begin at home with an internet search that brings a remote site to life through text, photographs, and videos. Creative collaborations can occur earlier with greater specificity using email, text, and video conferences for exchanging, reviewing, and revising digital files. The process of acquiring permits and insurance is becoming less reliant on in-person visits or even phone calls to a specific person or institution.

In 2020, Covid-19 accelerated the pace of change and the need to adapt. As theaters, museums, and restaurants closed or opened only at partial capacity, artists were forced to explore new ways of bringing art to the public. The results have been more virtual creations via platforms like Zoom and outdoor events in alternative spaces. Site artists are uniquely prepared to contribute to these efforts and meet the challenges of enabling audiences and performers to safely navigate sited productions.

Although much has changed, the essence of the art remains the same. Site artists continue to be inspired by design, architecture, history, and how a site is inhabited, used, and viewed by a community. The beauty and power of this work and its potential to alter everyone's perspective still depend on a set of tools and techniques that site artists have used for decades. These tools and techniques are the focus of this book.

When I started to create site-specific work, the community of site artists was small. Aside from Anna Halprin, who brought her movement practice into many different environments as early as the 1940s, and the early site work of Trisha Brown and Meredith Monk (both students of Halprin) in the 1960s, Merce Cunningham's *Events* that toured the world outside of the proscenium, I and others of my generation had few role models or books to guide us. Since then, the number of site artists has grown, as has the literature about site work—theory, history, analysis.

Interviewing many of these artists and writing this book allowed me to think more deeply about site work. I was particularly struck by how white the field has been, and I realize how much I have taken my privilege for granted. I never had to consider the role that my skin color might play in my access to funding, sites, and permissions (both official and tacit). Privilege can take many forms and influence a myriad of contingencies. Site artist Olive Bieringa of BodyCartography Project wrote in *Site Dance*: "I have the privilege of being white and can therefore choose my invisibility and maybe my 'craziness.'" In contrast, an African-American audience member commented at an earlier BodyCartography event: "Man, I just scratch my nuts and they take me to jail. What do you clowns think you're doing?" (Kloetzel, Melanie; Pavlik, Carolyn, *Site Dance* 2009: p.139) Fortunately, site creation has begun to attract a more diverse group of artists, audiences, and activities. This book aims to support, encourage, and increase site production to develop a greater diversity of voices in the field.

On Site: Methods for Site-Specific Performance Creation explores methodology, best practices, and strategies for any artist—performing or visual—interested in making art that interacts with a specific place. It is a practical book that identifies factors to consider before, during, and after a project: selecting sites, securing permits for public use/performances, designing the audience experience, developing an artistic vision, and generating content (movement, sound, imagery) inspired by a site. Also covered are real-world production issues in urban and natural environments, definitions of the different production roles, collaborative techniques, promotion, marketing, and documentation.

Although the book is mainly based on my own experience and practice, I have included the works and voices of other artists, producers, and writers. Scattered throughout the book are quotations taken from many hours of individual interviews that I conducted with 24 professionals. This cohort is not intended to represent the field; they were selected in part for their sustained commitment to producing site work over time, and they speak about some of their best practices and offer you their advice. The book does not promote a particular aesthetic or style or favor one theory about site work over another. The examples of my productions and those of other artists are included only to illustrate a particular idea or method. Art is personal and highly individualistic, so *adapt* the tools and suggestions you find here to your *own* vision and needs.

All sounds so neat and tidy, doesn't it? It's not. Giving advice is easy; following it can often be difficult. As recently as this past year, I haven't always followed my own advice. The chapters pertaining to contracts (Chapter 6), collaboration (Chapter 11), and documentation (Chapter 17) describe methods and best practices that, occasionally, I have forgotten or ignored—which I later regretted. Sometimes, circumstances, preoccupation with success, or impatience can derail the best of intentions. My hope is that this book will help you pause and consider the many available options when you embark on a site project so that you become increasingly confident in the individual process you develop for *yourself*.

Following the Acknowledgments are short biographies of the contributors I interviewed. I encourage you to delve deeper into their work through the links included in each biography. The links in the book's appendix to other artists and other online resources attempt to give a more diverse snapshot of current and past activity in site-specific creation.

Acknowledgments

I thank the hundreds of artists (dancers, actors, singers, composers, costumers, lighting designers, media artists, visual artists) for their trust, creativity, and collaboration throughout the process of making site-specific works over the past three decades. We have learned together and taught each other.

Eternal thanks to Denny (Alden S. Blodget) who has served as the primary editor, reader and sounding board for this book. His skills as a writer and editor along with his experience as a theater director and educator ensured that I stayed on track while striving for clarity. I am grateful for his keen insight, brutal honesty, and consummate friendship.

Special thanks to Norm Hirschy, my editor at Oxford University Press, for his caring feedback, wisdom, perspective, and sensitivity. His encouragement sustained me. Also, a thank you to Brid Nowlan for her precise copy editing, Dena Davida for creating the index and Hinduja Dhanasegaran for support during the book production process.

Heartfelt thanks to the artists, producers, and scholars identified in the Preface who gave their time to talk with me and contributed to this book. Their work and generosity are a source of inspiration and revelation.

Thanks to all of the photographers and artists whose images enliven the pages of this book.

To Naomi Jackson for the invitation to participate in the *Jews and Jewishness in the Dance World* conference at Arizona State University (2018), where I first met Norm Hirschy. To Julie Fox for her early encouragement and contributions to this book. To Jill Holman Randall for her comments on each chapter. To Sara Hook, Tony Giovannetti, Nel Shelby, Judith Smith, and Silva Laukennen for their valuable feedback. To Wendy Perron and Joanna Haigood for their advice and encouragement.

Gratitude to The Rockefeller Foundation for providing early support and the sublime experience of working as a fellow at The Rockefeller Foundation Bellagio Center Residency Program in Bellagio, Italy.

Thank you Norton Owen and the Jacob's Pillow Dance Festival for providing time on site as a Research Fellow.

Thanks to the California Institute of the Arts for the opportunity to create the Coursera online course, where the early structure for this book took form in 2013.

Given *On Site*'s focus on the relationship between producing and creation, I want to acknowledge some producers, associate producers, and rehearsal directors with whom I've had the honor of working over the past thirty-plus years. The collaborations with these colleagues and friends have shaped me as an artist and directly informed this book.

Profound thanks to Elise Bernhardt, Founding Artistic Director/Producer of Dancing in the Streets, for showing me the path of site performance before I could see such a path.

To Val Bourne (founding artistic director, Dance Umbrella Festival, London), Laura Faure (former director, Bates Dance Festival), and David White (former executive director, Dance Theater Workshop), who provided multiple opportunities to bring my work (on-site and in the proscenium) into the world.

To Richard Colton, Aviva Davidson, Jacqueline Davis, David Diamond, Simone Ferro, Stefan Hilterhaus, Jean Isaacs, Donna Leiberman, Fareed C. Majari, Gianni Malfer, Sam Miller, Susan Petry, Janice Roberts, Judith Smith, Amy Spencer, Liz Thompson, and Sixto Wagan for their creative vision and past commissions.

To some of the associate producers/project managers for their vital partnership, support and patience (with me): Carol Anderson, Hassan Christopher, Betsy Gregory, Sara Horowitz, Abbie Katz, Andrea Lillienthal, Lara Lloyd, Carole Magnini, Jana Morlan, Gregory Nash, Mara Penrose, Debs Ramser, Andrew E. Wagner, Yvonne White, and Mary Anne K. Williams.

To some of the rehearsal directors/assistants I've had the pleasure of partnering with for their creative energy and sensitivity: Savannah Ashour, Clair Beckett-Sargeant, Alexandra Beller, Annie Boyden, Christina Briggs-Winslow, Teresa Chapman, Ann Sofie Clemmensen, Gregory Dorado, Julie Fox, Cinnamon Halbert Smith, Sara Hook, Judith Howard, Sara Joel, Heather Klopchin, Silva Laukkanen, Sara Lloyd, Jessie Lyons Miles, Anne C. Moore, Liz Pavey, Carla Perlo, Jeffrey Peterson, Mary Ellen Schaper, Jane Shockley, Karen Stokes, Heather Sultz, Lily Kind, Luc Vanier, and Jeramy Zimmerman.

To my wife Jane Otto and daughter Sarah, who fill my life's journey with love and laughter.

Guest Biographies

Elise Bernhardt (New York) was founder/executive producer of Dancing in the Streets (1983–2004) and was the CEO of cultural organizations including The Kitchen, Foundation for Jewish Culture, and Brooklyn Youth Chorus; she is currently an arts consultant, floral designer, and teacher. www.fleurelisebkln.com.

Martha Bowers (New York) works as a choreographer, producer, and educator in communities and creates performances that allow audiences to uncover latent meaning in familiar surroundings. hookarts.org.

Carol Brown (New Zealand/Australia) is an interdisciplinary choreographer working in dance, music, image, place, and architecture. Her choreographies and collaborations question and probe space, belonging, agency, and environment and have toured internationally. www.carolbrowndances.com.

Mark Dendy (New York), choreographer for dendy/donovan projects, creates dance-theater, multimedia works that value all forms of design with a political sensibility and searing social satire. He won awards for work on and off Broadway and at the Metropolitan Opera and American Dance Festival: Obie, Bessie, Alpert. dendydonovanprojects.com.

Laura Faure (Maine) is a producer/consultant; she was director of the Bates Dance Festival (1988–2017) and developed the festival into a contemporary dance program known for its artistic excellence, curatorial vision, and a commitment to building community.

Tony Giovannetti (New York) is a lighting designer/technical director who has designed for theater, dance, and site-specific productions with Meredith Monk, Martha Bowers, Stephan Koplowitz, New York Philharmonic, and Dancing in the Streets. He was head of electrical construction at the Metropolitan Opera (1984–2017). agiovannettielectric.com.

Joanna Haigood (California), choreographer/artistic director of Zaccho Dance Theater, creates work that uses natural, architectural, and cultural environments as points of departure for movement exploration and narrative. www.zaccho.org.

Anne Hamburger (New York) is the artistic director, producer, founder, En Garde Arts, a nonprofit theater; she pioneered site-specific theater in the 1980–1990s and is currently producing theater with social change at its core, encouraging artists to explore storytelling through theater, music, movement, multimedia, and site-specificity. www.engardearts.org.

Sara Hook (Illinois) is a choreographer, performer, educator who makes work that both honors artistic forebears and enlivens the experience of contemporary culture. www.sarahookdances.com.

Debby Kajiyama (California) is the co-artistic director of NAKA Dance Theater. Her artistic practice includes an attention to story, objects in relation to the moving body, and the liminal state between the conscious-unconscious. nakadancetheater.com.

John King (New York) is a composer and has received numerous commissions (including Kronos Quartet, Bang on A Can). He is a primary collaborator with the Merce Cunningham Dance Company and has written operas, songs, and music for theater and dance. He is a co-curator of weekly telematic performances with musicians and dancers. www.johnkingmusic.com.

Melanie Kloetzel (Canada) is an artist, scholar, and educator who creates works for stage, site, and screen. Director of the dance theatre company kloetzel&co., Kloetzel employs practice-as-research methodologies to devise, perform, and then analyze her works for scholarly publication. www.kloetzelandco.com.

Noémie Lafrance (Canada/New York) is a site-specific choreographer and film director/producer known for her work in public spaces and dance films, and for engaging in public interventions. sensproduction.org.

Rosemary Lee (United Kingdom), choreographer/director and filmmaker, works in a variety of contexts and media, including large-scale site-specific works with cross-generational casts and video installations. Her interest is in both portrait and landscape and in our relationship with the environment, urban and rural. www.artsadmin.co.uk/profiles/rosemary-lee.

Debra Loewen (Wisconsin) has created 35 site-specific performances since founding Wild Space Dance Company in 1986. Her improvisational practice guides ensemble collaborations, with dancers and musicians contributing equally as instigators and co-creators in the creative process. www.wildspacedance.org.

José Ome Navarrete Mazatl (California) is co-artistic director of NAKA Dance Theater. He works in depth with local communities to facilitate mutual understanding through art-making with the goal to embody visibility by reclaiming public spaces and reconfiguring traditional performance venues. nakadancetheater.com.

Jennifer Monson (Illinois) is a dancer and choreographer who explores strategies in choreography, improvisation, and collaboration in experimental dance with a focus on the relationship between movement and environment. www.ilandart.org.

Sara Pearson and Patrik Widrig (Maryland) are the artistic directors of PEARSONWIDRIG DANCETHEATER; presenting internationally since 1987, they were described as "appealingly subversive, engaging, wry, and deeply affecting work" by the *Washington Post*. Both have been professors at the University of Maryland School of Theatre, Dance, and Performance Studies since 2009. pearsonwidrig.org.

nibia pastrana santiago (Puerto Rico) is an artist and dancer and develops site-specific "choreographic events" to experiment with time, fiction, and notions of territory. Her work was performed at the 2019 Whitney's Biennial. www.nibiapastrana.com.

Nel Shelby (New York) is owner of Nel Shelby Productions and the video producer for Jacob's Pillow and Vail Dance Festivals. She preserves and promotes dance by documenting live performances, producing livestreams and virtual programs, and creating marketing videos and documentary films. www.nelshelby.com.

Judith Smith (California) is the founder and artistic director emerita of AXIS Dance Company (1997–2017); she helped launch AXIS in 1987, grew the company to be the nation's leading physically integrated dance ensemble, and commissioned more than 35 works. www.axisdance.org/advocacy.

Amara Tabor-Smith (California), the artistic director of Deep Waters Dance Theater, describes her experimental dance theater work as Afro Surrealist Conjure Art. Her dance-making practice uses Yoruba spiritual ritual to address issues of social and environmental justice, community, identity, and belonging. www.deepwatersdance.com.

Susanne Thomas (United Kingdom) is a choreographer, producer, and director of Seven Sisters Group. With designer Sophie Jump, she creates immersive and site-specific works that focus on communicating contemporary issues through new and idiosyncratic works that defy labeling. www.sevensistersgroup.com.

Nancy Wozny (Texas) is a writer; editor-in-chief of Arts + Culture Texas and a writer and contributing editor at Dance Magazine, since 2010, she has been Scholar in Residence at Jacob's Pillow. artsandculturetx.com/tag/nancy-wozny/.

This Book's Evolution

As a site artist and arts educator, I've shared my excitement for site work with students from everywhere. I started as a teacher with high school students at the Packer Collegiate Institute (Brooklyn) and with college and graduate students during my tenure as dean and as faculty at the California Institute of the Arts (CalArts). In 2006, I wrote a chapter for the first book about site dance in the United States: *Site Dance*, edited by Melanie Kloetzel and Carolyn Pavlic, published in 2009 and still in print. That experience kindled a desire to write this book about site production. In 2013, while at CalArts, I taught the first Massive Open Online Course (MOOC) designed to create dance and performance: *Creating Site-Specific Dance and Performance Works* (on the Coursera platform, 2013–2016). The research for and experience of this, and the enthusiasm with which several thousand committed students from 154 countries responded, inspired the creation of this book. I realized that many artists, including young artists embarking on their careers, feel isolated in their efforts to make work no matter where they live. This book aims to support the notion that you are not alone in your desire to create something new using the world as your inspiration.

Stephan Koplowitz

Introduction

Inspirations and Definitions

Why Make Site-Specific Work?

> There's something exhilarating when I'm outdoors producing a show and thinking, my stage is as high as the sky and as far as I can see. And then while watching the show, all of a sudden on the horizon, I see a cruise ship go by precisely at the right moment! It's that kind of element of surprise of real-life colliding with fantasy and creativity in ways you could never expect that is magical.
>
> Anne Hamburger

Photo Introduction.1 *Stonewall, Night Variations* (1994) conceived and directed by Tina Landau, 1994, Pier 25, En Garde Arts production, New York, NY.
Photo William R. Rivelli, courtesy Anne Hamburger and En Garde Arts.

Artists tend to seek new challenges. As an artist, I often start a work by asking, "What if . . . ?" Site work consistently poses that question and promises tantalizing new

On Site. Stephan Koplowitz, Oxford University Press. © Oxford University Press 2022. DOI: 10.1093/oso/9780197515235.003.0001

opportunities. Creating a site work requires overlaying a new reality on reality— like a palimpsest—placing a fictional space over a real space. Rather than creating a world in what theater director Peter Brook called "an empty space," site artists find the *subject matter of the work itself in the real, physical world of the actual place.* A site is already charged with meaning and context, and the artist's job is to transform both the space and the audience's experience of the space. The goal is to invite the audience to view real life with fresh eyes: to see the ordinary as extraordinary. An audience benefits from this transformation, but the artist's perspectives on art-making and life are also inevitably altered.

My artistic career started with dance concerts for the proscenium stage. Each time I created a new piece, regardless of the specific theater or the content of the work, the process followed the traditional physical path, from the studio into a theater, each possessing similar architectural characteristics to support the creative process (walls, roof, empty space, and equipment for light and sound).

When offered the opportunity to create a work for a nontraditional site, I felt an immediate jolt of excitement; the opportunity got me out of the house, as in, out of my usual wheelhouse. Debra Loewen captured this feeling when she said, "I like getting lost in the process of trying to figure out how a space speaks to me or would speak to an audience or could speak to someone passing by. Listening to the site leads to acts of discovery, and I have no idea what's going to happen. On the stage, you have parameters that are like a television; it's a box. Site work takes you out of the box." For me, the attraction was not just the physical experience of working outdoors or in a new physical place but the subjective experience of expanding my comfort zone, engaging with ideas, themes, and cultures that I would not encounter during my usual practice of making work for the proscenium. A site project requires me to travel intellectually and physically to places not always familiar or conventional, and that in itself is exciting. I have the opportunity to learn the history of those places, to understand how people use those spaces today, and to let these factors shape my choreographic and thematic decisions. In a sense, the detailed site-specific process of creating work for different locations becomes as important as the product, perhaps more important, and changes with each new site. I share Joanna Haigood's feeling that "an art practice is not necessarily about a product; it's a way of seeing and being in the world. It is a process through which we discover and understand ourselves and the world around us. As a site artist, I feel I have an opportunity to be an explorer in nature, in built environments, and in histories."

Working at London's Natural History Museum, the British Library, and a coke (coal) factory in Essen, Germany, required extensive historical exploration before creation. I delved deeply into the history of a building and the events that influenced its design and creation. The producers in Essen organized a two-day tour of the North Rhine Westphalia region so that I could visit other coal factories and two historical museums devoted to the history of energy and coal mining. Experientially, acquiring new information, new insights, and new perspectives of our world is exhilarating. In the short term, it expands the context of the site and the possibilities for art-making.

And then there is the thrill of the physical exploration of locations not originally designed as performance spaces: visualizing new sightlines, moving through natural landscapes or architectural structures that require adapting to surfaces and textures not found in conventional theaters, discovering the emotional effects of the human figure framed on the steps of a cathedral or within the narrow confines of a factory. This aspect of site work is the central motivation for many site artists. Rosemary Lee describes her childhood on the coast, where she "found the marshes, the coastline, the water, the sand, the mud, the reeds, and the sky as ever-changing landscapes to be magical and quite theatrical. As a choreographer, I'm interested in the human figure in a landscape. I'm interested in what I can do with that and what it might stir in an audience. We are creatures on this Earth. I like my conceptual choreography bare and stripped back and dead simple in a very rich landscape."

Melanie Kloetzel speaks of finding the essence of a site through a form of communion: "My investment lies in *learning* about sites; the deepening kind of relationship and appreciation of a site is by far the greatest joy. But as my work has progressed, I've started to realize that I need to listen more carefully to what a site is saying."

An antidote to isolation

The act of creation can feel isolating. The solitary nature of working in a private studio or concert hall nurtures focus and preparation, free from prying eyes or distraction. Working on a site and being observed by the public can seem, at first, disorienting. But the experience can feel liberating. During my first sited project, I discovered that I enjoyed sharing my "studio"—Grand Central Terminal—with hundreds of people, including, yes, the stationmaster, as they walked through or stopped to watch. The sensation of my artistic process integrating into the flow of daily life dispelled the usual sense of loneliness.

And there are other benefits. When artistic creation occurs in public places like train stations, libraries, swimming pools, factories, gardens—locations not typically associated with the world of art—artists can benefit from the exposure. Watching artists work in public can inspire people to consider the role of art in their community and life. Rehearsing in a public site allows people to see an artist making decisions and shaping a work, making the process less mysterious. The usual process of solving creative problems in private can reinforce the idea that art-making is part of a closed society. Demystification can create a feeling of inclusion that will attract larger audiences and help people understand the value of art.

> Passersby get inspired by the process; they dance along with you. Folks often write letters after they've encountered a rehearsal or a performance. One time in North Carolina, this young girl brought her mother back the next day after seeing us. She pointed to us, and screamed, "Do you see that, Mom? I want to do that! That's what I want to do!"
>
> Mark Dendy

Site work continues to inspire because of how it brings me into the world at large. Attracting new audiences—a public who attend arts events infrequently—also offsets feelings of artistic elitism. I enjoy engaging people who would never imagine that their place of work or leisure could host a performance. There is excitement in both inviting an interested public and, sometimes, surprising or confronting an audience whose daily activities bring them in contact with a chosen site.

> The central goal of site work is to go beyond traditional presentational modes to reach people and comment on our life and times. The power of site work is to enliven a space in a way that vividly alters the viewer experience forever. It changes the way people think about a place, art, themselves, and their world. I love that the audience often becomes an active participant. People who wouldn't necessarily attend a performance often collide with an outdoor rehearsal or performance by accident and become intrigued.
>
> Laura Faure

Bonding with a site and audience

The entire process of creating a site performance (or installation) imbues the artist with knowledge and experience of that place in an intense and lasting manner. Working with and at a site for a performance is often done in a concentrated timeframe, days or weeks of intense emotional work resulting in deep memories that can last a lifetime. A site artist not only is physically active, making decisions and taking creative risks at that location but observes and studies the day-to-day activities at the site. The history and many backstories of a venue forge a unique perspective, creating a bond and sense of *partnership*. This bond deepens the relationship to a place, to a community, to a city, and to a country and adds value to the artist's daily life.

> As a globe-trotting artist, I was getting more interested in the locale and working with the cities I visited—spending more time with people and understanding a sense of place. Place-based dance allows me to ask, what's my accountability when I go into these different places? I wanted to have more of a legacy experience there rather than just a performance that comes one night and has gone the next. I wanted to be more engaged with local communities.
>
> Carol Brown

When I return to places that hosted my site creations, it is impossible not to re-experience memories, images, and emotions of my work. Grand Central Terminal probably stimulates the most intense memories because I spent the most time there: choreographing two major works (1987 and 1999) and directing a short film inside the terminal (*Catching the 5:23*, 2001). Whenever I am in the neighborhood, I make a point of walking through the terminal to conjure those feelings and memories and, once again, experience the wonder of the architecture and space.

Creating a similar sense of partnership in an audience is another factor in my motivation for making site-specific work. This work deepens the relationship between artist and audience. You are providing new perspectives, eliciting new emotions, suggesting new meanings. Often, the most enthusiastic audience members are the site stakeholders: people who work in or use the site regularly and who already have memories of the site. These audience members are intrigued by the possibilities of an original site-specific performance. Their comments always fuel my joy in creating this kind of work: "Thank you for giving me a new view of my town." "I will never look at those windows the same way again." "I had no idea the building I work in could inspire that."

Designing a new audience experience presents an added creative problem to solve and can bring much satisfaction. Creating site performances allows you to bring an audience physically in contact with the performance space in a more active manner than placing them in seats in a concert hall. Not only can you invite them to travel to the site, but you can also encourage them to physically explore the site during the performance itself. You can bring to life in exciting new ways a historical event or compelling contemporary issue that has deep connections to the site. As the artist, you are responsible for designing their specific journey through the site, a considerable distinction from the more conventional, sedentary concert-hall experience.

> I started creating work from a vision of using the public space as a stage and chose to work only outside the theater. I wanted to work with the immediate environment of our everyday life to rethink the relationship between audiences and performers and performance and real space. I also wanted to go beyond representation, as in the symbolism of staging elements or sets, and deal with, say, a real tree, a real street, a place, and explore the relationship we have to places and to elements of our environment by interacting with *their* life. Exploring a site and find its meaning or what it has to say.
>
> Noémie Lafrance

Ultimately, you will have your own list of reasons that inspire you to engage in this work. Chapter 1 (What Motivates Site Selection) delves into more specific, detailed visions and motivations for creating site projects. When I began to make site-specific art, I did not foresee that I would be embarking on a lifelong path. The challenges and pleasures of this work continue to inspire me and many other artists around the world. This book is a testament to that experience and compulsion.

> I think site-specific work brings great value. It takes something that usually happens indoors and can create a collision of people and art, one that people didn't necessarily choose. I think we want that to be part of it, just the way public art is part of a city. We want public dance or performance to be part of a city. Why not? It has just as much right as a statue does. In terms of a city's vitality, it's central.
>
> Nancy Wozny

Defining Different Forms of Site-Specific Work

When choreographers describe their work as "site-specific," do they all mean the same thing? What do site and specific suggest? What factors make a work site-specific? The term is used broadly for many non-conventional performance works, a catch-all classification for any art event presented outside of a traditional theater or gallery setting. The casual use of various labels has increased over the past 20 years as artists have created more work in alternative spaces. Many artists who create site-specific work field all kinds of responses and questions about how to define their work. People frequently label my work "environmental art" or "installation" or "flash mob."

In 2006, the artists and scholars Melanie Kloetzel and Carolyn Pavlik invited me to contribute a chapter for their book, *Site Dance* (Florida Univ. Press, 2009). Inspired by my experience with different definitions and classifications of site work, I focused on creating a rubric that delineates the different types. Several years later, these terms are *still* in flux and debated by many artists and scholars. My perspective has changed. I care less about labels and more about their definitions, especially how definitions can inform an artist's or audience's experience of a work. Sharing a vocabulary helps us investigate how each defined category reflects and affects an artist's creative process when starting a site project.

For a work to be considered site-specific or sited, it has to have a connection to a particular place or be inspired by an aspect of the site, and audiences should experience a purposeful interaction between the site and the content of the artwork. *Where* the art is being experienced is vital and shapes our understanding of the content of the art. When we encounter a sculpture placed in a garden or park, we automatically connect the contours and images of the art to the contours and appearance of the surrounding landscape. It is natural to combine the two, thus shaping our response to both the sculpture and the natural surroundings. Likewise, in a live performance, when a performer actively includes the environment in the performance, either through touch or focus, the audience begins to perceive the performer and site as one. If a work with a theme such as freedom, illness, or evolution, takes place in a prison, a hospital, or natural history museum, the audience's sense of the theme is affected by the location; in essence, theme and location become one entity.

Proposed here are four distinct, general categories that identify four types of site work (I will add some hybrid examples later in this chapter). Each of these categories is defined in terms of the *intentional* connection between artistic content and site, and they are listed from the most significant connection to the least: (1) site-specific; (2) site-adaptive; (3) site-reshaped; and (4) site-reframed. The four categories are informed by a central question that speaks to design, production, and audience experience: What is the intention of the work? *What is the back story for the choice of this site?*

Category 1: Site-specific

Exploring a site through its design, history, and current use is the method I have used to create many of my works. For example, I began my first site creation, *Fenestrations*, in Grand Central Terminal, by researching the architecture and conducting an inventory of the characteristics of the three grand windows spanning four floors. I measured the distances between the windows and the width of the glass catwalks that connect them. The inventory directly informed my decisions about how many performers were needed, how they would enter and exit the site, how I could create visual patterns. The physical world of the windows became a partner in the thinking and designing of the performance content and narrative.

Although I researched the history of the terminal, I decided to focus on one aspect of its current use as inspiration. In 1987, several of New York City's homeless population sought shelter in the terminal, many permanently. Anyone passing through the terminal could see them, and they became an inspiration for my art. Thus, I chose home as the guiding concept for the work. Commuters pass through the station on their way home, and it is literally home for the unfortunate homeless citizens of the city. I did not choose Grand Central with these ideas already in mind. They revealed themselves to me only during my research. They inspired all my decisions as I created the piece: the sound score (which incorporated the song *Home on the Range*) and the choreography, which suggested walking through a home and resulted in staging the performers to emphasize a communal experience. My decision to fill the space with 36 dancers allowed me to give the impression that the space was being fully occupied or lived in by the dancers. Everything was a response to either the physical design of the windows or the current use of the terminal.

Category 1 site-specific work is wholly inspired by the site itself and cannot exist as a performative experience in any other location. It is a work for which the artist has not made any creative decisions without first researching the physical design, the history, and the current use of the site. Transferring the work to another location would erase its core meaning and resonance. Category 1 work is the purest and most potent expression of site-specificity because the art is entirely dependent on the site in structure and content. The only way to experience this work is to be physically present at that unique place at that moment in time.

There is no one right way to create Category 1 work. Artists will always create their own paths based on their own experiences. However, Category 1 site-specific work suggests a powerful closeness between the artist and the site, and making this work involves a rigorous process. The artist must approach a site without preconceived ideas, biases, or agendas and allow the site to influence all creative decisions, including theme, number of performers, and structure—the entire artistic vision. This disciplined approach demands considerable effort, time, and patience. My methods and techniques for making this work are explained in detail in subsequent chapters.

Category 2: Site-adaptive (feature specific)

The term site-adaptive suggests that a work can be adapted to different locations in a variety of ways. A particular feature found in multiple locations—a subway, a beach, a staircase, a quarry—can inspire the creation. Initially, your approach mirrors the process used in Category 1—taking inspiration from the design, history, and current use of the original site—but you focus primarily on the feature that kindled your interest. Once completed, the piece can be replicated in similar locations that contain this feature, though each location will likely result in different interpretations.

My work *The Grand Step Project: Flight* (2004) was conceived in such a fashion. I created it for grand staircases, no matter where they were located. We performed *Flight* at six magnificent staircases found in New York City: the dramatic indoor stairs at the Winter Garden of the World Financial Center, the sunlit entrance steps of the Cathedral of St. John the Divine, the New York Public Library steps at 42nd Street and Fifth Avenue, and the steps on government sites in the Bronx and Brooklyn. The inspiration stemmed from the design and use of steps located in grand public spaces. I was attracted to the physical limitations imposed by performing on steps, the social context of public staircases, and the ways people engaged with these steps. I researched people's motivation for using the steps and wrote a list: to meet someone, rest, contemplate, eat lunch, conduct business, gain access—all the mundane activities of living. *Flight* became a celebration of these spaces, which tend to be taken for granted as merely incidental to other activities rather than the focus of an event. Staging a site-specific work brought much positive attention to the spaces and attracted thousands of people to witness a new use for these public steps. At its core, the work was an evocation of the human spirit through movement in a specific urban setting. Within the 15-minute work, all the daily uses of steps were captured in choreographic form through movement and staging. The title *Flight* was a wordplay on a flight of steps, the imagery of the opening sequence of dancers flying down the stairs, and the soaring physical energy found in the choreography. These concepts, combined with the physical design of steps, inspired the choreography for *Flight*. Because the choreography was to be adapted to six different sites, it needed to be both specific to the characteristics of these grand public staircases and generic so that it could be performed on any other public staircase in the world, while retaining its original effect.

Category 3: Site-reshaped

Dance producer and founder of the company Dancing in the Streets Elise Bernhardt proposed placing one of Merce Cunningham's *Events* on the floor of Grand Central Terminal (*Grand Central Dances*, 1987). She believed the regular pedestrian activity in the terminal aesthetically and visually echoed Cunningham's performance creation. The specific image that resonated with Bernhardt was the controlled randomness of the pedestrian movement in the terminal, which struck her as akin to Cunningham's version of controlled randomness. *Events* has a specific choreographic structure and time limit, as designed by Cunningham. No structural changes were made to the chosen *Event*, and Grand Central served as an intentional frame. Bernhardt constructed a temporary stage at one end of the terminal floor, and the Merce Cunningham Dance Company staged this *Event* precisely as they had for 23 previous years.

In Category 3, the site becomes secondary to the inspiration of the art. Here, a previously created piece is brought intentionally to a specific site that did not originally inspire it. As part of the process of wedding the site to the work, the artist can make changes—reshape it. Although not the origin of the piece, the location is selected because its history, architecture, or current use is connected to the subject matter or simply adds a desired visual effect. Artists or producers who engage in this type of reshaping must make a host of decisions affecting how the work and the site will relate to each other; however, the original construction of the art remains intact, even with the changes inspired by the new site.

Merce Cunningham was a master of Category 3, bringing his work to alternative spaces throughout his career. *Ocean* (1994), one of his most monumental works, was designed to be seen in the round, first in Brussels at the Cirque Royal, then at Lincoln Center (2005), and finally, before his death, at the Rainbow Quarry in St. Cloud, Minnesota (2008). I saw *Ocean* at Lincoln Center and then, a few years later, at the St. Cloud quarry. The experience of seeing this dance in two different venues was illuminating. At Lincoln Center, *Ocean* was memorable for how Cunningham and composer John Cage designed a nontraditional placement of musicians and dancers inside the theater, which created an immersive visual/sound experience. Musicians were lined up on the top rows of the theater along both sides of the hall, and dancers entered from all sides of the stage. I had the feeling of the art washing over me from every direction. *Ocean* was conceived with the simple idea of circularity, inspired by the water and ocean images found in James Joyce's *Finnegan's Wake*. It suggested a sense of "heightened three-dimensionality," according to *New York Times* critic Alastair Macaulay (2008). In Minnesota, the performance of *Ocean* began as one approached the St. Cloud quarry by either bus or car. As the height of the canyon-like space came into view, the quarry's scale created a sense of immensity. Cunningham's choreography, itself an abstraction of an ecosystem, was engulfed within an even larger ecosystem, reshaping the work to create the impression that the audience was immersed inside one big ocean. *Ocean* in St. Cloud was so visually imposing that my memory of the Lincoln Center production is faint.

Category 4: Site-reframed

In 1979, I experienced a concert by singer/songwriter Joni Mitchell in Boulder's Red Rocks Amphitheater, and the combination of seeing and hearing her music at this beautiful outdoor stage pavilion was extraordinary. My memory of the concert is inextricably linked to the site where it occurred. I have seen hundreds of concerts, but this one was significant because her performance was framed by extreme physical beauty. It imbued many of her songs with a sense of new possibilities, new horizons influenced by the amphitheater's outdoor, big-sky setting. The physical landscape added a sense of a song becoming part of a physical journey. On Mitchell's part, there was no thematic intention to place the performance in that location or to create an environmental experience. The venue was part of her multi-city tour; the union of the Red Rocks Amphitheater's natural beauty and Mitchell's formidable creative talent was a serendipitous occurrence with lasting effects.

Like Category 3, this category involves transferring a previously created work of art to a new site. Often, the piece is initially presented in conventional venues—galleries, concert halls, theaters, opera houses—and then placed in a new location without any *intentional*, overt, or implicit connection to this new site. The work is reframed, but that is all. It is not reshaped; the presentation is unaltered from the original. This transference allows an audience to view it from a new perspective, even if the piece itself is already familiar. The new frame elicits new responses by chance. The more unique the performance space, the greater the impact on the audience.

The unintentional mash-up between a site and an artist's work is common in the performing arts. There are several unique performance spots in the United States, such as Wolf Trap Farm Park (Virginia), Tanglewood Music Center (Massachusetts), Jacob's Pillow Dance Festival (Massachusetts), and the Gorge Amphitheater (Washington). The success of these venues is the result, in part, of how their environment frames the performances they present. Audiences experience unique architecture or natural beauty, and the art is seen in a new light and with added force because of the design features of the new structural or environmental frames.

Blurring the Boundaries: Categories in Flux

Conceptual site-adaptive

For conceptual site-adaptive works, the original theme and structure are retained when the work is transferred to new sites, but the new sites inspire new content specific to each new place. The process is akin to bringing an identical container to a site but filling it each time with something different. The artist creates a unique wine bottle and then fills it with new wines in different regions.

An example of a conceptual site-adaptive work is my performance event *Off the Walls* (1993) for the Portland Museum of Art (Maine) that I then reproduced at the Hudson River Museum (New York, 1996). I designed *Off the Walls* to explore how the public consumes art; it satirized the art-speak of some curators and museum docents; it brought to life specific paintings through performance and costumes and highlighted architectural design elements of the museum by staging performances in specific locations; it created new visual frames, such as looking down from a gallery or using the seating in a gallery as props for a dance. The two versions were rigorously identical in terms of structure, theme, the creative process, and production, but the content of each was different.

In its first iteration, *Off the Walls* included several discrete performance pieces (4–5 minutes long) inspired by specific locations and artworks found in the Portland Museum. Guides (actors) introduced these discrete events to the assembled audiences and performed soliloquies inspired by the individual artwork. The performances referred to the lumberjacks, postal workers, and abstract art of painter Abby Sahn, all found in the museum's collection. The Hudson River Museum has a different collection and different architecture, so the performances there reflected those differences and focused on trains, ghosts, and the cosmos, all tied to artworks and a planetarium housed inside the museum. The structure of both events—from audience design to the length of individual performances to the use of guides—was the same. And, although the content of each was a unique response to each museum's architecture and collections, the audiences' experience in both was similar, bordering on identical.

Another example of a conceptual site-adaptive work is *Night Light* (2000) by artist Ann Carlson. Inspired by historical archival photographs, *Night Light* first took place in the Chelsea neighborhood of New York City and took the audience on a walking tour to witness eight different tableaux vivants, each recreating archival photographs taken at the same site by using identical costumes. Carlson repeated that same concept in different locations with different pictures drawn from the photo archives of each new location. Her term for this kind of work is "series." And like a series, each site called for different subject matter collected by using the same process of archival research and choreographic recreation. *Night Light* in each of its versions always brought the past into the present through the physical presence of real people recreating these historical photographs. It made real what is typically viewed as lifeless, old, and two-dimensional.

Hybrid works

Other examples of site-adaptive works illustrate how porous and fluid the different categories are and how they sometimes contain aspects of multiple categories at once. Given the fluidity of these categories, you might ask why I bother creating and defining them. Their real usefulness is in providing artists and interested audience members a conceptual framework for understanding the genesis and intention of a work. Rather than rigid, pedantic boxes into which performances can be placed, I created these categories to suggest the breadth of possibilities for working on site. One category is not better than another; they are all just different and suggest different levels of engagement with any given site. *That is all.* Artists will decide what kind of site work most interests them. An awareness of the possibilities can expand the world of available options, and these categories can provide a vocabulary for thinking about and developing the works themselves.

Melanie Kloetzel, in her article "Site and Re-site: Early Efforts to Serialize Site Dance" (*Dance Research Journal*, April, 2017), analyzes many different approaches to site-adaptive works or, as she calls them, site works that are "serialized" in some manner. Kloetzel discusses the work of artists Ann Carlson, Sara Pearson/Patrik Widgrid, Eiko and Koma Otake, and me. All these artists have created variations of site-adaptive works, continuing to perform an original piece in varied locations, not necessarily similar or identical but still allowing either the concept or content to be repeated. For example, a quick look at *Ordinary Festivals* (1995) by Pearson/ Widrig reveals that the work began in a black-box theater. It was later transferred to various locations on the Bates College campus and other sites around the United States. Thus, this work started as site re-shaped (Category 3) and was then moved to a variety of other sites that could house it, except the sites did not have an identical feature as with a site-adaptive (Category 2) work. The core elements of the content that originated on stage found multiple new lives on tour.

Kloetzel's article also discusses performer/choreographer Eiko and Koma's *Caravan* (1999) project, which is housed in a specially designed vehicle (a caravan) and travels to different locations like a Category 2 work. The performance was created for the physical design of the caravan, not for a specific location. *Caravan* is an excellent example of a Category 3 (created off-site) work that is repeatedly moved and reshaped by new sites.

One motivation for working on site-adaptive works in general is their replicability. While they can have considerable labor and budget challenges, the bulk of the creative material is completed on one site, so new incarnations elsewhere require less labor. This asset can be attractive to presenters, providing an additional cost-effective inducement to repeat the work. After many years of making ephemeral Category 1 site-specific performances, I found the lure of touring and reaching more audiences attractive, even though creating a site-adaptive work is no guarantee that subsequent iterations will occur, a lesson I learned several times.

As the categories start to merge, works that began on one site can inspire or become part of the creative process that inspires another work. My *Genesis Canyon* (1996) in London featured a grand staircase. When I returned to New York City, the images, excitement, and challenges of making movement material on stairs stayed with me. During my regular excursions around town, the massive New York City staircases seemed to jump out at me, and a few weeks after my return, the concept for *The Grand Step Project* (described earlier in this chapter) came to mind. The two works had nothing in common except that I learned techniques about creating movement for steps and saw how bodies look navigating that space. This experience in London inspired me to work on new stairs and involve a large cast. The motivation, the content, and the impact of the new work were completely different, but *The Grand Step Project* (Category 2) stemmed directly from *Genesis Canyon* (Category 1).

Another example of categories in flux occurs when a Category 1 site-specific work becomes a Category 2 site-adaptive work unintentionally. When *Fenestrations*, created for the windows of Grand Central Terminal, premiered, producer Elise Bernhardt was unaware that a few hours south, inside the 30th Street Station in Philadelphia, there were similarly designed windows, with multi-level catwalks. Four years later, Dancing in the Streets brought me to Philadelphia to adapt *Fenestrations*, without much alteration of content, into what became *Fenestrations 3.0*. We were surprised and delighted that a work of the scale of *Fenestrations* could find another apt space and create a similar impact.

Flash mobs and site work

Between 2003, when Bill Wasik initiated the first flash mob (he called it "the Mob Project"), and today, when flash mobs are more numerous, many people came to equate these two events. People tend to refer to site works as flash mobs. When I am rehearsing in public or performing on-site, passersby increasingly assume they are witnessing a flash mob (one reason that I provide programs at my performances or carry printed information to distribute when I am rehearsing). In fact, the term "flash mob" has several definitions that are often debated. For example, Improve Everywhere, a group that has fine-tuned the art of flash mobs, rejects the name: they prefer to call their work missions or projects (Gailey-Dissertation, 2015).

Flash mobs by nature are performances that happen outside of traditional theaters. Flash mobs typically involve a predetermined activity (e.g., choreography, action), and they tend to be task-oriented for the performers. Flash mobs can utilize pre-choreographed and sometimes intricate movement material that requires extensive rehearsal. Dancers, musicians, and actors with varying degrees of training and experience can be cast. But tasks can be as simple as holding a pose for five minutes (Improv Everywhere's *Frozen Grand Central*, 2008), or having performers arrive at a destination wearing or not wearing a specific piece of clothing (Improv Everywhere's *No Pants Subway Ride*, 2002) or carrying a specific object (*Bristol Lightsaber Flashmob*, 2010). In flash mobs, the concept of the performance is often the inspiration for selecting a site. Staging a freeze performance doesn't require a train station, but for the task to be seen properly, a crowded (as opposed to an unpopulated) public space is needed for contrast, so a performance might be placed in a train station. Improv Everywhere has also created a whole series of retail-based flash mob performances targeting specific establishments. One performance took place in a Best Buy store and required that all the participants wear clothing that resembled the uniforms of Best Buy employees. The performers' task was to enter the store, disperse, and act friendly to disrupt shoppers' ability to identify actual employees. One core concept of flash mobs is disrupting reality. Usually, the concept or task inspires the choice of the most effective location to realize that concept, but the site is not what inspires the flash mob. If Improv Everywhere's concept is to disrupt the retail world, it then finds retail locations to accommodate the idea.

Many flash mobs rely on social media to organize performers, disseminate instructions, and, ultimately, document the performance for maximum online exposure. A flash mob's secondary audience, often by design, is online. By its very nature, there is no advance publicity or marketing before the event; thus, video documentation increases its reach. The element of surprise to an unsuspecting (captured) audience is the aim regardless of the content, theme, or site, and the documentation often captures both the performance and the audience's reaction to the mob.

Flash mobs are distinct from other site-based performance works in that their task-oriented performance experience relies for inspiration less on narrative content as inspiration with a definite beginning, middle, and end. However, they share with site-specific works a desire to place content and actions to achieve maximum impact within their chosen sites. Flash mobs continue to have a cultural impact, and both the contrasts to and commonality with other site-specific performances create its power to attract attention and engage audiences in the moment and on the internet.

Immersive theater and site work

Another popular cultural phenomenon overlapping site-based performance is the world of immersive theater. This art form has gained traction and attention during the past 15 years. Immersive theater may or may not depend on a specific location to create an immersive experience. Immersive theater can use a site to contribute to the immersive experience or construct the immersive world around the performance. The Punchdrunk production of *Sleep No More* (New York City, 2011) utilizes a constructed world and, therefore, is not a site-specific creation. It requires an empty multi-level warehouse space, but its theme and content are entirely disconnected from the building, location, or history. *Sleep No More* consists of an elaborate set that gives the illusion of a place (a hospital, a cabaret, etc.). Two of the primary thematic and narrative inspirations for the work are Shakespeare's *Macbeth* and Alfred Hitchcock's *Rebecca*. The work is akin to walking onto a movie set. Viewers are made to believe they are in a real place, and the performances respond to this manufactured space. The excitement of this constructed environment is that people can feel as though they are interacting within an actual, functioning movie or play.

However, an immersive theater work that depends on a chosen site is site-specific. One of the most memorable experiences I've had was Deborah Warner's immersive theater piece *Angel Project* (2003) in New York City. It was staged at nine different sites and designed to be seen by one person at a time. Solo audience members journeyed (in 10-minute intervals) by walking or taking the subway and even the Roosevelt Island tramway to different locations as part of a sequential visual narrative experience. *Angel Project* was marketed as an installation/

Photo Introduction.2 Nun (performer) with audience member, *The Angel Project, A site-specific Performance Installation* (2003) by Deborah Warner, Produced by Lincoln Center Festival, Times Square, New York, NY.

Photo © Konstantino Hatzisarros, by permission of Deborah Warner.

performance, and this designation refers to the visual tableaux created by the artifacts and performers found in each site. Warner made careful use of each space—its sightlines, architecture, and views. The effect was wholly immersive. Besides the constructed environments, the experience relied on the juxtaposition of being in two simultaneous realities: the fictional world of *Angels* and the real world of the surrounding city. At one point, an audience member was instructed to walk to Times Square and stand at a specific corner. It was difficult to distinguish a performer from a passerby (Photo Introduction.2). *Angel Project*'s simple premise was that angels stuck on Earth were waiting to return to the heavens, and we, the audience, were tracking their whereabouts. Warner described the work in wholly abstract terms, wanting the audience to bring their own stories to her very-real-but-constructed reality. This creation was engaging because of Warner's masterful use of her chosen sites.

Last Thoughts

Definitions and categories can be useful, but it is the art that matters. The audience experience and the artistic process of making the work are the sources of excitement and inspiration. Artists and scholars can debate how to catalog a work; the categories I present are not intended to be the final word. If this topic interests you, I recommend further reading of works by scholars such as Fiona Wilkie, Victoria Hunter, Melanie Kloetzel, Bertie Ferdman, and others (see Appendix 2: Additional Resources). They have spent considerable time analyzing site work and provide other descriptions and definitions. You will find terms like "site generic," "site sympathetic," "site inspired," "site-versatile," and others that eschew the word site altogether, like "environmental art," "outdoor performance," "street theater." Create your own methodology and rubrics or combine others to fit your vision. I offer these categories as tools to deepen your research and the development of your work.

PART I

HOW DO WE START?

1
What Motivates Site Selection?

In the middle of the rehearsal process for a site project in Milwaukee, the cast and I were walking from the parking area to the site, when one of the dancers, sounding both excited and exasperated, asked, "How *do* you actually select a site?" That simple question kindled thoughts of all the inceptive pathways to past sites and projects. How exactly *did* I pick them? Or did *they* pick me? A more practical question would be: What is my *process* for selecting a site? Do I even have a process? Looking back, I see that my unique experiences and path have influenced my perspective and prejudices when looking at sites. Only relatively recently did I develop a conscious awareness for site selection.

Influences in Selecting a Site

Within the first five years of my career as a site artist, I was commissioned by Dancing in the Streets (founded in 1984 and the first producing company in the United States dedicated to site-specific dance) to create six works, all on a grand scale and in public locations. The experience of working on such a scale during that relatively short period had an indelible effect on many subsequent projects. It influenced how I looked at space, architecture, and place as potential platforms for creativity. Additionally, these experiences established my preference for selecting sites that attract large audiences, that have a social/political context, that have unique physical designs, and that inspire a specific theme. I also discovered that site selection could result from two other factors: personal connections to a location and invitations from site administrators who have their own motives.

How? What? Why? Where?

How did I get here? What am I doing here? Why am I doing this? And why am I doing this here? For any creative project, all of these questions need answers. Selecting a site often involves several factors, some immediately conscious, some more emotionally subconscious that you discover only after you begin to explore the site and really analyze your attraction to it. For example, my initial excitement about *The Grand Step Project* derived from the size of the potential audience and the visual rhythm created by the open spaces of the grand urban staircases. But as I studied the sites, I also became increasingly conscious of my attraction to all the varied human

On Site. Stephan Koplowitz, Oxford University Press. © Oxford University Press 2022. DOI: 10.1093/oso/9780197515235.003.0002

activity. I realized that my choreography had to encompass as much of this human experience as possible and that I would need a large cast to capture this narrative. The conscious mixture of these factors—audience size, the scale of the steps, the social/human activity—resulted in my decision to focus on themes involving play, commerce, and meditation.

A clear understanding of your motivation for selecting *where* to work will enable you to make coherent artistic and production decisions and to communicate effectively with funders, collaborators, and production personnel. Although your initial attraction to a site may derive from a single factor, it is important to be mindful of any others that might be influencing you. Being intentional and communicating your intentions require conscious understanding of the factors that have formed your intentions. Although I have separately highlighted some of the most common factors in this chapter, it is their interactions that will ultimately shape your creative process and the work itself.

> I don't make work in a site that I don't have a relationship with. I've never chosen a site that didn't call to me in some way, whether it's a pre-established relationship or historical relationship or whether it's a relationship that I've been forging currently. And I do not make work in a community that I am not a part of without being invited by those inside that community. So, I spend a lot of time getting to know who lives in that place, getting an understanding of not just the history but also what my relationship is to it even before thinking about the art. What is my relationship to this place? Why am I here? Why me? Why do I need to do a piece in this place? All of that factors into a decision. I'm never looking at a site as a canvas that I'm painting on; rather, I'm figuring out how to merge with the wall, merge with the ground and have something come out of me into the site.
>
> Amara Tabor-Smith

Audience size

> I realized that, actually, you do take the work to the people rather than the other way around.
>
> Susanne Thomas

As you visit possible sites, you, too, may find large ones especially attractive. The opportunity to reach and communicate to thousands (in public places) as opposed to hundreds (in small black-box theaters) can be appealing. Some artists cannot resist the lure of performing for stadium-size audiences. However, if audience size becomes an intentional, determining factor in your decision, it is essential to be aware of the benefits and the possible disadvantages in such a choice. Unless a work is produced in a sports stadium, the most likely locations for large audiences will be heavily trafficked public spaces. These require engaging captured audiences—people who frequent a site in the ordinary course of their daily activities and are not aware that a performance may be scheduled at that location. The risk of working with this particular audience is that people can feel inconvenienced by the sense that their space has been hijacked—an issue I will discuss in more detail in Chapter 3 (Designing the Event and Staging the Audience).

On the opening night of *Grand Central Dances*, 6,000 people were situated on the terminal floor. Many had come to see works by six different artists, including the Merce Cunningham Dance Company and high-wire artist Philippe Petit. However, a subset of those 6,000 people were 2,000 tired, harried New Yorkers trying to catch their rush-hour train home on a Friday night. These commuters were performing their daily routine and were unhappy about navigating through the throngs of 4,000 people who seemingly, without notice, appeared out of thin air. I encountered several angry outbursts from the commuting public whenever they became aware of my affiliation with the production. Luckily, many commuters, despite being inconvenienced, elected to take later trains and stay to watch the unique event unfolding before them. In this project, the palpable tension between the two types of audiences, captured and invited, worked itself out. But as dance critic Anna Kisselgoff wrote in her review for the *New York Times* (October 11, 1987): "The fantasy that commuters hurrying home (the event began at 8 P.M. and ended at 10:20) would merely pause to look at the dancers and then go on, ran up against the reality of crowd control . . . Many of the spectators, packed in rows, had obviously come for the event. Those who did try to make a train plowed undaunted through the huge mass of onlookers."

One year later, another Dancing in the Streets production took place at the public Astoria Pools in Queens, New York (1988), an Olympic-size pool. The site-specific event occurred on one of the hottest, most humid days of the summer and required the audience to exit the pool and watch performances in the water for an indeterminate length of time. Initially, everyone reluctantly complied. As the performance progressed in the stifling heat, the audience erupted in an all-out mutiny because they had no sense of when it might end. People stormed the "stage" and re-entered the pool; nothing could stop them. In a flash, a human curtain came down. The audience had spoken through action. It was a surreal moment and a great reminder of the potential danger of engaging a captured audience. In a review of the event, Jennifer Dunning of the *New York Times* deemed the entire production "a mistake."

With proper planning, the potential risks of working with captured audiences can be minimized. An empathetic anticipation of how long people might tolerate an interruption to their natural movement through a space and a good plan for creating breaks in the performance structure can alleviate oppositional responses. When *Fenestrations* was invited back to Grand Central Terminal (and titled *Fenestrations²*), it was the only work to be programmed three times within three hours. At a length of 15 minutes, whatever interruptions or distractions the performance presented to the public were short-lived and allowed for a free flow of movement for the majority of each evening the work was scheduled. Ultimately, a well-crafted work that grabs the attention of a captive audience without excessive disruption to their normal activities has a powerful appeal that can make audience size a compelling reason for selecting a site.

> If you're going to make a work that's at all disruptive to a community, especially those who live around the site, be clear about what you need to do that could be disruptive, that's beyond the idea of "this would be so perfect for the piece." Because if it's not working in harmony with that community, you need to ask yourself what is my intent versus the impact?
>
> Amara Tabor-Smith

Making a social/political statement

The historical or contemporary significance of a site can be a source of inspiration, encouraging you to explore a social theme or highlight a particular topic. Artist and dancer nibia pastrana santiago was inspired by the now iconic site featuring statues of US Presidents (Paseo de los Presidentes) in San Juan, Puerto Rico (Photo 1.1):

> For my work *the presidents step on, or commemorating the invisible, or I want to be a sexy iconoclast* (2014), I found it so unbearable to see and walk by that site that I needed to do something disruptive. In a way I let the site speak to me and started to consider: How can

Photo 1.1 *The presidents step on, or commemorating the invisible, or I want to be a sexy iconoclast* (2014) by nibia pastrana santiago, Paseo de los Presidentes, San Juan, PR.
Photo © nibia pastrana santiago.

I do something radical without getting arrested? Local politicians are the ones responsible for funding this monument, so it's like colonial trauma. These are human-scale statues of US Presidents. It's an imperial historical site! I observed how the site conditioned visitors' behavior—basically people take selfies and pictures of themselves with the statues. I remember performing with a regular camera, which made it look very touristic. It was an intervention . . . a touristic intervention, a performance event. I made a score for myself: I won't speak, and if I speak, I speak in Spanish, and I'll take selfies in absurd and erotic ways. I believe there is empowerment in using one's body to reclaim space. Movement was a way to contest all these tropes and stereotypes about tropical women. The idea that the Caribbean is hot and is sexy produces all these fantasies of entertainment projected onto Caribbean bodies . . . As a result, the fact that I was doing sexy postures while taking pictures with the presidents' statues felt like I was vandalizing them. I thought I'm doing "corporeal vandalism." In a way, I'm insulting these statues, this monument, but nobody can stop me because I'm just acting weird and have a camera. I'm kind of dancing, and who's to know for sure that I am being offensive?

Site work tends always to influence public dialogue. When a work is performed in public, it *is* a political act, regardless of content or overt intention. The act of disrupting the normal flow of public activity forces people to see their surroundings differently and confront a new way of navigating a space, both conceptually and physically. This new perspective creates a tension that sparks thought and dialogue about the site itself and the larger issue of the relationship of arts and creativity to our society and daily life. Regardless of content, a performance in a public space suggests issues of open access and freedom of movement and expression.

Architecture and design

Site selection can be influenced solely by the visual design. Design is one of the most potent initial attractors to a site, and often my first entry point. The power of evocative and striking architecture or the beauty of the natural world is hard to resist if your aesthetic is visually oriented. Unique audience sightlines alone could make a site appealing, as though the site beckons you to explore the spatial possibilities.

The grandeur of the windows in Grand Central Terminal inspired Elise Bernhardt. At the American Museum of Natural History in New York City, I was initially wowed by the life-size replica of the largest mammal on Earth: the blue whale found suspended in the grand Hall of Oceanic Life. The visual impact of the grand entrance hall of London's Natural History Museum was also hard to ignore. The same was true of the Round Reading Room (inside the British Museum), or the Moshe Safdie-designed Salt Lake City Public Library (a site on my wish list).

Although other factors will likely play a role in ultimate site selection, visual design is an inevitable factor.

> I often find that perhaps what I would call "non-sites" can be exciting. It's not just the really dramatic sites like Grand Central Station, for example, which of course is amazing, but you also have to live up to that space. Sometimes, it can be wonderfully intriguing to find this sort of underground corridor or this nook in a house. I find that nearly any site can be a great site.
>
> Susanne Thomas

Purpose and themes

Sometimes, the purpose of a site suggests an exciting theme. For example, the invitation to work in an Olympic-size aqua center was irresistible because I found the idea of working with swimmers and water attractive (*Aquacade for Asphalt Green*, 2000, NYC). A more recent work in a cemetery (*The Beginning*, 2018, Northfield, MN) stimulated a desire to work with the emotional tension between life and death—grieving a death and celebrating life. In both sites, it was impossible to ignore the visual aspects (water, pool, gravestones) and the essential functions (swimming, end of life, internment) and not create a work that embodied or referred to the activities associated with the site. For these works, the locations generated the theme.

Another source of inspiration for site selection can be an initial desire to explore a specific theme; finding one or more sites that capture it then happens later. In 2008, I had the opportunity to assemble a site-specific touring company and was asked to create work in Los Angeles and Plymouth, UK. However, no specific site was identified. As I thought about them, my interest in water ultimately determined the sites I chose in those cities and inspired my search for other sites relevant to water. In Plymouth, I chose Smeaton's Tower, a lighthouse that had been moved inland as a memorial to seafaring, and in Los Angeles, I selected the Original Farmers Market to suggest the connection between water and the food that nourishes us. Since 2000, choreographer and performer Jennifer Monson has dedicated her work to an investigation of "the relationship between movement and environment," leading to "inquiries of cultural and scientific understandings of large-scale phenomenon such as animal navigation and migration, geological formations such as aquifers, and re-functioned sites such as the abandoned Ridgewood Reservoir" (ilandart.org). Choosing to start with a thematic focus can inspire possibilities for discovering content and selecting new locations.

Personal history

Sometimes, site selection results from more personal inspiration: the artist's experiences or memories or associations with a particular place. An experience linked to a particular site can be a strong catalyst. Artists Joanna Haigood of Zaccho

Dance Theater and Olive Bieringa and Otto Ramstad of BodyCartography Project have made site-specific works inspired by and taking place in their homes—the places where they live. A student from my online Coursera class designed an entire project for her backyard, enlisting family members as performers. Our domestic life, our home, can contain a concentrated positive or negative emotional history that can be a rich source of creative inspiration.

A person's experience of loss might inspire a project in a cemetery, or nostalgia for drive-in theaters could motivate creation in one of those few remaining sites. Inspiration might arise from a desire to work in a particular region, city, or natural environment—a personal affinity for the desert, the ocean, forests, lakes, or a specific city like Boston or Miami. A vacation or any kind of travel can result in unintended site research and discovery. The possibilities are endless, and the pull of personal experience can be a strong selector.

Invitations come in all forms

Site selection can also be initiated by an invitation from someone who has a particular motivation. A request might come from an arts presenter familiar with your past work who wants you to create a new piece at a specific location to celebrate a municipal or institutional event—such as an anniversary or building opening. As site-specific productions have become more ubiquitous, merely cutting a ribbon seems dull in comparison. The power of a public performance to bring increased attention to the new building can result in an invitation. The British Library celebrated its inaugural year in 1998, when I was asked to create *Babel Index*. The re-opening of the New York Public Library at Lincoln Center in 2001 resulted in an invitation to create *(In)Formations*.

An invitation to work on a site can also be motivated by the stakeholders seeking to change the perception of the site, to reintroduce the site because of negative word-of-mouth reports, or because the site is not known or frequented by the public. The event created for the Wexner Center of the Arts (The Ohio State University) in 1988 by Dancing in the Streets targeted the center's residential neighbors. The new building's architectural plans had generated a fair amount of public curiosity and some consternation given its radical design. The university wanted to invite the general public and its neighbors to see the building and experience a free unique cultural event. The British Library administration invited me to work in the newly opened building, motivated by the criticism that Prince Charles voiced about the library's design, saying it looked like "an academy for secret police" (BBC News Online, June 25, 1998). *Fenestrations* was invited back to Grand Central Terminal to introduce the New York City public to the then-novel concept of the terminal as a destination for food, shopping, and culture.

Site producer Elise Bernhardt invited many artists, including Merce Cunningham, to various venues during her career not only to re-educate audiences about sites but to alter their perception of an art form: "When I was in college, we always had to go see Merce Cunningham, and I would go, and I would feel nothing. I'd be like, what's the big deal here? Then I was in France, and I saw Merce's company in Avignon, outdoors, and it was an entirely different experience. That's when I thought if a girl from Long Island can get it because the work is in a place that's not a theater, perhaps many others could have a similar experience."

Finally, the desire for new educational experiences can result in an invitation from a school, university, or arts organization that may want its students or community members to learn from participating in a site-specific production. These invitations can be phrased in different ways: "Come to our community or campus, get to know us, and tell us what would interest you in terms of making a site-specific work." Or, "Come to our community because we would like you to make a work for this particular location." Once an initial invitation is made, a conscious selection process, using some of the filters suggested here, such as design and history, can allow the process to move forward efficiently.

Last Thoughts

Consciously understanding your motivation and selection criteria when considering sites will enhance the creative and production process. The more intentional your decisions, the more precise the path to completion, and the greater the shared sense of purpose will be.

2
Permissions, Permits, and Insurance

Most people would prefer to avoid the process of gaining access to sites and procuring permits. The prevalent impression is that securing permits is complicated, confusing, costly, and, ultimately, too time consuming. Even so, the access and permission process is an essential requirement for professional site work and can result in many benefits.

When I collaborated with DiverseWorks, a multi-arts presenting company in Houston, Texas, to create *Natural Acts in Artificial Water* (2012), I researched water-related sites, specifically public fountains, all over town. After interviews with four different fountain-site managers, I chose to work with Uptown Houston, the company that manages the Gerald D. Hines Waterwall Park. Getting permission to turn the large fountain on and off at precise moments was important to create a dramatic visual effect. When the engineer at Uptown Houston granted this request in our first meeting, it was evident that Hines Park offered not only impressive architecture/design but a willingness to accommodate special artistic requests.

The experience with Uptown Houston made clear that the process of getting permissions can add true and unique value to a project by uncovering unknown possibilities of a site. Had I decided to work at the park without permission, not only would I have missed out on the opportunity to turn the water off and on, the idea might not even have occurred to me, thus greatly diminishing the artistic potential of working at that site.

Official permission bestows professional recognition on the production: it sends a positive message to the public and allows you to freely publicize the event (to attract large and diverse audiences). It also establishes a collaborative partnership that can result in your discovering and gaining access to parts of the site that are not usually open to the public, which can contribute to your artistic vision. And this collaboration helps to prevent misunderstandings and reduce the potential for lawsuits if something goes wrong. You and the manager can discuss safety and liability issues and ensure that you and/or the institution has proper insurance coverage to protect your creative team and the audience. A lot of work and hours are invested in a project, and no artist or producer wants to be shut down at any point in the process, let alone the day of a performance, for lack of permission or liability insurance. Bypassing the permitting process out of fear of rejection is a risk that could limit both the success and development of the project.

On Site. Stephan Koplowitz, Oxford University Press. © Oxford University Press 2022. DOI: 10.1093/oso/9780197515235.003.0003

Getting to the Right Person and Asking the Right Questions

> If you want to get access to a building, learn what the building means to the owner or caretaker.
>
> Debra Loewen

There is no simple formula for procuring access to and permission to use a site. You might find the right person quickly by picking up the phone and talking to whoever answers, or you might need to make many phone calls, send several emails, and go to lots of meetings to find that person. The process can begin with online research to determine the site's staffing or with a visit to the site to ask someone whom to contact about permissions and access. Sometimes, you might think you have found the right person, only to discover you have not.

When the Dance Umbrella Festival commissioned *Genesis Canyon* (1996) at the Natural History Museum in London, we began the permission process with a phone call. After explaining the nature of the inquiry, we were directed to the person in charge of renting the museum's grand entrance hall. We made the appointment and believed we were on the fast track to getting access. However, after we made the presentation, our host pulled out a lovely leather-bound book with an extensive price list and photos of past events in the museum spaces. Our plans would cost $25,000 simply for access.

We then knew we had met with the wrong person. This initial museum contact was from Corporate Relations/Fundraising. When we balked at the price, he encouraged us to contact someone in the Education Department who would be more interested in our request and wouldn't assume we were paying partners. The idea of purchasing access was antithetical to the budget and the philosophy of bringing the work to the public itself. The aim was for the museum to appreciate (support) the educational and artistic value of the project because it aligned with the museum's own stated goals as an educational and creative institution. Luckily, the Education Department contact at the museum embraced our vision, and we embarked on a successful and productive partnership resulting, almost a year later, in the premiere of *Genesis Canyon*.

An organization may not view your artistic plan for a performance as part of the site's normal, day-to-day routine. The easiest answer for any organization to give when confronted with a request that may disrupt its normal reality is a simple no. Therefore, once the initial presentation is complete, try to phrase subsequent access questions in a manner that does not invite a simple yes/no response. Questions pertaining to the process of gaining access are potentially more effective: "What steps do I need to take?" "What concerns do you have?" A question such as, "Can I turn off the fountain?" might best be posed as, "If we wanted to turn off the fountain, with whom should we speak?" Rather than making demands, ask discussion-based questions that establish a basis for collaboration and invite conversations about creative ideas, possibilities, and processes.

For the First Meeting, Be Prepared

It is essential to come to these meetings prepared to present your artistic vision for the site and establish your willingness to work toward meeting requirements for any access and permissions. Bring a specific list of other requests needed to fulfill the plan: Will certain areas of the site need to be cleared of people? Do the cast and crew require on-site parking? When is best to hold rehearsals—before or after regular business hours? If security is needed during rehearsals, who will pay for this? Access to a site for rehearsal, creation, and performance encompasses many factors. Distinguishing between the essential and nonessential will help you navigate the conversation.

Some questions in this meeting will be dictated by the budget (paying for security might strain the budget), while other questions will be driven by the artistic vision (wanting to gain access to a specific location within the site). Regardless, it is important to stay focused on the big picture. Don't argue or debate if secondary requests are denied. Remember, the organization has agreed to allow you to use its site. Some items can be revisited when all parties have developed a good working relationship.

> It's important to know how to talk to people. It was one of the big lessons I learned when we did a series of performances in the rooms of at the Chelsea Hotel. We were shut down by the fire department and had to move the remaining performances to a loft on 16th Street. I learned that you can't talk to a firefighter the same way you talk to an artist. You have to go into a meeting and be mature enough to understand the perspectives and concerns of the people you're speaking to. If it's property owners, they want to know about insurance. Don't go on and on about your vision; talk to them about insurance. If you don't know how to do it, make sure that you have somebody on your team who does.
>
> Anne Hamburger

Navigating and Addressing Concerns from the Inside Out

Getting to know not only the stakeholders of a specific site but others who have jurisdiction over elements that may affect your performance can make a big difference. Production manager and lighting designer Tony Giovannetti describes his approach: "If you're not in your hometown, you have to talk to local people and find out who's really calling the shots in a particular neighborhood. In the residential Upper West Side of Manhattan, the police department might have a lot to say about what's going on regarding noise levels of amplified music, or in another neighborhood, it might be the community board for street closures or the Business Improvement District for sidewalk use in proximity to businesses."

Once you have established positive relationships, continue to develop them. Anticipate specific issues that might arise, and address them. If an issue requires the involvement of other departments within the host organization, ask your primary contact to assist you. For example, my two *Off the Walls* projects, made for the Portland Museum of Art (Maine) and the Hudson River Museum (New York), were approved by my contacts in the museums' education departments. However, one concern was how to sell the project to other members of the curatorial staff. My contacts suggested that the museums' curators would fear potential damage to works during the rehearsals and performance. We addressed these concerns using three strategies: (1) We would avoid any galleries designated as off-limits. (2) We explained that professional dancers and actors are trained to have body control within a space. (3) We respected requests establishing exact distances between performers and specific works of art. Being as straightforward as possible is always helpful, and having someone from the inside voice potential concerns was essential in brainstorming ideas to address those concerns.

> Even when you have permission, you have to keep treading carefully to maintain the relationship because you can lose it as quickly as you get it. I had an early experience in my project at the Waterloo Station. After long negotiations, we got permission to rehearse in the forecourt of the station. I was still short one dancer, so I auditioned someone during that first rehearsal. During the session, the dancer did this very loud and outrageous improvisation to impress us. It was too much for public consumption, so we lost permission. We should have eased into our process with more care because we were working in public view. If they knew we could be careful and considerate with their customers, they would have perhaps given us more space. We learned a good lesson.
>
> Susanne Thomas

In general, most demands institutions make when considering a site performance are reasonable. Taking the time to uncover the reasons behind a "no" is essential. Of course, sometimes you just have to walk away. If authorities impose too many restrictions during the initial meetings, you should consider withdrawing your proposal. At what point do the conditions alter the original vision and make it unrecognizable? Understanding the true and primary reason for selecting a site will make that decision easier.

> In certain situations, you may have to be prepared to move to a different site. With a deep analysis of what's there, people who have decided on a particular site may be able

to find another appropriate site that retains a key characteristic or theme expressed in the original site.

Melanie Kloetzel

Being Present as an Artist and Producer

The pool project (Agora, 2005) didn't only involve art-making. It involved managing a contractor, dealing with the community board, understanding what the community had invested in that site. Many of these involvements, which ended up shaping my creative process, I did not see coming. In the end dealing with the inertia of city government was my biggest challenge.

Noémie Lafrance

As the artistic director, your presence at permission meetings is essential in making a final site selection. Besides learning more about a site, being present provides firsthand knowledge and the opportunity to assess the true depth of commitment an organization offers. Your presence at these meetings also establishes another aspect of your role. Site artists are more than artists; they are bona fide producers (or co-producers when working with an organization's producer). It is essential to embrace your role as producer, not just when negotiating permits and access but when other producer issues arise: marketing, creating audience design, negotiating documentation, and fundraising. You will want to be treated as an equal producing partner with whoever has commissioned your work.

Going Rogue

We learned during public performances and rehearsals that when the police arrive, you need to move out. So, whatever you are doing needs to be mobile. That's how we developed putting our sound system on mobile bikes, yes, even a projector.

José Ome Navarrete Mazatl

Deciding to proceed with a sited project without permission means going toward a guerilla-style performance. There may be compelling reasons for making such a decision. You may not have a budget to cover the insurance or security costs that would be required if you sought permission, not to mention the costs of marketing or any other contingencies. Or the site might be difficult to access or too small for a large audience, so your marketing plan might target only a small, private network of supporters. Perhaps your intended aesthetic experience relies on surprising a public audience of passersby. Or, and this is potentially a disastrous reason, you feel you don't have time to obtain permits because the performance is scheduled with little lead time.

Some site artists, such as Olive Beringa and Otto Ramstad of BodyCartography Project, have successfully produced works without permits both in urban and more rural locations, including performances on public transportation, on buses in San Francisco (*Market Street Transportation*, 1999) and at a beach in New Zealand (*Freyberg Beach*, 1998). Melanie Kloetzel has experienced increasing frustration with navigating permits and the increasing commodification of public space and has staged rogue works as an act of protest with what she calls a site-versatile work, *It began with watching* (various locations, 2016).

Choreographer Amara Tabor-Smith has created several works in Oakland that take place in the streets and are processional in nature (Photo 2.1): "For the processional work, we don't get permits because we're constantly moving. We just do it. I've just never felt the need to deal with any bureaucracy that I don't have to." Her idea is that if the performance is constantly moving through a space, without disrupting the normal flow, a permitless event is more likely to evade detection.

Pushing forward with a production with little lead time is always a risk, but circumstances can make the risk seem worthwhile. Whatever the reasons or circumstances, if the project is going rogue, it's best to know what specific factors contributed to your decision and to anticipate any unwanted consequences.

Photo 2.1 *House/Full of Blackwomen,* episode_*Now You See Me (Fly)* (2016) created by Amara Tabor-Smith in collaboration with Ellen Sebastian Chang, downtown Oakland, CA. Photo © Robbie Sweeny, courtesy Amara-Tabor Smith.

Last Thoughts

The process of gaining access and procuring permits will take time and effort. Investigate, research, probe creative intentions, and allow time for the collaborating institutions to discuss concerns. An open and honest dialogue will strengthen the creative process and the final product. Engage in this access/permission process fully, embracing your dual roles of producer and creator, knowing that the process will protect the entire collaborative team and the creative work.

3
Designing the Event and Staging the Audience

When arriving at a theater to see a concert or show, most audiences are well trained. They pick up a ticket, enter the theater, find a seat, read the program, chat with seatmates, and wait for the lights to dim—the ritual is simple, straightforward, and comforting. Attending a site-specific event can upend the usual expectations of this experience. Where does one find tickets or a program? Where are the seats located? Arriving at a site to attend a performance can seem disorienting.

Audience design (staging the audience) is an essential part of creating a site-specific production because how the audience physically encounters the art influences both the experience and meaning of the piece. As a result, site artists must include the audience's perspective in the conception of the work. You must decide *how the audience will experience the physical site and where they will be situated in relation to the performers*. You must make these decisions even before rehearsals have started in order to formulate your production plan, so the audience design becomes part of the *concept* of the performance. Safety considerations also influence audience design; for example, physical distancing protocols to minimize transmission of Covid-19 have added a significant factor for artists and audience design, affecting site selection and the creative content.

> With *Bird Brain*, audience participation was important, and the audience's experience was foregrounded. I had an environmental education focus in this project. Every performance had a movement workshop with the audience to get them actively using simple sensory and spatial awareness exercises. This guided them into a sensitized state to observe the environment and the dancing. I asked them to watch the dance as though they were watching the rest of the environment, with the same curiosity. I invited them to move closer to us or to move further away, just like they might with a bird, animal, or other parts of the environment.
>
> Jennifer Monson

Staging the audience can support the work's intention, emphasize the site's physical properties, and create the best viewing sightlines for the performance. The site is the subject matter of the work, so how you design the viewing of the site must be woven into the fabric of the performance experience. Will the work's intention be more effective if the audience has a more intimate view of the space? Or is a broad and more distant perspective more appropriate? Does the site inspire the use of multiple locations that can only be seen if the audience is mobile? At different moments

On Site. Stephan Koplowitz, Oxford University Press. © Oxford University Press 2022. DOI: 10.1093/oso/9780197515235.003.0004

of a performance, you may decide to change the audience's perspective, in which case you may need a hybrid design.

> I hadn't planned for the audience to be such an important part of the show in the train station because it was my first work with a big public presence. It was such a busy public site with a natural choreography of people crossing and waiting. We infiltrated the site with performances that showed up in different places in the station, and at some point the passers-by became as important as the performers. The whole area became this playground, this field for performance. The audience experienced what one reviewer referred to as "spectatorial self-consciousness." As a spectator, you became aware of your role in the viewing.
>
> Susanne Thomas

At this early stage in the process, the physical design of the space, safety issues, and the need to provide the most unobstructed sightlines may be the only reasons to create an audience design. You may not develop a clear idea of the theme, narrative, or the meaning of the work until later in the process—once rehearsals have begun or you have spent more time investigating the space. But your audience design will ultimately either enhance or hinder your audience's response to your work. As you begin planning, try to imagine several audience designs to test different possible narrative scenarios and open up other creative possibilities. Working from the outside (how things are organized) to find the inside (the theme, the story) can be facilitated by first delving into audience design. For example, a promenade performance invites a more intimate view of your site that might suggest a more personal, theatrical storyline that focuses on an individual performer. Considering a more formal, distant perspective could inspire a more abstract narrative.

Keep in mind, too, specific practical considerations: Audience design should be part of the discussion when negotiating with a commissioning producer (if there is one). You must be sensitive to producers' concerns about the audience's comfort and treatment during the event. Additionally, you may have no choice but to create an audience design that adheres to official health guidelines. In 2019, The Wooden Floor (an arts and dance-based youth development non-profit in Santa Ana, California) contacted me about creating a work for the summer of 2021. The producer wanted something that would utilize the building—three large studios, a courtyard, office space, and classrooms. Before the pandemic, my initial design involved an intimate and immersive audience pathway through the building, allowing close contact between audience members and performers. But Covid-19 safety protocols changed this plan; performers and audiences would have to maintain a specific distance from each other. I also had to limit the number of audience members per performance and the amount of time people stood in one place in any indoor space. The challenge was to create material that would enhance my vision for an appropriate site-specific creation and instill confidence in everyone involved that our shared health concerns were being addressed. As we approached the premiere of *Passage/Home* in mid-July, 2021, Covid-19 protocols began to relax and we were able to make further adjustments to our audience plan (we increased capacity) and even their pathway within the work.

Audience comfort and sightlines matter. If audiences feel unsafe, for any reason, no matter the appeal of the work, they can become angry and even leave the site. If audiences encounter viewing difficulties, they will struggle to understand and appreciate the work. It is that simple. When people buy a ticket for a performance in a traditional theater and the box office does not inform them that a seat is partial view, they are frustrated and disappointed. Even purchasing a known partial-view seat is an exercise in compromise. The negative emotional response resulting from discomfort will affect a viewer's artistic experience, and the art will suffer.

Seating

Should you use chairs? Although this decision may appear trivial, it could have aesthetic implications. Will the introduction of a new element into the space affect the experience and design of the work? I have designed some projects without chairs because chairs would have affected the theme, the feel, or the intended experience of the work. If the performance takes place in an ancient or distinctly historical location, the introduction of modern chairs may interfere with your intention to evoke a feeling of the past. Or the arrangement of seats might feel incongruous with the visual design of the site. However, accommodating audiences with a range of abilities (like senior citizens and others with durable medical equipment) is more important than strict adherence to aesthetic choices that might result in preventing some people from attending your work.

Audience Design Models

What follows are specific design models, all of which can be modified and altered during the rehearsal process and performances. During preproduction, ascertaining projected audience size and designing the audience in relation to a chosen site will help with decisions such as the number of performers, the stagehands needed, the length of the performance, and other production issues that will be addressed in later chapters. At this stage, creating a plan is all that is required.

Frontal or proscenium design

This audience design suggests that the performance has a front that requires it to be seen from that perspective, similar to a conventional proscenium theater.

However, a site artist needs to make other decisions: Are audiences meant to stand or sit? Lie on their back, looking up? Sit on the ground or in a provided chair? If they are to sit in chairs, how many are available? Within this one model, there are many variations and many options. Will audiences include people with physical needs requiring access to a chair or space for a wheelchair? Regardless of the audiences' physical capabilities, if the performance is to be viewed standing, it's essential to anticipate the length of time people can stand before becoming uncomfortable. I suggest not to make audiences stand in one place for more than 30–45 minutes. You should imagine your comfort zone when considering running time and audience comfort and the anticipated audiences' age range. One way to extend the standing time is to allow the audience to move about the space. Giving the audience a task, like walking and actively engaging with their surroundings, can enable you to extend the performance time to 60 minutes or more.

Fixed place, pivoting audience

In this format, the audience's location remains constant, but their orientation changes as the work requires small shifts in their position. *Genesis Canyon* was designed with this structure. For 50 minutes, the audience stood (some sat on the floor at times) in one area of the grand entrance hall, and, at different moments, the staging of the work required them to pivot left or right. With each pivot, the audience focused on another part of the space—the stairs, stone bridge, balconies—in an order determined by my narrative. This design can be used in several ways and is an easy strategy for refreshing the audience's perspective on a site—and can be as effective as having them walk to another location.

Fixed audience, multiple views

This design creates multiple audience locations in one performance space. Each audience member selects or is placed in one section and stays there for the duration. The design provides people different views of the same performance, depending on which location they occupy. Two popular examples are arena staging (theater-in-the-round), which places the audience in sections surrounding the performance space, and double-front orientation, which sets the audience in two areas on opposite sides of the performance. There are variations of these, but the constant is that the spectator selects or is placed in one location and remains there. In the first section of my work *Babel Index* at the British Library, the audience was situated not only in different locations around a fixed performance space but on different levels. This option offered the opportunity to experience lateral and vertical vantage points, giving some the impression of looking at a flat surface, like a writing tablet or piece of paper. I took advantage of this perspective by creating movement that suggested ink on a page or carvings in stone, tracing the development of writing through the ages.

Mobile audience/promenade performance

In this format, the audience walks from one place to another in a prescribed order. They might stand or sit once they arrive at each location, but walking to different areas, no matter how many, makes the performance a promenade.

A variation of the promenade divides the audience into smaller groups, and each begins a journey to one or more locations using staggered starting times; one group starts at one o'clock, and 15 minutes later, the second group begins—and so on. Site artist Martha Bowers' *Safe Harbor* (1998) used this structure. Although this design asks more of the performers because they must repeat their performances for each new group, more people can view a work without scheduling additional performance dates.

Selecting a promenade design is often motivated by the artist's desire to use multiple locations within a larger site. In *Night Light* (2000), Carlson worked from photographs, and each site corresponded to the exact location found in a photograph. For *Invisible Wings* (Photo 3.1), Joanna Haigood moved the audience to different places to illustrate a new chapter in the underground railroad narrative. *Safe Harbor's* multiple sites each spoke to another aspect of a fisherman's life and culture.

Photo 3.1 *Invisible Wings* (2007) by Joanna Haigood, Jacob's Pillow, Beckett, MA.
Photo © Nancy Palmieri, courtesy Joanna Haigood

Self-directed promenade with unified conclusion

Another variation of a promenade performance invites audience members to walk to multiple sites choosing whatever path each wants to take in any order and then to assemble in a specific area at the end. My *Off the Walls* museum project began as a self-directed experience, during which audiences chose their paths and then gathered for the finale. Promenade performances are popular and effective. Asking audiences to move through a space over time creates a sense of going on a journey. It immediately enhances the sense of interactivity and gives the work an instant temporal and physical narrative. The action begins here and ends there; the selection of the starting and ending points should be made with an idea of how these points reinforce the concept of the work. My design for *Babel Index* led audiences through the British Library's grand entryway, but I did not highlight the scale of that space. Instead, I placed performers in two different small locations that would distract people from looking at the space in its entirety. Then, the sections of the work took place inside the building in enclosed areas. The finale brought the entire audience together back in the entrance hall, where I placed all 54 dancers spread out over three levels of balconies to capture the height and breadth of the space. I wanted audiences to experience the prior sections as single works—each as one book in the library—and by the end to feel the enormity of all the collections housed in this building. The finale suggested the 3,000-year history of the collection and its influence on our culture. Capturing the scale of the grand entry hall in a unifying audience experience after their self-directed promenades was the essence of my concept.

Mobile audience in moving vehicles

Another variation of the promenade structure is to move the audience using some type of mechanical conveyance—bicycles, skateboards, electric scooters, cars, buses, public transportation. In San Diego since 1999, Jean Isaacs of the San Diego Dance Theater has produced a site-specific series called *Trolley Dances*. It is a time-staggered performance during which the audience rides trolleys or other public transport to experience different performances throughout greater San Diego. I took part in *Trolley Dances 2015* as one of six artists featured in different fixed locations. Each site welcomed a new audience every 30 minutes over a period of six hours.

In 2013, I worked with public transportation as a means for an audience to promenade a site-adaptive work called *Red Line Time*, a five-minute site-adaptive work performed sequentially at fourteen Red Line Los Angeles Metro stations. The performance began with the five-minute dance (performed by eight dancers) at Union Station. With each subsequent metro stop, the audience gained a new spatial experience as they viewed the choreography against different backgrounds in different locations and from different sightlines and angles. Each performance was timed to allow both the performers and the audience to catch the next arriving train. At times, the performance at a particular station was cut short to enable everyone to return to the train platform. I wanted the audience to experience how their perception of time and space could expand and contract as a result of these temporal and spatial changes, all dependent on the train schedule and the next stop. Another variation was Ann Carlson's *Geyser Land* (2008), during which the audience was *on* a train the entire time. People could see performances inside and outside the train as it traversed the Montana landscape.

Extended promenade performance

This variation challenges the audience to experience a work over a longer time, usually over several days. Meredith Monk created *Juice* (1969) and *Vessel* (1971), both of which used this design. Monk, a true site-specific pioneer, continues to explore alternative audience designs. *Juice* (Photo 3.2), the third in a series of promenade productions made for museum spaces, took this format one step further by premiering new sections at different sites over an entire month. After its performance

Photo 3.2 *Juice: a theatre cantata in three installments* (1969) by Meredith Monk.
1st installment, Solomon R. Guggenheim Museum, New York, NY, photo V. Sladon; rehearsal photo, Meredith Monk loft, New York, NY, photo Monica Moseley; third installment, The House loft, New York, NY, photo V. Sladon. Photos courtesy Meredith Monk/The House Foundation for the Arts, Inc.

at the Guggenheim Museum on November 7, 1969, it continued at Barnard College's Minor Latham Playhouse from November 29 to December 1. The final section was at Monk's downtown loft on December 7. Monk selected this temporal design to make a specific point, as described by Nat Trotman on the Guggenheim Museum's website:

> For her, the progression from public to domestic space resembled the movement of a zoom lens, offering closer and closer scrutiny of her performers with each installment. For much of the first part, Monk used the vast space of the Guggenheim's rotunda to physically separate viewers and performers, often entirely obscuring the latter from view. At Barnard, she suggested greater closeness by incorporating personal stories into the scripted action and using only four performers from the first installment, who remained isolated on a proscenium stage. By the finale, the live performers were absent entirely, appearing only in close-up shots on a video monitor amid a display of objects and costumes from the previous installments. By that point, of course, the first installment of Juice was nearly a month past, so audience members could only experience the entire piece through the timeframe of their individual memories. Thus, as visual proximity increased, so did a sense of detachment and irony, creating a rich tension between space, time, and states of intimacy.

For the *TaskForce* projects in Idyllwild, Los Angeles, and Plymouth, UK, I invited audience members to follow, over an entire week, a series of site performances, all on the theme of water, within a specified geographical area. Each day, audiences could visit a new site to see an entirely different work. I wanted audiences to experience a physical mapping of their city or region through the water theme while altering their sense of space and time. By mapping these water-based sites, the audience could begin to consider the many, often-taken-for-granted ways water touched their life.

My site-adaptive *The Grand Step Project* took place over two weeks at six different grand staircases in three New York City boroughs. There was no expectation that audience members would follow the performances over time and distance. Still, those who did experience how the different locations framed the work discovered new meanings. When the work premiered at the Winter Garden, a few yards from 9/11 Ground Zero, the bodies rolling down the stairs took on one meaning. When they rolled down the Saint John the Divine Cathedral steps, those same bodies suggested other, more spiritual images of floating, ethereal bodies, and communal rituals, among others.

Simultaneous performances

This design entails producing simultaneous performances in different locations and giving an audience the choice of which to attend. The sites can be near or separated by miles; they can be identical (all by a river or all on identical tennis courts) or completely different (share no physical characteristics). One of the most extensive works of this kind is Marylee Hardenbergh's *One River Mississippi*

(2006), seven simultaneous performances at seven Mississippi River locations. This structure allows hundreds of people, separated by miles of the river, to experience similar work simultaneously. The work is marketed so that audiences know that they are participating in a shared experience in real time over a great distance. The title captures Hardenbergh's intentions to bring specific river locations to life and highlight the seamlessness a river creates as water connects one place to another. To quote Hardenbergh's mission statement: "Through simultaneous Mississippi River performances, to bring national attention to the river, its health, and its shared culture."

All of these audience designs have many variations and combinations. My purpose in providing these eight is, once again, to provide a framework and vocabulary to help artists develop their work. The process of designing the audience begins from the moment of conception, but your choices can change during your rehearsal/creation process and even on the day of a performance, as I will illustrate later in this chapter.

Audience Size/To Ticket or Not

I don't make work to be "stumbled upon" by an audience. I am looking for my audience to have a more voluntary and focused experience. To achieve that I often create a symbolically enclosed space. Audiences pay for tickets, which represents for me a form of commitment to the experience. The enclosure can be delimitated by light or by the natural elements of topography but is not necessarily enforced; however, it is always understood and respected. In many ways, the performance itself establishes its arena in how it uses the space in relation to its audience and how it creates focus.

Noémie Lafrance

Projecting the audience size is a crucial step in conceiving and designing the audience structure. Your audience design is determined, in part, by the size of the space: How many people will the space comfortably and safely accommodate? Should you add more performances, each with smaller audiences to reach more people? Ultimately, it is wiser to design an event that can be seen by *more* than the expected turnout. You cannot always accurately predict attendance. If the audience size in relation to your site's capacity is of no concern, your marketing campaign can take whatever form generates the most interest. If you wish to restrict the number of people for fear of crowding and discomfort, the marketing plan must reflect that reality.

Besides any health and safety issues, your initial discussion with the presenter/producer of your project will often focus on a desire to reach a certain number of people, especially if the budget depends on ticket sales. Expectations of audience size might also derive from promises you made in grant applications or from your own expectations and/or those of your presenter. If a chosen site can accommodate only 50 people and 500 people are the desired total audience, then designing the performance to be performed 10 times could be the best solution.

You can control audience size by using either reserved free or paid tickets. If working in a public site, make sure you understand how people generally access it. If it is usually free and open to the public, asking people to pay or denying them entry to an event could cause confusion and even anger. The ticketing decision you and your producer make will affect the audience design and experience, so you should always participate in deciding how *many* tickets or reservations are to be sold or made available. Choosing to ticket an event ensures that the maximum capacity will not be exceeded. If each performance can accommodate only 50 people, ticketing will prevent worry that 100 people will suddenly clamor for entry.

Creating a ticketing scheme for my work at Grand Central Terminal or for *The Grand Step Project*, both in large public spaces, would have been difficult. Those performances were designed as public art, which always allows the viewing public free access. Also, performances in public sites require an awareness that some people may resent the presence of a performance in their space. That is always a risk for site artists, as is overcrowding, which can also create problems. A chosen site's physical size and scale may be disproportionate to how many people can see a performance. The 8,000 people who converged on *Grand Central Dances* each night was a 5,000-person surprise. While this overcrowding was not a problem for my dance up in the windows, it did obstruct views of the constructed stage for the Cunningham and Childs companies. The placement of the performers will determine where the audience will be situated. If there is more than one vantage point from which audiences can view the work, you must decide which perspectives are best in terms of impact and intent. The earlier you, the producer, and/or other stakeholders clarify and agree on audience size, ticketing, and placement, the better.

At Lincoln Center, during the performance, people didn't circulate. We were above the fold in the *New York Times* Arts Section, and thousands of people showed up. The producers wouldn't print a program, so there were no notes. I announced that the work was like a treasure hunt, to travel and see different things. Not everyone understood. The second night was easier because half as many came. We thought we had a good plan for moving the traffic. In hindsight, we should have insisted on printed programs, perhaps tried to limit the audience, made a reservation list, done two shows a night. Still many critics and audiences loved it and had a wonderful time. If you were claustrophobic, it wasn't for you.

Mark Dendy

My work *Occupy* (2017) is an example of how the relationship between crowd control and ticketing can affect the performance. This project's informal reservation format left us no way of predicting how many people would attend on a given day. The Yerba Buena Gardens are centrally located and frequented by hundreds, sometimes thousands, of people. I conceived *Occupy* to be seen in a series of small, intimate spaces throughout the park precisely because the work explored how our humanity is affected by the constraints imposed by crowded urban and domestic spaces. The AXIS Dance Company, which commissioned the work, spent a good deal of time strategizing ways to attract a broad audience and limit each performance to a manageable number of people. We thought we had achieved crowd control by encouraging potential audience members to reserve a free ticket online before the event, allowing us to get an advanced sense of audience numbers. If too many reserved for one of the four performances, we would post online that the performance was sold out and encourage people to select another time or day.

Our efforts were only partially successful. The result of not offering *paid* tickets, which was not an option given the rules of the gardens, was that many people arrived without reservations and others already at the garden for other reasons saw the promenade audience members and decided to join them. By the end of the short run, we drew so many people that it became necessary to change the audience design to accommodate bigger crowds. This is not a common occurrence but a good reminder about the importance of having both foresight and *flexibility*. *Occupy* was originally sectioned in six designated areas in which the audience could stand (or sit). As the audiences grew, my site boundaries expanded with them. The increased audience made sightlines for certain sections challenging for some people to see any of the work, so I needed to make alterations to allow more viewing comfort. It was an exercise in flexibility.

Last Thoughts

The ability to imagine multiple audience designs for a site or an event is one of the advantages that site artists bring to any performance in a physical distancing climate, such as the ones resulting from the Covid-19 protocols. For many artists, thinking about and designing the audience's physical/visual experience before creating the work might have appeared to be putting the cart before the horse. Since 2020 more are discovering that careful audience design is integral to the work's original concept and continues to be essential to revealing that concept to an audience.

PART II
MAKING A MASTER PLAN
Paths to Research

4

The Site as Inspiration for Your Work

> Even though a site is a collaborator in the piece, it is a collaborator because of aspects that the site holds, and then there's what I bring to it. Recently, I've been referring to my work as site-responsive because I see it like a call and response with the site. I'm hearing and seeing something from the site, from the people and then I bring my response into it. I'm not making something that doesn't exist here; I'm going to focus on a specific aspect of that space's story.
>
> Amara Tabor-Smith

Creating site work requires a unique process. Most artists who operate in traditional forms begin with an empty page (a blank sheet of paper or canvas) or an empty performance space. But choreographers who create site work do not start with a blank page. Instead, they work in active, living spaces that already have a purpose, history, and physical life. While a blank canvas or page is meaningless until the artist imbues it with meaning, sites typically already mean something to those who live in, work in, or visit them. Consequently, the sites inevitably influence and partly or wholly inspire the ultimate creation of the art you present. The creative process is a partnership between the individual imagination and the site itself—a journey of artistic discovery.

This chapter explores that journey and introduces techniques as sources of inspiration for developing the conceptual structure for your work—four lenses through which you can consciously investigate a site: its physical design, history, current use, and community. Each lens involves a different approach, and each site may require that you use one or more of these lenses in your research and design. Site-specific (Category 1), site-adaptive (Category 2), and site-reframed (Category 3) works are supported by the observational, conversational, and text-based research the lenses entail.

> In my work I've had what I would say are two main strands; one is what I call "the site as the origin of concepts." I'm excited about a site and everything grows from the site. The movement material, the design, the sound, everything, and how the audience is placed or interacts. I've also done projects that I call "the site is the contextual container." Then I have an idea for a work, and I actually look for a site that can house this project. Again, not just as a backdrop but as an active agent in the work.
>
> Susanne Thomas

On Site. Stephan Koplowitz, Oxford University Press. © Oxford University Press 2022. DOI: 10.1093/oso/9780197515235.003.0005

Design/Architecture—Site inventory

As preparation for developing your concept and beginning rehearsals, a useful first step is to allow sufficient time to explore the physical site—to absorb visual information without judgment or bias. This approach allows you to discover details and aspects of a site that may not be readily apparent on a first or even second viewing. I call this process *site inventory*. Like any inventory, it requires an objective frame of mind that allows you to take stock of what you see, free of any preconceptions or artistic agendas. Resist the temptation to make judgments about the beauty or ugliness of what you see. Resist any impulse to attach yourself to metaphoric or allegorical images that may arise. Imagine you are a doctor examining a patient, free of emotional attachments, allowing for an objective view of the body at hand. Once you have absorbed the site's details, you can develop thematic ideas related to its design or architecture and make decisions about performance locations within the site, audience design, performer/audience capacity, and the best time of day or season to schedule the event.

> I start by feeling the space, like a meditation. Then, I let these questions come in, and I start to superimpose visuals of bodies in the space. I ask what does this space mean to people who use it? Who used it a hundred years ago? I like to think about all those ghosts. What are the human relations that make or made this space what it is today? What is its intended use or purpose? How did it not get used? Whom is it for, who has access to "public spaces" and who doesn't? What is invisibilized here or in the idea that this space was made public?
>
> Noémie Lafrance

A camera, a notebook, and an analytic mind

When doing a site inventory, it's important to explore the site with a walk-through and take photos and notes from different perspectives. Consciously making written notes and recording your observations will give you valuable data and develop your observational skills. The act of writing notes makes observation a more conscious process. These notes should contain concrete data: the number of items found in a site (windows, trees), the distance between objects, the size of objects, and simple diagrams and sketches as needed for illustration. My preference is to use a hardbound artist's sketchbook, which allows for both written notes and drawings/diagrams.

Photographing the site is an excellent complement to your notes and sketches because it provides a more complete record of your initial site experience. These photos can also be used for production discussions with collaborators and in grant proposals and project descriptions. The number of photographs taken is usually dictated by the size and complexity of a site. A complex site offers several different viewing perspectives and contains a multitude of different textures and surfaces spanning a great distance. The Tinside Lido in Plymouth, UK, was the site for one of my *TaskForce* performances. Conducting a site inventory was a challenge given its scale, multiple levels, and the number of views of the seaside pool, but the inventory process proved invaluable.

Videography is another tool to aid site inventory. Video footage of a site helps measure distance in real time. Recording a walk-through of a space is one way to capture distance, time, and physical features. However, video is not a substitute for photography, which can communicate visual information at a glance, while video requires more time to watch.

Ultimately, regardless of what methods you use, recording the distance and size of all things found on a site is essential to understanding and recalling the scale of your potential performance space. Knowing the exact feet/meters of a space or the distance between two design elements (windows, steps, columns, etc.) can determine how to place performers in that space. What are the right proportional numbers of bodies for a site? Site inventory provides the means to make calculations and decisions about the placement of performers and the size of your entire cast. In preparation for creating *Fenestrations* in Grand Central Terminal, I walked through the four stories of catwalks on which the dancers would perform, measured the windows' width, and ascertained three bodies, with arms fully outstretched to their sides, would comfortably fit inside each window. That measurement made it possible to calculate how many bodies would fill the entire performance area: three windows per floor, multiplied by four floors, meant engaging 36 dancers.

The first purpose of a site inventory is to immerse yourself in a site and experience its physical character. Getting exact measurements is useful, but, if possible, once you have completed your first or second site inventory, ask the stakeholders of the site to provide you with whatever architectural or topographical plans that are available. These official plans will help you make specific production decisions around any technical needs or will simply speed the process of visualizing the space once rehearsals and the production process have started.

Some prompts to keep in mind during the process:

- Are there any significant design elements found on the site that a performance could highlight?
- Are there any particular perspectives within the site that interest you?
- What are the varieties of geometric shapes within the site? Count and describe them.
- What are the site's elements and textures (i.e., grass, cement, sand, glass, rough, smooth, etc.)?

What constitutes a significant design element? Some cannot be ignored, given their sheer size (a staircase, a fountain) or placement within a space (window, column, tree). But are there other less obvious design elements (door handles, window frames, inlaid floor patterns) that can be considered significant when taken into account as a whole? Taking inventory and categorizing as many design elements as possible, including their geometric shapes, are strategies for making sense of a site. Once you have accounted for these shapes, begin to notice any patterns that link them. Does the design of the lamps relate to the door design? The goal is to get a clear image of the site by picking apart as many details as possible and then conceptually putting these elements back together into a new cohesive image. Finding interesting perspectives that can connect these elements to the audience will dictate how your performers are seen and what kind of movement or content they might perform.

Other aspects to consider are the types of surfaces. During site inventory, feel the surfaces and make a note of their textures and colors. This information was instrumental in costume decisions for *Genesis Canyon* at London's Natural History Museum. The grand entrance hall is full of different textures and surfaces of polished and natural terra cotta tiles and carvings. Craig Givens, the costume designer, selected colors and fabric choices to replicate these visual and tactile elements, allowing the performers to meld with their surroundings.

What sounds do you hear?

The ambient sounds of a space are another critical element to note. What is generating the different sounds? Are the sounds coming from the site itself, or are they nearby? Sound will affect aesthetic and production decisions. Sometimes, sites have ambient sounds that cannot be controlled (animals, fountains, nearby construction, or piped-in background music). The natural or mechanical sounds are as much part of the site as the physical design. Accounting for these ambient sounds in your site inventory is vital. For some sites, to complete a thorough sound inventory, it is best to visit at different times of the day or during the exact time that you anticipate having performances. Cataloging the sounds that may or may not compete with your performance could inspire the work's score.

During my collaboration with composer John King on the Alexander Calder stabile, *Teodelapio* (2012) in Spoleto, Italy, King recorded ambient sounds associated with the site (the sculpture was located on a roundabout in front of the city's train station) and extracted sounds from the Corten steel sculpture itself. His sound collections were incorporated in the work's final score, which blended seamlessly with the actual ambient sounds. The score made it *impossible* for any unintended natural sounds (car horns, bus engines, train sounds) heard during the performance to seem jarring or out-of-place. At times, it was difficult to distinguish the prerecorded sounds of those from the surrounding city.

Sometimes, it's not desirable to compete with the natural sounds of a site. The intensity of the fountain sounds at the site of *Natural Acts in Artificial Water* in Houston and for *Play(as)* (2015) in San Diego inspired my decision to allow those found sounds to replace a recorded or live sound score.

Are there lights in place or only natural lighting? Are there electrical hookups?

Answering these questions will help you decide the time of day or night for your performance. If your budget does not allow for artificial lighting, ascertaining the site's natural light capabilities is paramount. If you have a budget to rent lights or media equipment, knowing how much electrical power is available and where it is located will help determine how many instruments to rent and where to place them. You may also need power for other requirements, such as dressing rooms or safety and visibility conditions in non-performance areas.

Is the site covered or enclosed, or is it open to the outdoors?

Simple observation will answer this question, unless a particular indoor site has access to the outdoors that is not obvious. It's important to look carefully for surprises: walls that open up, windows that seem to open but are forever shut, etc. If you are using an indoor space, note any access to the outdoors—and vice versa. Taking inventory of these spaces can help with determining performance areas and/or pathways for audience flow. Ask questions; don't just rely on observation.

When I made a site visit to the Picnic House in Brooklyn's Prospect Park, the site manager demonstrated how the large space could be divided by a temporary wall that seemed to appear out of nowhere. This knowledge sparked the inspiration to create a visual backdrop for my performance. The REDCAT stage in Los Angeles at Disney Hall is a black box performance space that connects to a loading dock and a street visible to the audience if specific doors are left open. I have seen several artists use this feature when adapting their work for this venue.

What is the size of the location? Is it small and intimate or large and expansive? What are its total dimensions?

Answering these questions has obvious importance for their impact on your design and approach to a site. Are you working to make a large space intimate or a small one grand? Knowing the exact measurements of a site will give you the information needed to calibrate your casting decisions, sound requirements, and audience size. It is possible to treat a large site with a design for an intimate performance and, conversely, to transform a small and intimate site for a large-scale performance. The former can be achieved by limiting the size of the cast and the performance area, and the latter can be achieved by placing a large number of performers in a small space. *Occupy*, designed for a series of small sites found inside the Yerba Buena Gardens in San Francisco, was staged with large casts to give a sense of spectacle and power to each site.

How do visitors to the site normally interact with it? What areas are most frequented?

Suppose your site is in a heavily trafficked area and pedestrian activity is a concern. In that case, you must visit during the intended time and day of the week of the scheduled performance(s) to ascertain how the site is physically affected by regular use. If tourists, not just community members, frequent it, then the time of year could affect how the site is populated. These observations will inform you of any need to manage or alter public access to the site. For example, the Gerald D. Hines Waterwall Park performances took place during a weekend in May when many Houstonians use the park for leisure activities, not to mention as a stage for photos of weddings and quinceañeras, throughout the day. Given the flow of people, I had to make an important decision about whether to engage park security to keep certain areas of the park off limits during the performance. Site visits to the park during the weekend and weekend rehearsals guided my final decision to restrict access because I did not want random people to wander through the sightlines during the performance. It was also possible to alert the public in short 10-minute increments when they needed to move or wait during a specific performance portion.

What areas or locations within the site have potential as a performance field?

You can consider this question toward the end of your site inventory. Some sites will offer several different performance options, and you must decide how many and which specific ones you want to use. This decision is tied directly to several contingencies: budget (more areas might require a bigger budget), audience size (some areas might be too small to accommodate the audience you are seeking), weather (perhaps some areas are indoors and some are outdoors, and you wish to avoid outdoor weather, or you select outdoor sites because you do not want to incur lighting costs).

Some sites can feel intimidating because they present an enormous array of possible performance spaces. As part of a Florida site-commissioning program called *Grass Stains* (produced by Pioneer Winter, 2018), I consulted with dance artist

Sandra Portal-Andreu at the Hialeah Park Race Track near Miami. I was struck by the immense scale and volume of different potential sites found within the track's confines. Given the project budget, which meant working with a small cast, I encouraged her to consider more intimate sites located within the park's campus to avoid having the park's scale diminish the performance's impact.

Hang out, and make more than one visit to the site

> I look to see whether I want to "live" there for a little bit. I find people who have a con-nection to the site and listen to their stories. I have a camping stool that I can carry over my shoulder with my camera and notebook, and I just sit, sit, and sit.
>
> Debra Loewen

The best way to conduct site inventory is to just hang out in the space. Allocate enough time to be on site as a passive observer. Sit or stand in the site and let time go by. Put your phone away. Don't look at your watch. Allow yourself to conduct an open-eyed observational meditation. Allow the visual and physical site to become part of your consciousness so that your subconscious mind can begin to work and perhaps begin to make connections. Your mind will spontaneously formulate images that may have remained hidden after a prior short and cursory experience of the site.

I recommend multiple visits to a site, if possible. Different aspects will inevitably reveal themselves to you with each visit, much like reading a book or watching a movie more than once. With each reading or viewing, your thoughts about the in-tended work will be different because *you* are different, the time is different, even the world around you has changed. This transformation can happen with the passage of one day, one week, a month, or even years. Repeated experiences are never precisely the same; we invariably notice something new each time.

> In 2018, I did a project that was researching dawn. Once a week for an entire year, Mauriah Kraker and I (and sometimes the other collaborators) went to a bit of restored prairie in East Central Illinois, a half-hour before there was any light in the sky. There's something about these visits that produced a particular focus for me. Nobody ever saw us dancing on that site. From that research, we made a dance, which we performed at The Chocolate Factory in Queens, NYC. We asked how do the vibratory, planetary, atmospheric and weather systems shape the body and the choreographic structures? And how do we bring that knowledge and experience into the theater through sound, light, and movement?
>
> Jennifer Monson

If you visit a site for the first or second time without having secured permission for your project, I guarantee that you will see it differently once the site is confirmed—or surrounding circumstances connected to the site may have changed. When I conduct a site inventory before signing a contract, everything is theoretical, no matter how clear my observations of the site. Once the project has officially begun, everything theoretical has to become practical. The most extreme example of such a transformation occurred for The Wooden Floor commission of *Passage/Home* (2021). My first site visit to The Wooden Floor building was in 2019, two years before the premiere. My site research enabled me to create an artistic plan that would support the grant writing for the production (to the National Endowment for the Arts and California Arts Council) and communicate my artistic vision to the greater community. Eight months later, the pandemic brought sweeping changes. I was compelled to conduct several other site visits to research new possibilities for production and presentation.

My original plan for *Passage/Home* included live performances located in small sites throughout the interior of the building. I wanted audiences to experience the space by animating the facilities' less public spaces: administrative offices, the large dressing room (as large as many dance studios), connecting corridors, etc. I had also planned a short section of works around the exterior of the building.

Site visits during the pandemic resulted in a plan with more outdoor locations, and I discovered safe ways for the audience to experience the inside of the facility while also keeping the performers safe: Works could be staged inside and seen through windows or glass doors from the outside as audiences moved around the building. And the new plan inspired three new movement and several media installations—site-based video projections that replaced live performers so that small, controlled groups of audiences (masked and distanced) could move through some of the interior spaces to see these installations. Performers did not have to be stationed there. What did not change were the themes inspired by the history/mission of The Wooden Floor and the current use of the building.

Last Thoughts

Site inventory is one of the most critical steps in your creative process. Spending as much time as possible on this before you embark on your rehearsals will pay dividends and give you confidence in your conceptual approach. No matter how much you rely on the history or current use of a site for your inspiration and your conceptual framework, the physical site contains essential information and is ultimately the vessel for your work.

History

Site inventory is a great way to understand and internalize a site, but an equally useful lens is researching its history. Research as much as time and resources allow, regardless of the nature or scope of your project. Historical research for urban, human-made sites or for natural habitats not only will communicate to the various stakeholders your interest in understanding their culture, thus projecting a sense of professionalism, but will also spark inspiration for shaping your artistic plan. If your performance reflects past history, it can give an audience a feeling of being transported to another time. Your costume design, choice of music, movement vocabulary, and media projections can powerfully evoke this sensation. Your entire vision for the work or even your primary motivation for choosing the site could be tied to historical themes you discover during your research.

> I always do a lot of research, and for almost every project I've ever done, I will take multiple trips to that spot if I'm not already living there. I do lots of workshops in the community. I research the history or the associated artistic vocabularies connected to the project. For example, for *Safe Harbor*, we knew it was going to be about immigration, so we researched the immigrant groups who were part of this waterfront. The Irish were one, so, we found Josephine McNamara, who taught us Irish dance steps; we incorporated that. We found out that there were West Indian immigrants who arrived with all their traditions, African traditions, Brazilian. We learned music from those cultures. We wanted to look for the cultural vocabularies associated with the site's history.
>
> Martha Bowers

An approach

Historical research can begin by asking questions of the site's stakeholders: What makes this site unique? How has the site changed over time? The answers to such broadly phrased questions will give you insight into how deeply connected the site's current occupants feel to its history. If the selected site has historical significance (and attracts visitors for that reason), these conversations could start with more leading questions: What part of the site's history do you find the most interesting? What are some historical facts about the site that are not well known? The purpose of these conversations is to determine if the backstory of a site means something to the general public or local community and could lead you to information not customarily gleaned from internet searches alone. However, if your interviews prove fruitless, you should not abandon your goal to understand the site's past. The internet can also be a valuable resource for pursuing any discoveries that piqued your interest. The combination of online and in-person research can help create a list of books, articles, and visual sources that will create a more comprehensive portrait of the site.

During preproduction, spend as much time on historical research as possible. Even if you believe that your only interest in a site is visual, understanding the historical context of a site is necessary if you are working cross-culturally: outside your neighborhood, region, country, or continent. Gaining an understanding of the history will signal to everyone connected to your project that you are not using the site for your personal designs but are sincerely invested in creating work that responds explicitly to the site with knowledge and sensitivity. If a selected site appears to be remote or uninhabited, research could reveal that it was once a burial ground or the location of a decisive battle or protest. Knowing this information before production can help prevent you from working on site in a potentially inappropriate manner. Everyone who works with you from the surrounding community will have more confidence that you respect their past.

Site history, land use, and ownership

The evermore frequent practice of Native American land acknowledgment in the United States, which is more common in New Zealand, Australia, and Canada, contextualizes events or public social gatherings using information on specific site history. Indigenous land acknowledgment is a formal statement that commemorates and recognizes the distinct indigenous societies connected to the land. Its purpose is to raise awareness of colonization and honor the legacy of the affected indigenous people and their relationship to the land, signal a commitment to present-day dialogue around land ownership, and encourage new relationships with indigenous communities. Choreographer and director Emily Johnson of the Yup'ik Nation, whose company Catalyst (based in Lenapehoking, also known as New York City) has created a body of work that actively promotes "justice, sovereignty, and well-being," engages "audienceships within and through space, time, and environment—interacting with a place's architecture, peoples, history, and role in building futures" (www.catalystdance.com). Johnson's work, for both stage and specific sites, makes extensive use of history and community as foundations for creation. She has been a leader in expanding indigenous rights and culture awareness.

> I have a background in history, and I will always look at the history of the site first. Maybe that's visiting archives, finding out what was there apart from what's there now, what's underneath that history. So we'll be looking at the layers of history. I want to know who owns the land, what's the story of ownership. I also do my own physical mapping by going there and sitting, spending time watching people, observing the life of a place across time. I'll go at different times of the day to see how the light moves and the flows of traffic and people. That would be my primary research before I engage other collaborators or dancers. I also make recordings. I'll take photographs, video, and sound files.
>
> Carol Brown

For *Liquid Landscapes* (2009) in the Devon, UK, area, I selected two sites historically connected to Sir Francis Drake, the famous 16th-century explorer. He had lived in the area and was responsible for bringing water to the city of Plymouth. As a white artist ignorant of Black history, I didn't know that Drake was also a notorious slave trader. I failed to follow my own advice: I did not conduct thorough, objective research. In my eagerness to explore the theme of water in these popular locations, I limited my research to my theme and missed an opportunity to create a richer, potentially more nuanced and powerful production that would have been more sensitive to and respectful of historical truth. This embarrassing experience offers a cautionary tale that illustrates the importance and value of conducting proper historical research.

Architectural/design history

Suppose you are working in a site such as a park, garden, edifice, passageway, etc. In that case, a starting point is to research the designer/architect/urban planner and what motivated the design vision. What was the historical context that influenced the creation of the site? Did the site have specific functions? Did the edifice replace something else, or was the existing structure repurposed? What historical aesthetic forces informed the selection, the design, and the philosophical concepts it embodies? Delving into the designer's biography and the circumstances surrounding the design can be rewarding: The past can illuminate the present. Ascertaining the role that the site has had within the greater community over time is the aim of this research.

Environmental/ecological history

Researching natural sites can be more challenging, but no less critical. Looking at the ecology, geology, and biology of such sites will reveal their inherent nature and energy source. Additionally, the history of the location is pertinent. Was a forest always a forest? Or was it at one point submerged? What is the makeup of the earth beneath the trees? What kind of trees are found in that area, and why? Did humans ever use this site for habitation, war, exploration? Who owned the land in the past? Is it possible that the location was once a burial ground? An awareness of any indigenous land ownership results in a more thorough understanding of a site.

Historical events and use

For *Genesis Canyon* in London (Photo 4.1), the specific site was the grand entrance hall, which, when first visited, overwhelmed my visual sensibility. The initial fear was that any performance created for the space could never match its ornate decorative design. Putting those concerns aside, I decided to explore the rich history of the building and museum. I discovered that it was built as a "cathedral to nature" (nhm.ac.uk) and that it opened when Charles Darwin's theories and writings on evolution were first popular. The museum's mission is to catalog and illuminate the

Photo 4.1 *Genesis Canyon*, first section (1996) by Stephan Koplowitz, Natural History Museum, London, 1996.
Photo © Tricia de Courcy Ling.

history of natural life on our planet. The more I discovered, the more inspired I became to capture this history in my artistic plan. I decided that the narrative structure would follow the theme of the history of life; that three singing performers dressed in Victorian costumes, playing the role of tourists who, with an invented language, sang their conversation, would debate the concept of evolution; that the title of the work, *Genesis Canyon*, would reflect the idea of life beginning and evoke a spiritual and biblical connection. I could not ignore the building's history, and it guided the artistic vision, giving the audience a sense of history unfolding during the 50-minute performance.

Two years after the premiere of *Genesis Canyon*, I experienced Joanna Haigood's *Invisible Wings* at the Jacob's Pillow dance festival. This site-specific work was wholly conceived and inspired by Jacob's Pillow history as one stop on the 19th century Underground Railroad—a network of safe routes and houses for escaping slaves. Haigood's plan reflected her extensive research into the history of US slaves and how they navigated through the Berkshires and locations on the Pillow campus. Most people who walk through the fields and along the dirt paths surrounding the Pillow would never have known this history had it not been uncovered and rediscovered in her work.

Choreographer Amara Tabor-Smith delved into the more recent history of a person and a community with her work *He Moved Swiftly but Gently Down the Not*

Photo 4.2 Selected moments from *He Moved Swiftly but Gently Down the Not Too Crowded Street: Ed Mock and Other True Tales in a City That Once Was*, (2013) by Amara Tabor-Smith, Oakland, CA.
Photo Rami Margron, Beli Sullivan, courtesy Amara Tabor-Smith.

Too Crowded Street: Ed Mock and Other True Tales in a City That Once Was (2013, Photo 4.2). The five-and-half-hour site-specific event was inspired the life of a beloved Bay Area dance teacher, mentor, and choreographer, Ed Mock. The work, exploring an extensive history of San Francisco culture and events, touches on, in Amara's own words, "questions of legacy, lineage, and collective memory."

Last Thoughts

Using the lens of history should be an integral part of any site-specific project. History can both inspire and provide a more complete understanding of your chosen site. Allow sufficient time for historical research. Ignoring it could result in unforeseen complications or give the surrounding community and stakeholders the impression that you are attempting cultural appropriation.

Current Use

This third lens of inquiry is based on the current use and public perception of a site. How is it being used today? Are people using it as originally intended? If not, how did its current use evolve? What do people think of the site in terms of its practicality, accessibility, or management? What are people's hopes and dreams for the site? As with historical research, conducting interviews is one way to start the process. Speak with as many people as time allows: owners, caretakers, employees (from administrators to maintenance workers). If time permits, have discussions about the site with the local community and people beyond the immediate community.

Follow up the interviews with online research, viewing recent news articles, blog posts, videos, and pictures. The ubiquitous use of phone cameras has created unprecedented views of our world. Searching for images of a particular location or institution on Instagram or YouTube can reveal the plethora of ways in which people are interacting with a specific site. Using hashtags (#) makes it possible to see what hundreds and thousands of people say about a particular place. For example, #bryantpark (the site of one of my projects) has almost 600,000 posts on Instagram today, and a quick perusal of the posts offers, as the name suggests, instant perspectives of the park through pictures and words. Searches on YouTube for Bryant Park will provide thousands of videos that can make you feel almost like you are taking a walk through the park. Searching the visual media on Pinterest can also yield impressive results.

I have also used Google Earth, which is engaged in mapping both the exterior and interior worlds. One entire section of Google Earth contains visual records of the interior of many significant buildings, such as museums, around the world. I use this service for remote site visits either before or after an in-person visit. Online research, combined with the increased ease of uploading video and pictures, provides a useful investigative tool for understanding recent history and current use of a site.

Spending time on-site during your site inventory sessions will also give you a sense of how people are using a site. Multiple visits at different times of day will allow you to see who uses the site for what and when. When working at the Yerba Buena Gardens in San Francisco, I noticed many people coming to the park early to practice tai chi, yoga, or other physical activities. At midday, workers arrived with salads and sandwiches for their lunch break, and the afternoon brought parents and young children. Weekend activities were different from those of weekdays, and it was interesting to notice how weather influenced some activities and had no effect on others. All this information helped me assess the crowds' size and the activities that animated specific areas, information that aided my conceptual framework for the project.

Understanding how the public uses and perceives a site is essential and may be slightly more relevant than learning about a site's more distant past. The feelings and opinions of the current stakeholders could directly influence their relationship to your artistic plans. Knowledge of everyday use can help you understand administrative decisions on your request for permits and access. I was denied access to the Round Reading Room of the British Library when that library was still housed within the British Museum precisely because the library administrators wanted to avoid publicity. Highlighting the reading room, given the controversial decision that would soon see the library move out of the museum to a new and equally controversial building, made my request for access a complete non-starter. Ironically, two years later, I was invited to work at the new British Library expressly because the public had not yet accepted the new library's home. Now, the library administrators wanted publicity that might increase foot traffic to the new building.

In response to this invitation, I created *Babel Index*, inspired by the design elements of the space and the mission and collections of the library. This new building had no prior history, only the recent history of a few months and much debate. Therefore, I worked toward making art that highlighted the library as a unique repository of knowledge and transformed the physical space, showing the public its possibilities and beauty. Unlike my work at London's Natural History Museum, *Babel Index* had no narrative or overarching story; the work was abstract and purposefully immersed the audience in a promenade through the building lasting an hour and a half.

Remote natural sites

These stories of challenges you can face when working in buildings might suggest that it's easier to select an outdoor site. However, be careful: Selecting a remote location does not immunize you from societal scrutiny. A remote location may seem devoid of daily human activity, but that does not mean there is currently no activity in that space.

Large public parks and trails have rules and regulations that need to be followed: There are limits on capacity for both vehicles and people, as well as issues of access and permits or some environmental laws—all of which could affect your conceptual, performance, and marketing plans. Your first step should be to ascertain who manages or owns the land and to set up a meeting. Once again, the possibility of any indigenous land ownership should be part of your research.

During a site consultation with dance artist Jenny Larsson for *Grass Stains* (2016), we conducted a site visit at the Matheson Hammock Park (outside Miami, Florida). We entered the park on a long dirt path that cut through thick vegetation replete with local flora. For most of our time inside the park, we seemed to be completely alone. At the end of our almost two-hour visit, the topic of permits and access arose. We felt so alone that we briefly considered foregoing that step. We couldn't imagine an owner or the need for a manager. Still, we did know that undiscovered or unmanaged land doesn't exist in the United States. Fortunately, as we were exiting the park, we ran into a ranger who directed us to the office at the edge of the park, where we discovered that a substantial amount of paperwork would be required. The ranger also spoke of disagreements and tension among the dog-loving public and the hikers and birders. This all made sense when we heard it, but before our serendipitous encounter with the ranger, we had no idea about it. Ultimately, Larsson chose another site, specifically because the Matheson Hammock Park had very restrictive rules governing video/photo documentation and weekend activities. However, it would have been easy for us to assume that permits were not needed given the natural habitat's location and apparent emptiness.

Last Thoughts

Researching a site's current use and recent history is not a step you should ever omit, especially if your project requires official permissions. The permitting process can be a productive part of your research because you will inevitably meet people whose pride or sense of duty will prompt them to share valuable information and their own feelings about the site. These conversations will result in a deeper understanding of your site that can help shape your artistic vision and create an event that resonates with your audience.

Community

> The community we initially worked with were bird watchers whom we asked to do a breeding bird count of the area in and around the Ridgewood Reservoir. They hadn't realized that the reservoir was there and how rich it was for bird watching. And then we discovered that some people descended into the drained reservoir to play paintball. There was a kind of illicit or unprogrammed community use of the reservoir that shifted its ecology. All those things began to influence my research and to culminate in the project. We did a solstice performance from dawn to dusk, which was about 18 hours long, and we brought in members of the community to perform with 20 performers from my dance community. But most of the impact was just the kind of research that we did by going out there three times a week: our steady presence and the collaborations with scientists whom we brought to the site from the Parks Department.
>
> Jennifer Monson

Investigating and understanding a community requires that you spend time interacting with the people who live in a neighborhood, town, village, region—whatever geographical area that you feel constitutes the greater community of the site that interests you. This research requires that you set aside your preconceptions and discover what the local population thinks and feels about the place. For example, imagine that you are invited to do a project in Paris, and your predisposition is to create a work for the Eiffel Tower because of its popularity as a symbol and architectural wonder. You start chatting with Parisians in different locations around the city. These conversations will inevitably deepen your understanding of what the locals value about their city and how they think about the tower. The result might be that you discover a few other Paris sites that would be potentially more meaningful choices, choices that start to excite you more than the tower. Or your conversations might reinforce your initial attraction to the tower, but now your thoughts are more informed, more deeply imbued with a Parisian sensibility. The purpose of exploring a site through the lens of community values is to allow your vision to be influenced and shaped so that the production will ultimately resonate powerfully with your local audiences. In essence, you are initiating a dialogue between your aesthetic frame of reference and the local culture.

Long-term inquiry

During the last 10 years, a new generation of site artists have committed to creating site-inspired and site-specific works that are born out of a long-term (multi-year) investment in one specific place or community connected to their place of residence. NAKA Dance Theater (José Ome Navarrete Mazatl and Debby Kajiyama) and Amara Smith (Deep Water Dance Theater), both based in Oakland, California; Emily Johnson (Catalyst) in New York City; and nibia pastrana santiago in San Juan, Puetro Rico, to name just four, make environmentally sensitive site works that not only engage community members as performers but speak directly to social concerns that are both local and universal. They follow generationally such artists as Anna Halprin, Joanna Haigood (Bay Area, California), Heidi Duckler (Los Angeles, California), and Martha Bowers (Brooklyn, New York), many of whom continue to create and present site and environmentally based work in their home communities. Long-term commitments to a community, over years not months, bring new meaning to the term artist-in-residence and result in deeper sensitivity to the chosen environment.

Initial inquiry (first visit to a site)

Walk, drive, take whatever public transportation is available, and visit as many different parts of the community as possible. During your travels, meet and interview people, both through formal appointments and spontaneously during your journey. Ask questions: What makes your community special? What buildings or places reflect that specialness? What most matters to you and your neighbors? What locations, either currently or historically, represent the values of your community? What is the most important thing to have happened in your community? Where did it happen? Meaningful research requires several conversations and visits to all sites that are mentioned during your discussions. This process needs to occur over time and with as many people as possible. The exploration of community should not feel rushed. This research can seem time consuming and even labyrinthine at first, but the results will strengthen the specificity of the art and foster a higher level of immersion for both you and your audiences.

> A site can be a building, a park, but there's also who inhabits that site. So, ask, who are you and what is your relationship to those people in that site? Historically, find out who is missing from that site, what has been erased or invisibilized? Why are they missing? Find out who has privilege and who doesn't. The answers are deep and nuanced. The deeper you go, the more you discover. Finding the nuances within a community, that's what artists do.
>
> Debby Kajiyama

The process can begin before you have started to develop any specific artistic plans, or you may approach your research with a theme or concept already in mind. When I was working on *Liquid Landscapes*, which had water as a unifying theme, I spent several weeks, over many months, investigating different parts of the Devon region of the UK, concentrating on sites located within a 50-kilometer radius of Plymouth. Over two years, I made four, week-long visits to the area before starting rehearsals. Collaborating with a local producer, Lara Lloyd (working with Dartington Arts at that time), who grew up and lived in that area, was a huge advantage. This type of partnership is ideal for any project that occurs beyond your own home or region. In conversations with Lloyd, I explained in great detail my definition of what constituted a water-related site. I was interested in visiting sites with actual water and discovering sites with less obvious connections to water. Before each site visit, Lloyd scheduled meetings with people in places she believed would be relevant in our search. As both a producer and a member of the community that I was researching, she proved to be a powerful presence in guiding my exploration into the community of greater Plymouth, research that influenced the entire work and production.

The influence of community on site selection

Your understanding of a community and its values can influence your selection of sites. When Gustavus Adolphus College in Minnesota commissioned me to honor its 150th anniversary in 2012, rather than finding one or two sites that I thought would inspire me, I wanted to discover what had made the college and its community unique during its 150 years. I spent several days walking through the campus and interviewing students, faculty, and administrators. Lutherans founded the school, and I conducted interviews to understand how Lutheran values were embodied in the community and the physical campus. These discussions inspired the choice of each of the four sites that I ultimately selected for this project.

Amara Tabor-Smith, a resident of Oakland who is aware of the issues and values of that community, created *House/Full of Black Women, a work* (Photo 4.3)

Photo 4.3 *House/Full of Black Women* (2017) created by Amara Tabor-Smith in collaboration with Ellen Sebastian Chang, downtown Oakland.
Photo © Robbie Sweeny, courtesy Amara Tabor-Smith.

described on her website as "a site-specific ritual performance project that addresses issues of displacement, well-being, and sex-trafficking of black women and girls in Oakland. Set in various public sites throughout Oakland over a five-year period, this community-engaged project is performed as a series of episodes that are driven by the core question, 'How can we, as black women and girls find space to breathe and be well within a stable home?'" Each iteration of this project has taken place in a public site inspired by her research and connections to Oakland.

The influence of community on theme

> We don't pick sites like "Oh, that's a cool place; let me go do something there." It's more that we want to work with folks who work or live in this place and this happens to be the site that is most connected with them.
>
> José Ome Navarrete Mazatl

Site artist and producer Martha Bowers, who has dedicated much of her career to the Red Hook community in Brooklyn, described how working in Red Hook began:

"The very first work I ever did . . . in . . . Red Hook was called *On the Waterfront* and was actually triggered by an event. The local elementary school principal was killed in a shootout when he went to try to catch a student who was running back home. He got caught in a drug shootout, and it was, you know—it was just devastating to the whole community. I had been a teaching artist for lots of different organizations, so I just offered to teach a free performing arts program, and that became the seed. Then I started a program at the senior center, and so then it was like, Well, what? What do you all have to say about your community? What would you like to see changed? And so, the kids and seniors—it was—very clearly, it was about violence in the community in the aftermath of the crack epidemic. So that became what the piece was about.

Like Bowers, you will discover that an initial investment of time and energy in the community can result in unearthing themes that will inspire your work.

> I encourage artists to become part of a community. I think that's how you can contribute to political change. That's how you can have an impact. You can't really have a significant impact if you bounce in and out of places. If you stay in a place and you're committed to it, you get involved. I see a lot of new collaborations focused on COVID relief with people in my community right now. I've seen the wealthier, gentrified side of Red Hook work with those in need—seniors, people in public housing. I've seen those two communities come together more than I have in the past. So get to know your community. Show up; that's the biggest thing: Show up. Show up to things even though they're not an interest of yours. Show up if they're having a meeting about police and policing. Show up if they're having a townhall. Show up, and do more than just be an artist. Listen, and be engaged, and engage with things that aren't necessarily just about the arts.
>
> Martha Bowers

The influence of community on casting

Delving into a community can inspire you to involve its members to perform or participate in the creation of your work. Martha Bowers in that first site project in Red Hook ended up casting the children and seniors whom she was teaching during her initial introduction to that community, and "the content was really determined by them, and then how can we enlarge that—expand that, given the sort of enormity of the space that we had to work in." Her solution was to fill the space with her students.

Forklift Danceworks in Austin, Texas, is a site-oriented company that creates entire productions cast with only the specific community members hosting the work. The company has taken its community-based work to swimming pools, featuring the lifeguards, staff, and nearby residents of three Austin public pools; to college campuses, where they conducted a series of performances called *On Campus: Dances for College Campus Employees* (2018–2019), featuring dishwashers, custodians, physical plant staff, or maintenance crews as the sole performers in the works; and to many other sites and communities. The company spends extensive time researching a community through in-depth dialogue and site visits before embarking on a project.

Last Thoughts

Exploring and assessing possible sites using the four lenses defined in this chapter can yield real rewards. They are research tools that will help you organize your approach, deepen your understanding of sites, generate creative ideas, and strengthen your connection to your prospective audiences. Each of the four lenses has its merits and strengths, but you would be wise to consider using all four in some capacity for each project. The more time you can devote to this preliminary work, the more likely you will be to cast off your preconceptions, and the more your work will be shaped explicitly by the site.

PART III

FUELING YOUR VISION

5
Staffing Key Production Roles

When establishing new work roles or entering a group with already established roles, you must be keenly aware of inherent power dynamics in relation to your role as lead artist with collaborators and with the host producers. Such an awareness will engender more sensitivity in discussions about fee payment and workload assignments that each team member will absorb (all stemming from the requirements of your artistic/production vision). Conducting candid and specific conversations about your expectations concerning workload with everyone from producers to performers will help instill positive and productive relationships. This topic is even more pertinent in the next two chapters (Chapter 6 Negotiating Fee and Contract; Chapter 7 Planning Your Planning Budget) where your relationship to a potential producing partner and prioritizing needs in relation to funding are discussed.

This chapter defines various production roles that you can consider as you determine the composition of the production team you need to assemble (Photo 5.1). The number of staff positions you can fill will vary depending on the project's size and financial resources. Your job is to determine which roles are most important. To help you anticipate challenges that may arise in a project and prioritize your

Photo 5.1 Production meeting for *The Northfield Experience* by Stephan Koplowitz (2018) with lead producer and production manager Janice Roberts (at center), at St. Olaf College, Northfield, MN.
Photo courtesy Stephan Koplowitz.

On Site. Stephan Koplowitz, Oxford University Press. © Oxford University Press 2022. DOI: 10.1093/oso/9780197515235.003.0006

staffing needs, the following discussion will explore each supporting role's duties and responsibilities.

Executive Producer

As the lead artist, you should assume the role of a producer in some capacity in all projects. If you are working with another institution (a commissioning body or presenting organization), that institution will typically provide an executive producer with whom you will partner as a collaborating producer. The benefits of having outside executive producers are manifold. Under most circumstances, they will take the lead, with your support, in any grant-writing and fundraising activities. Or they will support you if you are leading the grant-writing process. Whatever the relationship, your partnerships with executive producers can offer a stronger platform for raising money from foundations or government entities. Additionally, working with another producer can open new avenues of funding possibilities because many producers have their own relationships with individual donors and foundations.

Working with an executive producer will also help define the project and formalize your role as artist and producer of the work. Because of their obligations to the commissioning body, executive producers will establish a budget cap, the length of the production and rehearsal period, and the amount of access you will have to the site. Although you will have a voice in all these decisions, your commissioning producer will have the final say. Unless these limits adversely affect your production's artistic integrity, you should treat them not as negative impositions but as another set of fixed factors to address when creating the work. A site-specific project is specific not only to the site but also to the needs, abilities, and mission of the partners involved in producing the work.

Increasingly, site projects are seen as part of community and audience development; often, commissioning partners will request that a project involve specific members of their community. My work with Laura Faure on *Mill Town* (2017) was a good example. She invited me to create the work simultaneously with a request that I engage specific members of both the greater Lewiston/Auburn (L/A) and Bates Dance Festival communities. In this instance, we involved the Bates Dance Festival Youth Arts Program (young students, ages 10–16, from the greater L/A region), local high school dancers, and several Bates dancers. This cast was augmented by eight professional dancers who came from both Maine and New York City. For *Aquacade for Asphalt Green*, the Asphalt Green Recreational Center required that I work with its community of middle and high school swimmers and athletes and an ensemble of invited Olympic swimmers and divers. The instructions were quite specific: to use 90 students and create at the swimming center a 30-minute performance containing a specified number of dives and laps to be exhibited by the five Olympic athletes.

The job description for the executive producer (presenting/commissioning organization) is as follows, with annotations:

- *In consultation with the artist, hires and oversees the project manager/associate producer, rehearsal director, and all other host production team members.*

Typically, hiring the essential personnel is a collaborative effort involving you and the executive producer.

- *In consultation with the artist, creates the budget, including the artist's fee and all project costs, and oversees fundraising.*

Although the executive producers usually take responsibility for raising funds to meet the budget, they will ask you for support.

- *Keeps track of all line-item expenditures in the budget.*

The executive producer has the final say in how money is spent and needs to be consulted if any changes are made to the working budget.

- *In consultation with the artist, creates and funds a marketing and press campaign/plan.*

The marketing campaign is the means for communicating the project to the wider world, and executive producers ensure that the messaging reflects the mission of the host institution.

- *In cooperation with the project manager, coordinates all major aspects of the project, especially securing all site permissions and required insurance.*

Hiring a project manager who is compatible with both the executive producer and the primary artist is essential, given the many negotiations that a site project requires.

Like primary artists, executive producers serve as production cheerleaders to motivate and energize the entire team through their enthusiasm and commitment to the project. It is important to start any project with a clear, positive relationship with your executive producer and to maintain honest and timely communication during your project.

Project Manager/Associate Producer

Once you and your executive producer have agreed to embark on a creative partnership, you will need to discuss who will coordinate, manage, and support the project.

After you and your producer have developed a list of production needs, you must decide whether to divide this list between you or to hire a project manager. A project manager is either someone already on staff at the commissioning institution or an outside professional from the broader community. If the candidate is already on staff, you will have to hope you are paired with a compatible person. If the job is to be posted, then insist that you take part in interviewing candidates.

Working with a project manager can expedite resolution of the many production challenges you will encounter before and during a project's creation. Sometimes, the biggest challenge when working on a site away from your own community is locating and meeting the right people. You will need to forge partnerships with site administrators, individual artists, and community organizations that can help with finding performers and building audiences.

The first step in forging a productive relationship is to make sure that your vision and needs for the work are thoroughly communicated and understood. This relationship is intensely collaborative, and sharing your past work, overall artistic vision, and mission will help any project manager work with you more sensitively. When I work in communities far from my home base, the project manager helps me navigate the local culture and politics. This person will sometimes make the first contact with others whom you may want to involve in your project.

Unless you or someone you have hired (if you are self-producing) fills this role, project managers will have a dual loyalty. As employees of the commissioning organization, their role is to protect that institution and shield other employees from spending time on the site project. At the same time, they have a responsibility for the integrity and success of the project. They are working to help you realize your vision. This dual role doesn't have to create a conflict of interest, but it is a dynamic that you need to understand so that you treat your project manager sensitively. Good project managers/associate producers will give you honest feedback and advice when they perceive your artistic plans as counterproductive or politically/culturally insensitive to the greater community. Creating an honest and open exchange of ideas with project managers is extremely important. Unless you possess firsthand knowledge of the issues in question, do not ignore their advice.

Over the years, I have worked with many different project managers, but two stand out in tackling large site projects: Lara Lloyd, who single-handedly helped produce the entire *TaskForce* UK project throughout seven sites around Plymouth; and Janice Roberts, who not only initiated *The Northfield Experience* (2018) but coordinated and produced the project. In both instances, Lloyd and Roberts were employees of the host presenters (Dartington Arts and St. Olaf College, respectively) and also members of the local communities, and both exerted significant influence on their communities. A project manager who lives and works in the area can help you avoid unnecessary conflicts or roadblocks and help solve such problems if they arise.

During our preproduction site visits in Northfield, Minnesota, we presented our project to the Northfield City Council, seeking financial support and city services (police, parking) at no cost. At one of those meetings, Roberts spoke not only as the lead manager of the project and a professor at St. Olaf College, but as a taxpaying homeowner in Northfield for over 25 years. As a parent of two children, she knew the town's infrastructure, educational offerings, and culture and had contacts within the community that proved invaluable. We were successful in securing both funding and the vital cooperation of city services. Similarly, Lara Lloyd was a resident of Devon, UK. She grew up in that area, understood the region's unique characteristics, and had specific knowledge of towns and cities near Plymouth. She also had a network of valuable contacts that went beyond her employment at Dartington Arts. Her community knowledge enabled us to secure permissions to several sites and discover new locations.

Both Lloyd and Roberts started working as project managers at the very beginning, when I had only a general idea of what I wanted to accomplish. My partnership with each of them helped actualize the projects. As you spend more time with your project manager, you begin to develop the ability to think together with a sense of synchronicity, a learned shorthand that doubles your ability to think through ideas and strategies. Finding sites, gaining access, locating artistic collaborators, forging community partnerships, securing rehearsal space are the results of the creative energy and problem-solving that project managers offer. They bring to life the artistic vision through their ability to channel the resources of the outside world.

The job description for project manager/associate producer is as follows, with annotations:

- *Works closely with the artist and is the liaison with the executive producer once the project is in motion; is good at multi-tasking, can handle delicate and time-sensitive negotiations, and has excellent interpersonal skills. All decisions and information about the project are coordinated through this person.*

Having a project manager who has solid experience that reflects these qualities is essential. For a smaller, less pressured project, you could engage a talented, less experienced person. Still, the best person for this position is someone who only needs to be informed of your vision and needs, not trained or requiring supervision to take initiative and make decisions.

- *Is the primary point-person for all aspects of the production at all times, does whatever it takes to make sure the production is moving forward, and ensures that the project adheres to the established budget and commissioning organization's policies.*

Progress requires a production schedule (usually created by the project manager, the artist, and the executive producer). The project manager ensures that all deadlines are met.

- *Directly coordinates all the logistics of the artist's site visits, including flights, accommodation, etc.; sets up a schedule of activities that will occur during visits, including meetings, etc.; and creates the master schedule for these visits.*

These duties ensure that a production stays on course and directly influence your working conditions. Before the start of rehearsals, you may need as many as three to four preproduction site-visits. Each of those visits has an agenda, and project managers are responsible for making that plan a reality. For example, they may need to organize an audition or set up interviews with potential composers, costume designers, or site stakeholders. Any specific needs you have pertaining to your accommodation are also usually handled by project managers. Their ability to find suitable housing in terms of size, cleanliness, amenities, and location can affect your morale and frame of mind while working. Ensuring that your time is fully maximized during these visits and that the priorities of the production are being addressed are the main goals.

- *Assists in locating potential artistic collaborators in consultation with the artist and executive producer.*

Some project managers will have their own contacts within an artistic community; if not, they should be comfortable making cold calls to introduce the necessary number of artists to the project.

- *Coordinates dialogue as needed among all artistic collaborators.*

Once a project has begun, the project manager can facilitate discussions and meetings among collaborators. A smaller project may not require this function, but with constant deadlines and long rehearsals, having someone else coordinate meetings saves you time.

- *Attends all meetings during the artist's site-visits unless explicitly asked not to participate.*

I recommend that you allow project managers to shadow you during all meetings in order to understand your needs, the needs of the other artists, and the progress or lack of progress being made. By fostering a sense of partnership that invites a free exchange of ideas and impressions you can get honest feedback about your interactions with others.

- *If directed by the executive producer and/or artist, instigates, negotiates, and coordinates all permissions for site/performance venues.*

This aspect of the production becomes more important if you are working over several sites or if the site has an extensive administrative bureaucracy. If permissions have been obtained before hiring production managers, their responsibility is to maintain good relationships with site administrators.

- *Coordinates with the artist and executive producers all aspects of marketing, including programs for performances. Works in tandem with press and all other relevant marketing personnel.*

Managing the marketing campaign from afar (if your site is distant from your home) is not always possible, so your project manager is better positioned to ensure that deadlines are met and solve problems that arise.

- *Ensures that all collaborators have necessary information at all times and is the agent who will deliver that information if needed.*

The project manager (with your input) is the primary source of keeping everyone informed and connected to the pulse of the project.

- *Coordinates the scheduling and procurement of rehearsal space, costumes, technical needs, and hiring of personnel (both paid and volunteer) for the production. Works closely with the technical director on these duties.*
- *Keeps track of all expenditures as dictated by the budget to provide accurate and timely reports to the executive producer and artist.*

The executive producer and artist must always have up-to-date information about production expenses to make any necessary revisions to the budget. However, production managers make no budgetary allocations without first consulting with the artist and executive producer. Some budgets include funds for unforeseen emergencies (caused by, for example, weather or a sudden loss of personnel) when budgetary decisions need to be made quickly. Project managers facilitate but do not make these decisions.

- *Keeps clear records of the project's progress and is ready to give verbal or written reports on the status of the production at any time to the artist and executive producer.*

Project managers should schedule weekly production meetings with all primary production and artistic collaborators. These meetings can expedite communication and help to facilitate problem-solving.

- *Coordinates hiring and firing deemed necessary by the production team.*

As an agent of the executive producer and in consultation with you, project managers ultimately create all contracts for each new hire, usually in concert with either the institution's lawyers or members of the human resources department. If terminations are necessary, they sometimes deliver the news to the employee with you and/or the executive producer present.

- *Is frequently on site and is present daily during the last two to three weeks of the production, or as needed.*

As the premiere approaches and more people become involved, especially technical (sound, lights, video) and front-of-house (audience, ticketing, etc.) personnel, the project manager must be present daily. On the other hand, once these roles are filled and the project is moving smoothly on schedule, the technical director may be able to take on some of the work load and reduce the need for the project manager's constant presence. You and the project manager can make that decision.

- *Is physically present during all technical rehearsals (as deemed necessary by the artist and/or technical director) and all performances and dress rehearsals.*

The best way to gauge a work's status and help troubleshoot problems is to attend key run-throughs (usually scheduled by the artist) and be present at all performances.

- *Owns or has 100% access to a car (unless the project is taking place in a city with high-density public transportation, e.g., New York, Paris, London).*

Project managers must respond rapidly to sudden problems and manage full schedules of daily meetings that might occur at distant locations. How project managers are compensated for using their own car is negotiated as part of their fee.

Ultimately, the project manager's job is to protect the artist and the executive producer from distractions that interfere with their primary focus—the artistic creation of the project and the integrity of the commissioning organization. The best project managers have the experience and ability to anticipate needs and work proactively.

Rehearsal Director and/or Rehearsal Assistant

Project managers have no responsibility for the performers. Rehearsal directors oversee and manage the rehearsal locations and schedules and are the primary contact for the entire cast.

The main difference between the titles of rehearsal director and rehearsal assistant depends on the jobs you trust them to perform. A rehearsal director is someone you rely on to conduct rehearsals in your absence. Rehearsal assistants take on the organizational and liaison duties but lack the experience to run rehearsals on their own.

It is also possible to engage both a rehearsal director and rehearsal assistant if your production is large enough and has sufficient funding.

Working with a rehearsal director is a luxury and a necessity if your project involves simultaneous events and a large cast that needs to be rehearsed in your absence: an extra pair of eyes allows you to be in two places at once. I usually request support with the rehearsal process if I am working with more than 15 performers, regardless of the number of sites selected.

Your relationship with your rehearsal director (or assistant) is the second most important relationship after the project manager and directly affects the creative process. I always seek experienced artists capable of giving creative feedback that can help me make decisions and save valuable time. As with your project manager, maintaining clear communication of your artistic intentions and sharing past work will ensure that your rehearsal director understands your motivations and vision.

Other essential qualities and duties of the rehearsal director are as follows, with annotations:

- *Is experienced at directing rehearsals, and has the choreographic or theatrical directing experience relevant to your project. A person capable of giving you honest feedback, is well organized, can take precise notes, has a good memory for details, is an excellent communicator, and is approachable.*

Seek to work with rehearsal directors with solid teaching experience, which is even more applicable to the role than creative experience alone. Given the many pressures felt by most casts during a production, you should select someone who is empathetic and sensitive to the workload of the entire cast. You want someone who can tell you (and speak freely) if the rehearsal workload/process seems unhealthy for your cast, for example, if rehearsals are too long with insufficient time for rest. Your rehearsal director should make sure you are working in tandem with all safety protocols in terms of the physical and emotional needs of your performers.

- *Meets with the artist during preproduction and pre- and post-rehearsal times as needed for planning and coordination.*

Your preproduction meetings with the rehearsal director are important to ensure a clear understanding of the project's goals, the physical challenges the site may present, and how these will affect the rehearsal process and safety issues.

- *Rehearses the ensemble of performers to ensure that the performers are executing the performance material in line with the goals of the work.*
- *Is present at all scheduled rehearsals whether the artist is on site or not.*
- *If possible, assists the artist with the auditions for performers.*

I attempt to engage rehearsal directors as early in the process as possible, primarily because I want them to be involved in auditioning and cast selection. Their early presence establishes a sense of partnership in the process and with the chosen cast.

- *Keeps track of performers' attendance.*

The rehearsal director is the contact person for the performers and should know if they will be late or absent.

- *Leads warm-up sessions before each rehearsal (length to be determined by the artist).*

The rehearsal director is responsible for keeping track of each performer's physical needs or past injuries and, when leading a warm-up, keeps this information in mind.

- *Assists the artist during rehearsals as needed (gives feedback if asked, keeps track of changes, etc.).*
- *Is in charge of keeping detailed, legible notes of the creation process.*

The rehearsal director needs to take careful notes, which serve, when required, as a means to recall or revisit creative material that has been taught or discarded. If you feel comfortable asking for feedback on your work, rehearsal directors can provide valuable perspective and ideas.

- *Keeps track of musical counts/structure and is prepared to communicate such information to the composer(s) and instrumentalists as needed.*

As a careful note-taker, the rehearsal director is indispensable when working with a composer who is creating an original musical or sound score and should communicate to various collaborating artists the number of measures and beats, how passages are being counted or tracked, and the length of passages or sections.

- *Attends collaborative and production meetings as necessary.*

It is wise not to burden your rehearsal director with too many meetings; so, if you need to communicate creative material to other collaborators (especially composers), try to schedule those meetings close to or even during already scheduled rehearsals.

My role was to translate the dancers' experience to the choreographer. I reminded him of things like a hard floor or a repetitive motion that was hard or stressful. I remember helping him and the composer by making the music cues more obvious so that the dancers could hear them in the midst of all that they were doing. I think I was like an ambassador for them. I had to caretake the section that had just been created and help the choreographer continue to nurture their sense of pride about it. I occasionally gave him my opinion about something that I thought was not working or could be enhanced.

Sara Hook

Technical Director/Production Manager

These two titles are interchangeable given the similarities of their duties. The difference between production managers and technical directors is that the former do not design lights, sound, or media. A production manager can coordinate and manage resources, like ensuring the availability of storage or obtaining necessary permits or scheduling the timely arrival of deliveries, etc. A technical director is usually someone who has both overseen a technical crew and has experience as a technician in lights, sound, or media and can assume one of these technical roles in a production. A production manager will just oversee and coordinate the work of each technical department.

You will need a technical director/production manager if your production requires lights, sound, or media, in addition to the usual production needs (stage management, costume management, etc.). Once technical rehearsals begin, the technical director or production manager becomes the primary support of the work and the person with whom you will have the most contact.

It is customary to rely on your production manager/technical director to help solve production problems. When I was working on *Babel Index* for the British Library and requested 11 books that would appear to be illuminated from the inside, my first conversation was with the production manager, Simon Byford, who found the right people to fabricate and bring this concept to life. Byford was not involved as a lighting designer, sound designer, or projection designer but ensured that all of these departments worked harmoniously and efficiently.

I have worked on other projects during which a lack of coordination at the technical level allowed some technical team members to extend deadlines and work independently, and so interfere with the work of other collaborators. The bigger the project, the more complicated the potential conflicts, and if you do not want to direct both the production and the artistic side of a work, hiring a technical director/production manager is the best way to keep everyone and everything moving forward effectively.

The following job duties for technical director/production manager need no annotation:

- *Oversees all technical aspects of the production: lights (if needed), costumes, sound, and stage management.*
- *Performs any necessary technical duties if qualified (lights, sound, etc.).*
- *Collaborates with the artist and project manager in all aspects of the production.*

- *Hires personnel (as needed) in full consultation with the artist and project manager.*
- *Does not make any technical/artistic decisions without consulting the artist.*
- *Creates the master production schedule from the arrival to the return of equipment.*
- *Ensures that the production maintains proper safety standards.*
- *Attends all production meetings as needed.*
- *Is present for specific rehearsals and showings as needed.*
- *Is present for all technical rehearsals and performances.*

Production Assistant

A production assistant is invaluable when you are working on site. This position is seen as an entry-level job for someone starting in the field; it requires no specialized technical knowledge, just a good dose of common sense, positive energy, and the ability to anticipate problems and needs.

A production assistant's duties are varied and open-ended and depend on the nature of the project and its location. Some of the more common responsibilities include helping with security (e.g., keeping all the valuables of the cast safe during on-site rehearsals); interfacing with a curious public to prevent interruptions to rehearsals; transporting and setting up rehearsal equipment (sound, video playback, etc.); creating a clean and safe site for rehearsal (removing debris or unwanted chairs or any other moveable items that would impede the use of the site for rehearsal); in the case of injury, transporting and accompanying a performer to seek medical help as needed; assisting the rehearsal director as needed with note-taking or sound/media playback; procuring any necessary food and drink during rehearsals if requested; and during performances, helping the technical staff with installation and/or crowd control. The role entails a varied and valuable set of duties.

Other job duties of the production assistant:

- *Assists the project manager with different aspects of the production when not in rehearsals with the artist or rehearsal director.*
- *Functions as the project manager's eyes, ears, and legs during the creation/rehearsal process. Briefs the project manager of any important needs and information after each rehearsal. Runs errands for both the artist and project manager as needed during rehearsals.*

Stage Manager

During the last weeks of rehearsals, you may need to designate or hire someone to call cues for sound, lights, or media and to ensure that all performers are in place before a performance. Engaging a stage manager, not in the sense of the classic theatrical stage manager who serves the role of rehearsal director/assistant and then transitions to cue-calling during performances, but simply someone who works during technical rehearsals and performances, can be quite helpful. Several team members can assume this role depending on the scale and the budget of a project.

Last Thoughts

The six production roles discussed in this chapter highlight work that must be addressed no matter the size of a production. More than one person can assume some of these duties. But most importantly, you delineate all work that must be accomplished and make a realistic assessment of what is possible under the circumstances. What tasks are you willing to take on yourself? What do you need to delegate to others? Does the artistic plan need to be amended in relation to the available budget and labor pool? Be careful not to overextend yourself in your efforts to accomplish your goals, and be protective of the people whom you engage to support your vision.

6
Negotiating Fee and Contract

Approaching Negotiation

Asking for money, resources, and recognition is challenging at any stage of an artist's career, but when you are just beginning your career, contract negotiations can seem both a novelty *and* a luxury. They are far from either. The purpose of this chapter is to help you think about and develop a strategy for these negotiations. Conversations with potential producing partners will occur with more frequency as your career develops. You will discover that contract negotiations are essential in gathering the support you need and creating a planning budget for your work. Thinking about the terms and conditions under which you wish to work helps you understand your priorities, whether you are self-producing or working in partnership with a producer. The central principle of this chapter, as well as Chapter 7 (Planning Your Planning Budget) and Chapter 8 (Fundraising for Your Artistic Plan), can be summed up with these words: To receive, you must ask.

No one likes rejection. You can increase the likelihood that your requests for financial support will succeed if you prepare. You need to think carefully, specifically, and critically about your artistic vision and goals for any project. The more you work to understand your reasons for making a request, the more precise and unemotional contract negotiations will become. You must also research the organizations with which you intend to partner. This research can help you understand what sorts of projects an organization is likely to support. There are several arts organizations that have resources to help you with this process. In Appendix 2 (under *Additional Chapter Resources*) you will find a few of them to further support your research. Knowledge that can add perspective and build confidence as you prepare for the negotiation process. Knowledge can give you more power.

Working with Producers (keep your eyes open)

Establishing trust

Flexibility and transparency are crucial elements in establishing trusting relationships with producers. Find out what motivates them (and their institution) to produce site-specific work. How does a site project align with their long- and short-term goals? Will your project connect to their mission? Listening, learning, and communicating honestly before making requests will contribute to a more substantial alignment of shared goals in any negotiation.

On Site. Stephan Koplowitz, Oxford University Press. © Oxford University Press 2022. DOI: 10.1093/oso/9780197515235.003.0007

Understanding and being comfortable with your producing partner's perspective can influence your artistic plan and give you a realistic context for the decisions and requests you make. If your producer expresses an interest in working with specific community members or values history and tradition, your site selection or casting ideas may reflect those interests. *Make sure your and your producer's priorities are aligned before signing a contract.* If you discover that your personal and aesthetic priorities are not in alignment, finding alternative sites or institutions or even self-producing may be warranted.

Once you have created your artistic plan and vision for the project, you can begin to formulate the contents of the contract, which also leads to crafting a planning budget. Early discussions of your terms and needs provide a producer time to resolve any problems that might arise, find additional funding, or seek new sources of support without the pressure of looming production deadlines. Proper planning and anticipation of production needs will help establish a trusting and positive relationship with producers.

Don't assume the worst

> Ideally, a commissioner, like the Dancers' Group in San Francisco, says, "Hey, we are not going to tell you what to do or what to say. Tell us how we can support you." For us, it was like a dream.
>
> Debby Kajiyama

At the start of their career, artists often worry that others might not value their vision for a project. However, you can never know what people think or want without *communicating directly with them.* Talking with a producer will expose many shared beliefs, goals, and concerns, and strategies for achieving those goals will stimulate discussion and productive debate. Keep a balanced perspective and remember the following:

- *Producers would not have agreed to partner with or commission you without appreciating your value and unique creative qualities.*

Producers will research your capabilities and artistic accomplishments before making any overture to you. Keep that thought in mind as you continue to develop the dynamics of your relationship.

- *Like you, producers want to bring art and ideas into the world.*

Some producers have the title of artistic director of their department or institution and see their work as an extension of a personal creative vision. Regardless of title, producers, in general, perceive their work as a creative endeavor. When producers choose to collaborate with you, they are inviting you into their inner circle. Your work becomes an extension of their artistic vision and goals. This has positive repercussions as long as the producer maintains respect for your artistic vision.

- *Producers want to build a reputation for producing/presenting quality artistic experiences.*

You and the producer share a desire to create fully nourished and healthy work. Who wants to see unrehearsed performers, shabby costumes, or low-quality projections?

- *Producers understand that art cannot happen without honoring the labor of artists.*

Most producers chose their career because they love art and art-making. Remember that if conflicts arise. Sometimes, they do.

Work to avoid conflict

Producers want to present quality work, but conflicts can arise over the means of achieving this goal. Money tends to be the central issue, although artistic and social concerns are also areas of potential conflict. Your definition of "community engagement" may differ significantly from that of your potential producer. Take the time for thorough research and discussion with potential partners before making commitments.

If money (the budget) is the source of potential conflict, approaching negotiations with realistic expectations can help you avoid conflict. Some producers have a fixed amount in mind and try to fit your ideas into their funding reality. They expect you to make revisions and cuts, but they may not have considered the impact this would have on quality. Your job is to help them understand this impact.

Avoiding money conflicts also requires your willingness to understand and acknowledge the fiscal limitations of your potential producer. Researching producers' past and current commissions and projects, and talking with them, will provide insight into their aesthetic and production experience. If the producer works for a nonprofit institution, look at the publicly posted online tax forms to gain insight into annual budgets and expenses. Do not start a project without an understanding of a producer's external/internal pressures and history. Producers may have positive reasons to commission you and want to see a site project realized, but they may not have experienced the economy of scale in working outside the concert hall. Do not move forward in the hope that you can renegotiate a signed contract once a project has begun. Before making any new requests once a project is underway, consider their feasibility and importance carefully.

Anticipating possible challenges

- *You want to gain access to a particular site but worry about rejection or highly restricted access.*

Many iconic sites are mandated to allow access. For example, Grand Central Terminal allows all legitimate film companies, at little or no cost, to use the terminal as long as these companies agree to adapt to its policies and schedules. Many sites actively seek ways to attract new community members, and site-specific projects are well suited to achieve this goal. A site's commitment to your project is an indication that the stakeholders want the public to see something memorable and want you to have the access you require. Safety (for all) and, of course, budget concerns are two reasons sites restrict access, but both of these factors are negotiable.

- *As you begin collaborating with producers, you might anticipate that they will want to spend as little money as possible.*

If the producer has no prior commissioning experience, especially with site-specific projects, you might be correct. To address this issue, discuss, as early as possible, the essential aspects of your project that might require special funding and explain the reasons that they are so important to your vision.

- *You worry that your comfort and safety while working on a project are not a priority to your producing partner.*

Remind your producer that access to healthy living and working environments affects everyone's physical and mental wellbeing during the creation process. Your requests for safety measures, your choice of housing, and freedom from anxiety over per diem costs are all a part of this equation.

- *You assume everyone you meet will understand your vision for a site-specific project.*

Do not make this assumption. Err on the side of caution; be prepared to explain in as much detail as needed how your ideas and visual imagery will animate the site.

Determining Your Fee

Some questions to answer when deciding what your fee should be:

- *Do the circumstances support your asking for a fee for this project?*

The answer to this question depends on how the project is financed and whether a commissioning organization is involved. If the latter, there is no question that you deserve and need to negotiate a fee.

If you intend to produce the project and raise the money yourself and want payment, the budget you create for fundraising must include your fee as part of your overall fundraising goal. You earn the fee, in part, by raising money for the project. Unfortunately, not all artistic projects will reach their funding goals, so you may have to decide what is more important to you: doing the project or receiving a fee. As a self-producing artist, you might find it useful to raise money for everything except your fee or put your fee as the lowest priority. This intentional strategy will communicate your passion and commitment to the project, regardless of whether you get paid.

For some of my self-produced projects, such as *Revealed* and *Webbed Feats* (1997), I was the lead fundraiser and decided to relinquish my fee in order to cover unforeseen production expenses. Like many who start businesses and forego a salary, I believed that not taking payment was a good investment that would pay off in the future as people got to know my work. At that time, I was a full-time teacher, so I was not dependent on a fee to pay monthly living expenses. Not everyone is in that position. Although the decision to ask for or forego payment will depend on circumstances, do not abandon the attempt to garner compensation too soon. A commissioning producer with funds to support a project will ask about your fee early in any discussion.

Generally, there are only a few producers who have experience commissioning *and* producing site work. A discussion of your fee will inevitably be included in early conversations because your fee will give producers a good indication of a project's overall cost. Once this discussion has started, attempt to complete your planning budget before finalizing and naming a specific fee. Your fee should reflect the size and scope of the project. If the producer in your initial conversations shows signs of worry and insists on pinning you down to name a fee, then clearly state that you use a sliding scale based on project size. Emphasize your flexibility depending on the scope and ambition of the work. Then mention a fee range, explaining that the low figure is for a smaller project requiring commensurately less time; do not commit until you have researched the potential cost of the overall project and the commissioning institution's financial resources.

- *What kind of institution is commissioning the work? Is it a small, medium, or large entity? Is it a for-profit or nonprofit institution?*

If the site work is for commercial or marketing purposes, your fee should align with that industry's standards.

- *What is the commissioning and project history of the producer and the institution? What kind of artists have they commissioned? Are they young unknowns or established artists? At what level have past productions been funded?*
- *How comfortable are you talking about money?*

Determining a fee may seem complicated in part because money discussions around self-worth can be emotionally charged. As an artist, defining your value without some practical or emotional support can feel daunting. Some artists have managers, agents, or gallerists to negotiate payment, but many artists represent themselves. The most effective strategy for building your confidence in negotiating your payment is to feel prepared through your research so that you can bolster your discussions with facts and figures about both the project and the commissioners. Knowledge will make you feel more confident.

- *What is your time worth?*

From conception to performance, there are physical and temporal demands made on you and your team. It is great to love your work, but love doesn't alter the labor equation. Your time is money, and big productions require a more significant allocation of your time. How many hours, days, or weeks will it take to make this work? How much labor will be involved? In your initial planning process, you are either *estimating* your time commitment based on experience or know exactly how much time the project will require (in days or weeks) and the number of performances scheduled. Do not forget to include the periods between rehearsals, which often demand more time as you follow up on feedback sessions with collaborators and deal with marketing and other production-related contingencies.

Understanding the production history will give you some guidance and context for your production requests. If possible, contact other artists who have worked with the institution or other producers to ask about their experience. Creating a budget and discussing your fee (and the fees of others involved) are requirements for any project. The goal is to make a payment request informed by the producer/presenter's commissioning history and appropriate for your resume and needs.

Two strategies for determining your fee

After determining the entire production budget, one approach is to take a percentage, 10–15% of the budget, to establish a preliminary figure for your fee. Other fields such as architecture, construction, and public art use this method of fee calculation.

Another method to ensure proper compensation is to divide a project into different periods, each with its fee structure. When a commissioned project has an extended development process, sometimes as long as three years, I will ask for smaller fees paid during the preproduction activities, such as site visits and production or fundraising meetings. Some producers will schedule meetings without committing to the project or to compensation. When this situation arises, you have to decide how much work you are willing to provide on spec. I have started several projects without any guarantee of payment, motivated by a belief that my participation would result in a contracted commission.

Conversely, I have started projects by asking for a fee for research and travel time. If an educational institution is requesting my time, I will propose payment that includes some teaching so that my participation in meetings and other preproduction activities coincides with my giving master classes and lectures to students. If you are comfortable with those activities, this strategy becomes a win-win proposition for everyone, making the institution more apt to agree to pay a fee before project confirmation. Producers do not usually ask you to travel at your expense (beyond your region) to discuss or research a possible project. Unless there are highly unusual circumstances, you should always ask, at minimum, for reimbursement for travel and lodging. Ideally, you will also be compensated for your time.

The next section provides a more detailed breakdown of your options when a commissioning organization first approaches you.

Initial commissioning inquiry

When a producer contacts you with an inquiry for a possible site project, your first action is to make a site visit to determine whether the project interests you. Will you seek compensation for the time, energy, and expenses required for this first trip? Your options are: (1) Make the site visit, and be reimbursed for expenses only. (2) Make the site visit, and, in addition to expenses, charge a fee for the time involved. (3) Make a site visit and make no monetary requests.

Select the last option if: (a) The site is close to your home. (b) Coincidently, you have other compelling reasons to visit that location. (c) The person inviting you is someone you trust who has no budget but does have a sincere desire to start a project with you. This last scenario suggests that you may be investing in a relationship with another person with whom you could start a producing partnership. The person contacting you may not be directly associated with an institution but, like you, may share an interest in and enthusiasm for site work.

But, do not agree to start a project with others, even in an exploratory phase, without a clear understanding concerning compensation for your time and travel expenses.

Get It in Writing: Topics to Consider for Inclusion in a Contract

During negotiations, suggesting contract clauses based on your needs should not be fraught with tension. As mentioned earlier, be forthright and honest. Create a list for yourself of the most important areas—items that you might want to ensure are included in your contract, such as audience design, selecting collaborators, housing, marketing, documentation, fees, etc. Even if you have an agent or a manager to participate in your negotiations, you should always be present for any discussions that affect artistic issues.

During contract discussion, take careful notes so that you can help draft the contract. The final agreement does not have to rely on legal jargon. Accessible language, understood by all, is preferable, but, ultimately, you would be wise to have someone you know and trust review whatever you are about to sign.

The following contract topics are suggestions for discussion and/or inclusion depending on your project and circumstances. Ask producers if they prefer that you present suggestions before they draft a contract or in response to their first draft. An initial in-person meeting to discuss contract requests can save time and create the opportunity to negotiate in a constructive, relaxed manner before anyone invests effort and emotion in creating the actual document. Ideally, the contract negotiations and signing will be complete before auditions. Holding a public audition is a threshold that signals the production is officially moving forward. If a contract is unsigned, you are in jeopardy of negotiating without sufficient time for discussion and revisions.

Contract riders

Contract riders are a set of requests or clear demands that accompany a contract. Sometimes, a rider is simply an amendment to an already written contract. Sometimes, a rider is presented before a contract is even written. For example, some A-list Hollywood actors seeking to increase diversity and inclusivity now require riders with specific guidelines for hiring production personnel. Choreographer and director Emily Johnson requires producing partners to sign a "Decolonization Rider," which specifies a series of actions and behaviors including land acknowledgment and seeking permissions and involvement from indigenous members of the host community. Johnson wants to encourage Black, Indigenous, and People of Color (BIPOC) involvement, as much as possible, in the production process. The full details of the rider can be found at www.catalystdance.com/decolonization-rider.

You should discuss riders that include nonnegotiable demands (yours or your producer's) early in your relationship with site stakeholders or producing partners. Often, such discussions will have a significant positive impact on how a work is created and produced. Some of the topics considered next could be addressed in riders if they are particularly significant or complex.

Taxes—independent contractor versus employee

A discussion about how fees are taxed or excluded from taxes should occur at the onset of any negotiation. You should do your own research, either through institutions that support artists or with a tax accountant, to understand fiscal tax options as you move forward with your career. As you negotiate with presenters, producers, and potential individual donors, you must decide how you will present yourself as a taxpayer to federal, state, and city governments. The source of funding for your project will determine your relationship to taxes. Below are three possible scenarios.

Scenario 1
You are an independent artist: Your fee is paid to you as an independent contractor with the host organization. You will receive the entire fee, and at the end of the year, a 1099 tax form will be sent to you, which states that federal and state taxes have not been withheld from your fee. It is, therefore, your responsibility, as an independent contractor to file and pay whatever taxes are required. The state of California recently passed strict laws concerning how independent contractors are defined. It is essential to research the tax laws of any state (or country) of employment.

Scenario 2
You are deemed an employee of the host institution. Your fee will be subject to all local and federal taxes (including Social Security), and you will receive an amount that reflects those deductions. When you file your taxes, it may be possible to claim deductions to recover some of the taxes that have been withheld.

Scenario 3
You can have your fees paid directly to a nonprofit entity. This entity could be your own, formed to support your work, or one that you have joined so it can act as an umbrella organization. Fees paid directly to a nonprofit are not subject to any taxes or withholdings. However, if funds are then paid to you as an individual, you will have to pay taxes on that income.

At some point in an active career, many artists wonder if they should go through the process of creating a nonprofit corporation to support their work. This subject needs careful research and discussion. In the Appendix, under resources for Chapter 8 on Fundraising, there are links listed to help with this process.

Topics to consider when working in another country

- *Do you want the contract or one version of it to be written in your native language?*

A shared language will prevent misunderstandings. If you are required to translate the contract yourself, confirm that all parties agree with your translation.

- *Do you want the producer to pay any foreign income taxes resulting from your fee?*

Foreign taxes are a reality to keep in mind. If an international producer cannot pay your taxes directly, you can request an increase to your fee. To avoid having to revise your initial fee request, inquire about taxes *before* you sign a contract. Remember, too, that your home country will tax your income.

- *Do you want the producer to reimburse you for visas or work permit fees?*

Foreign visas and work permits can take valuable time to acquire; find out if you need them ahead of time, regardless of who is paying. Ask your producer or do your own research.

- *Do you want your fee paid in the currency of your country of residence or that of the host country?*

Fluctuations in the currency exchange rate could increase or decrease your fee. If you receive your fee in the host country's currency, and if the exchange rate falls below an agreed-upon level, do you want the producer to make up the difference?

Schedule of fee payment

- *Do you want your fee paid in three installments coinciding with three production thresholds?*

The first payment occurs upon signing the contract (ideally, before the first audition); the second payment is at the midpoint of the production timeline; and the third is after the project's premiere. You should also discuss the amount of each payment. Most producers like to pay the largest portion of the fee at the end in case unforeseen circumstances force a cancellation. One suggested division of payment: 20%/30%/50%.

Force Majeure

A *force majeure* clause in the contract frees both parties of any obligations under circumstances beyond anyone's control, such as a terrorist attack, severe weather events, or a pandemic. It is a common clause that is often overlooked.

- *Do you want alternatives to automatic cancellation of your contract (and fee payment) under a force majeure circumstance?*

Taking the time to discuss alternatives to outright cancellation and loss of expected fees can mitigate economic hardship for both you and the artists you have contracted. One strategy for salvaging works for site-specific performances is to create online experiences in the form of site films. When all performing arts events across the United States were cancelled due to the Covid-19 pandemic, The Industry (an experimental opera company that creates immersive environmental performances) and Heidi Duckler Dance (a site-based dance performance company), both based in Los Angeles, created and distributed filmed versions of their cancelled productions in

2020. A discussion of alternatives to catastrophic cancellations can allow producers to achieve some of their goals and protect you against loss of fees.

Per diem and travel expenses

A per diem is an agreed-upon amount paid in advance to the artist to cover daily expenses or in reimbursement for these expenses. Typically, the per diem covers food (breakfast, lunch, dinner) but not local transportation, which is a separate expense.

- *Do you want your fee to be separate from any per diem or other reimbursable costs?*

When you sign your contract, you cannot always know the exact costs of some expenses. Airfare, food, and housing prices fluctuate, so it makes sense to have the producer agree to reimburse you directly for these expenses soon after their purchase. If this is not possible, a flat fee for all these projected expenses can allow you more control and flexibility in arranging travel, accommodation, etc.

During negotiations, you might also want to consider other possibilities: perhaps asking for a fixed daily per diem that accrues for each night you are not at home and which also includes the costs incurred on the day you travel to the site; or perhaps asking that all transportation costs (including airfare and travel to and from airports and any rental cars or public transport during rehearsals and site visits) be reimbursable.

Housing

- *Do you want to have input on all your housing arrangements?*

The type of housing you require or prefer should be considered and included in your contract. Is it a hotel, short-term rental, guestroom in someone's home? How close do you want to be, by car or public transportation, to both rehearsal and performance sites?

Complimentary tickets (if applicable)

- *Do you want to receive a certain number of complimentary tickets for each performance?*

Some producers and presenting organizations have standard complimentary ticket policies that apply to their concert hall productions. It is best to review those policies to ensure that they make sense in a site-specific context. Producers who usually work with a set number of seats restrict complimentary tickets in proportion to availability. A site project may accommodate hundreds of more audience members, and the ticket policy should reflect that fact.

- *Should you and the producer, together, create a list of invited VIP guests (e.g., other producers, journalists, donors, etc.)?*

This conversation avoids replicating names from your personal complimentary list.

Rights

- *Do you intend to retain the copyright to your work?*

Allowing artists to retain their rights to their art is standard practice. If the producer wants the right to remount the work, insist on further negotiations so that you have agreed that the remounting will occur within a set timeframe after its premiere. Remounting site-specific work is rare, but possible if you have created a site-adaptive work. Request that any remounting of the work include your input and supervision.

Working within a fixed budget

- *Do you expect to collaborate with the producer to reallocate funds as needed?*

If specific budget lines show a surplus while other areas are in deficit, having a say in reallocating funds will keep the project on track. Chapter 15 (Working with a Set Budget after Fundraising) has a more in-depth discussion of working with a final budget.

Selecting collaborators and performers

- *Do you expect to choose or approve all artists associated with the production in consultation with the producer, or do you want sole control of auditions and interviews?*

Some of my projects began with a producer promoting or making strong recommendations for specific collaborating artists and performers, a scenario that requires delicate handling. Sometimes, your involvement in a project is even predicated on working with someone the producer has already chosen. Once again, early discussions are essential for setting expectations and avoiding conflict.

- *Do you expect the producer to take responsibility for providing adequate publicity announcing auditions for the project?*

Everyone associated with the project wants to attract the most qualified performers for the work. Strong marketing of an audition helps to ensure maximum attendance.

- *Do you need to ensure that the producer will hire the agreed-upon number of performers in a timely fashion, with no loss of rehearsal time?*

During one project, I selected performers whom the producer never officially hired (performers received phone messages but nothing in writing). When I returned to start rehearsals, only a small percentage of my original choices were still available to work. If you partner with an organization or producer with no previous artistic or commissioning experience, you should consider the need to include this requirement in the contract.

Audience design

- *Do you want to make clear that once the audience capacity is agreed upon, you will decide, in consultation with the producer, how the audience will view the event and that any increase to the size of the audience could require revision to the audience design?*

This request goes to the heart of the discussion in Chapter 3 (Designing the Event and Staging the Audience) and establishes your dual role as artist and collaborating producer. A producer's desire to sell more tickets or accommodate more people could also upset the delicate balance between site capacity and audience comfort in relationship to performance sightlines.

- *For promenade productions, do you wish to have sole responsibility for training guides or establishing training protocols?*

The pressures of production week can delay or even cause people to overlook training for guides. If you are not present to instruct guides, they could receive incomplete or erroneous information that will affect your audience design.

Off-site rehearsal space

- *Do you want to ensure that your producer has procured rehearsal and studio space before the start of rehearsals and that the producer has agreed to provide an off-site rehearsal space if inclement weather prevents the use of the site space?*

The need for both these requests is obvious, and these alternative rehearsal spaces must be clean, safe, and readily available to avoid loss of productivity.

Marketing, programs, documentation

Chapter 16 (Promoting and Marketing the Work) has a more detailed discussion of how to market a site-specific project. Before initiating any marketing campaign, a review of your role in designing the campaign should occur. You or the producer should inform all marketing staff or graphic designers about all contractual clauses that pertain to you and the work's marketing. Marketing, like the quality of the project itself, affects your reputation and your ability to get future commissions or grants. The considerations in this section are not frivolous or egotistical; they are essential to your livelihood.

- *Will it be important to ensure that you approve all publicity/promotional materials and that you do so far enough in advance to meet required marketing deadlines?*
- *Do you expect your name to be included in all publicity materials that mention your project (articles, advertisements, banners, posters, brochures, postcards, websites, voice messages, etc.)?*
- *Do you wish to ensure that contracts with any collaborators (music, lights, sets, costumes, etc.) will not stipulate that if your name is on any publicity material the collaborator's name must be included, but rather that collaborator credits will be included at the sole discretion of you and the producer?*

If you include this last request in a contract, collaborating artists should be informed of it before signing their contracts.

This suggestion comes from an early experience of mine. I had neglected to discuss or include any marketing clauses in a contract for a highly public, well-funded, large-scale site-specific creation. The marketing campaign included a large poster and giant advertisements placed in subway stations. The poster was designed and printed without my input, and I had seen it only after it had been designed and printed. The poster featured the title of my work in large letters, a quotation from a *New York Times* review of a previous production in the *New York Times*, the producer's name, the dates and place of the performance, and the logos and names of all the significant funders. To my surprise and disappointment, my name was missing. When I inquired about this omission, the marketing director indicated a clause in one collaborating artist's contract that stipulated that his name had to be included if my name appeared on any publicity. In response, based on concern about lack of space and the graphic designer's fear of a crowded visual design, the marketing director chose to leave all artist names off the poster. Ultimately, after learning of my disappointment, the producer overruled the marketing director and had all posters put through a second printing with my name and *all* primary collaborators listed.

My insistence on including my name was important: This was a high-profile project, and the production's success would benefit everyone. A negative reception of the work, no matter whose name was on the poster, would not deter the producers from funding their future seasons, but responsibility for negative reviews would be mine. My reputation would be tarnished. So my willingness to put my name on the poster reflected the artistic and professional risk I was willing to take (for better or worse). In addition, I was creating a public work for a famous historical site that had never presented such work in its long history, so a failure to recognize the artists in the marketing materials would also have signified that the artists were secondary to the production itself—that it was created by nameless people working in the background. That experience underlined the importance of thinking through all aspects of the commissioning and creation process before signing a contract. I then began my practice of collecting topics for possible inclusion in future contracts. With every new project, new issues arise, so my collection of topics is likely to grow.

Publicity photos

- *Do you expect producers to schedule publicity photo shoots so that you are always present to direct the staging of the photographs?*

Your direction at these sessions helps ensure that the photographs are accurate visual representations of your work. Chapter 16 (Promoting and Marketing the Work) contains a more in-depth discussion of the role of publicity photographs.

- *Do you want the authority to select the publicity photos for marketing and to provide the producer with a selection to use?*

Giving the producer a choice of photos that you approve rather than insisting on just one or two images fosters a sense of collaboration. I usually provide three to five options.

Rehearsal and performance photographs

- *Do you want a voice in selecting photographers to document the work?*
- *Do you expect that all publicity, rehearsal, and performance photo files will be made available to you at no charge?*
- *Should you ensure that any photos must be credited to both you and the photographer and include the title of the work?*
- *Do you expect to share the copyright of all photos taken or to be given full rights to future use of photos for your publicity purposes without payment of royalties as long as the images also credit the photographer?*

If you neglect to make these requests, future use of photos for your marketing or publicity purposes could result in complications and a bill from the photographer demanding payment. Make sure that all rights for future use are spelled out and that photographers understand and accept them.

Press releases and the title of the work

- *Do you want to approve all drafts of press releases before they are disseminated?*
- *Do you expect to have sole control over both the working and final titles of the project?*

Chapter 16 (Promoting and Marketing the Work) discusses the importance of a press release, and these requests will ensure your control over your work.

Program

- *What information do you want included in the printed programs: names of all collaborators, performers, and technical/production staff; an artist's statement; your biography and the biographies of any other collaborators or core dancers; a special-thanks section that you write; funding credits?*

Chapter 16 (Promoting and Marketing the Work) contains a more detailed discussion of the program as a marketing tool.

- *Do you need the producer to collect and give you a minimum number of copies of all printed marketing materials at the end of the project?*

Maintaining a proper archive and record of your work is essential; do not rely on your ability during the final busy weeks of production and performances to collect all of this archival material. You will need this documentation for future marketing purposes on your website and to show future producers examples of previous marketing campaigns. Chapter 17 (Documentation) has a more detailed discussion of the importance of archives.

Interviews

- *Do you expect producers to schedule press and media interviews to avoid, as much as possible, interrupting rehearsals?*
- *Will producers give you audio or video files of all television or radio interviews?*

This last request will support your goal of collecting the many artifacts that help document your work for archival and future marketing purposes.

Video documentation of commissioned work and rights

- *Do you expect to approve, in consultation with producers, all videographers hired to document the work?*

Many videographers have experience documenting concert and proscenium productions, but very few have direct experience with site-specific performances and events. It is essential to participate in the selection process to ensure that the videographer has relevant experience.

- *Will you need to collaborate with the hired videographer on setting camera angles and establishing a shooting schedule at least two weeks before the first technical rehearsal?*

Before signing a contract, you should discuss with producers the minimum equipment and personnel required to document your project effectively, and you may also want to make these part of your contract. Your goal is to create a final document that employs film and film-editing techniques to capture the essence of the work for the screen. Chapter 17 (Documentation) discusses this topic in more detail.

- *Is it important for you to direct or participate in editing the performance footage and to retain final approval of the edited work?*

Your knowledge and comfort with video editing will determine if this is a request you should make.

- *Do you wish to retain full copyright of video documentation or share the rights with the producer?*
- *Do you want to require that contracts for your performers and collaborators clearly state that all broadcast rights belong solely to the video copyright holders?*

If you do not clarify this issue in writing, any future broadcasts of your past work as part of a news story or documentary will require signed clearance agreements from all performers.

- *Do you want to request that, at no extra charge, you receive copies of all master video files of the production and the final edit?*

The goal for inserting in your contract all requests for copies of marketing and documentation materials, including future access to photographs, is to prevent your having to pay for materials generated by your creation.

Last Thoughts

Many of the topics listed here may not be relevant to your specific project or may be unimportant to you. However, keep the list in mind as you navigate the development of new projects. Each project will be different, but the final contract between you and your producer will support both your and the producer's artistic vision and career goals if discussed, negotiated, and written with patience and care. Creating and producing can be stressful, but solid agreements that reflect shared goals and outcomes contribute to a more peaceful and nurturing journey.

7
Planning Your Planning Budget

This chapter aims to guide you as you develop a project budget that you can use for preproduction planning and fundraising. Identifying the specific production needs as you create your artistic vision has many benefits:

- It requires that you think through different contingencies and scenarios and consider the cost implications. (Use the topics presented in Chapter 11, Collaboration and Collaborative Elements, as you discuss and develop your planning budget.)
- It will enable you to prioritize your production needs in terms of funding.
- It will anchor your project in the economic reality of what you can afford.
- It will communicate your fiscal professionalism to a producer/presenter and any potential backers.

This chapter explains line by line how to build a generic budget for a site-specific production and discusses your responsibilities as artist and producer. Whether self-producing (acting alone) or partnering with an executive producer, the work involved in site inventory (Chapter 4), site selection (Chapter 1), permitting (Chapter 2), and audience design (Chapter 3) illustrates the inevitability of your dual role and its importance in reducing obstacles to realizing your best work. Completing this planning budget will require research, negotiation, and patience.

Later, once all fundraising is complete, the planning budget becomes the working budget, which is discussed in Chapter 15.

Planning Budget Breakdown

In the header of the budget document, write the name or the WORKING TITLE of your project, the name(s) of the originating ARTIST(s), and the name(s) of the PRODUCER(s)—you alone or you and your partner. If you are seeking a producing partner and none exists at this stage, leave it blank.

Assumptions

NUMBER OF PERFORMANCES

How many days of performances? How many performances each day? Include the confirmed or projected dates.

On Site. Stephan Koplowitz, Oxford University Press. © Oxford University Press 2022. DOI: 10.1093/oso/9780197515235.003.0008

NUMBER OF PERFORMERS

How many performers will you need?

OTHER

You should supply any other relevant information that will provide a context for understanding the budget, such as time of day or if the budget is predicated on a minimum/maximum number of attendees.

Budget Code	Description	Amt	Units	×	Rate	Total	Notes
	Artist Fee						Usually a flat fee.
	Artist Producing fee (optional)						Usually a flat fee.
	Travel Lodging Food/Per Diem	---------	-------	------	---------	------------	If the artist is working away from home.

If you are creating several possible budgets for a single project (e.g., a large version, a small version, etc.), each one with different assumptions (or variables), this format makes it possible to insert different numbers and label each version accordingly.

Determining Your Fee—A Short(ish) Primer

Fees for the artistic team are usually at the top of a budget, with the first lines for the originating artist.

As the artistic director your time is allocated to multiple responsibilities, and your fee is based on the time that all these responsibilities require for any given project.

(Originating) Artist: The artist role requires that you create the vision and devise an artistic plan for the work. Your plan will guide the entire creation process. You must be physically present to do the work in rehearsals, meetings, and feedback sessions with collaborators, directing and developing the project's technical/production elements and overseeing any post-production needs.

Producer: Your role as producer supports your role as the artist. If you are self-producing, you will run meetings and make all the artistic and financial/marketing decisions. If you have been commissioned and are partnering with a producer, your role as producer is collaborative. The point is that you should take some degree of responsibility for producing the work and should be compensated for your time.

Ultimately, you are one person with multiple responsibilities, each requiring considerable time and labor: site selection, navigating the permissions/permitting process, preproduction meetings, phone calls, emails, writing artistic plans, creating budgets, hiring the creative and technical teams, implementing a marketing plan, being available for press interviews, creating marketing materials (photos, text, poster/postcard design), establishing a social media presence, creating an audience design, fundraising (grant-writing or in-person solicitations), and post-production activities (overseeing the editing of the documentation and final reports required by outside funding sources).

Your roles are reflected explicitly in the first two fees listed in the budget document: an artist fee and a producing fee. If asked to present just one fee, I explain that my one payment includes all my responsibilities as artist and producer. I want to dispel the perception that a fee appears too large and to highlight to commissioning organizations and funders the value I bring to the process. It's essential to make sure everyone is clear about the amount of time the product and process will entail. Some producers do not assume or understand that an artist would want or be qualified to contribute and collaborate as a producer. I encourage you to address your multiple responsibilities in detail *early* in these negotiations.

> We realized many years ago that we are mostly producing the work ourselves because site work has such different demands than theater-based performance. We've had bad experiences when a commissioner hires a producer, and we still do all the work because the producer just doesn't have enough experience with site production. This can create conflict and difficulty and, ultimately, more work. We often need to tell them what to do—basically, doing their job—which defeats the objective.
>
> Susanne Thomas

Expenses

The other three budget lines (travel, lodging, per diem) are needed if you are working away from your home. Some presenters will want to bundle your fee with your expenses and offer one figure. Only agree to this offer if you have thoroughly investigated all the costs for travel, lodging, and per diem for the area in which you will be working. Expenses associated with your work are not income, so bundling them into your fee may have tax implications when you file a return.

Production Fees/Salaries

PRODUCTION MANAGEMENT TEAM					These positions are not necessarily tied to the performance dates, and are paid weekly or flat fees.
Producer (in addition to the artist)					
Project Manager/Coordinator					
Technical Director					
Rehearsal Manager					
Other Management/Support					

This section of the budget pertains to your production management team. Please refer to Chapter 5 for a detailed description of these roles and duties.

Some of your projects may not warrant or be able to afford support staff. Lack of funds or expediency could require you to assume these production roles. Artists often assume multiple roles when creating work, and completing your planning budget compels you to acknowledge whether those positions are required or not.

Partnering with an institution

If you are commissioned and partnering with another institution, the institution may already have on its staff a paid producer, project manager/coordinator, technical director, etc., who can be assigned to your project and covered by the institution's yearly operating budget. However, many institutions or producers want to account for their employees' time and include the costs of their time in grant applications and fundraising initiatives. All nonprofits want to raise money for general operating expenses, and grants in support of your project might be an opportunity for them to cover some of their yearly administrative costs. The grant organization sometimes mandates this budgetary practice for institutions (e.g., the National Endowment for the Arts) because these granting institutions want to ensure that both artists and institutions account for the project's operating costs. Inclusion of these costs can seem onerous as it increases the overall budget, appearing to make fundraising more challenging.

When the planning budget becomes a working budget, after the fundraising period is over (discussed in detail in Chapter 15), producers will generally forego using the recently procured production funds to cover salaried staff if the fundraising effort has fallen short. However, staff essential to the project and paid hourly may prove impossible to exclude. Be sensitive to the realities of your commissioners. But, if you are a freelance artist, you may be disappointed to discover during the initial meetings that you could be the only person not getting compensated, unless the project is adequately funded at some future, seemingly unknown date.

If a cultural center or festival is commissioning your work, the role of technical director may be an existing salaried position, so, if the presenter does not need your budget to account for this person's salary, you wouldn't need to include it in your budget line. However, your project may not fit into the in-house technical director's schedule. Therefore, you will need to add an outside technical director's fee in the budget line. A qualified salaried faculty member might serve as a rehearsal manager in a university, in which case you won't need to put anything in that budget line. The decision to include money in your planning budget or not depends on the salaried faculty's willingness to participate, their contract, their workload or the availability of time within their academic schedule, but never assume that an organization's salaried employees will or should work without some compensation.

The line for other management/support could include a marketing director, a grant writer, or anyone connected to supporting the project. You may have the means to hire your own marketing/fundraising personnel, or these may be employees of the presenting institution. If appropriate, this line could also include your manager or booking agent.

Collaborating Artists' Fees/Salaries

CREATIVE TEAM						
Composer						These personnel generally receive flat fees but may also get a day- rate for performances.
Costume Designer						
Lighting Director						
Sound Designer						
Video Director						
Etc.						

If the project does not need other collaborators, you will save money. However, if you hope to work with original music, costumes, lighting, etc., the first step is to include the necessary professionals with appropriate fees in your planning budget.

The need for a lighting designer is predicated on where and when the work is performed. Are you working with or without natural light, indoors or outdoors? Lighting requirements are potentially the most expensive part of a budget. They can include a designer, technicians to hang/focus lights, and rental costs for both lights and bringing electricity to a site. Lighting costs add up quickly. The sooner your lighting needs are known, the sooner you and your presenter will know if the project is economically feasible.

The position of sound designer is often misunderstood. The sound designer's job is to design how sound is amplified into a space and then manipulate the sound quality so that it is calibrated optimally for your location's acoustic dimensions. Your ability to hire this position (or a sound designer who is part of an audio rental package) for large spaces of any kind can make a significant difference to the quality of your work. Some composers may have knowledge and skill in this area, but sound design is a specialty art form, very much like lighting design.

If projections are part of your artistic vision, you will need a video director to ensure that the images are appropriately focused and edited for the specific projection surfaces. This need is unrelated to any video documentation of the work, which appears in a different budget line.

Performers' Fees/Salaries

My ethics are clear: If I have a grant, a commission, or a budget, I'm going to pay everybody for sure, and that's why people want to work with me . . . I've also done pieces where I've used my savings.

nibia pastrana santiago

PERFORMERS							Fees for performers are often divided between rehearsal pay and performance pay.
	Performers/Actors/Dancers						
	Core Company						
	Ensemble Performers						
	Musicians						
	Other						

Anyone who is performing in the proposed work is part of these budget lines.

At this point in your planning, performers' pay is either specific or estimated. For some projects, the number of performers needed is known and inflexible. After completing the site inventory, you should have determined a specific number of performers or a workable range. Try to avoid underestimating your needs. If you are uncertain, ask for more performers than you may need. Reducing a budget is much easier than increasing it once you have started production.

I use two performer budget lines for large casts, given my method of creation (discussed in Chapter 12). I engage a core company of 5–10 performers who help me develop the choreography for the work's narrative. After one or two weeks, they are joined by the ensemble performers, who learn creative material devised with the core company and continue building the work. Pay for the core members is higher, given their more substantial time commitment. For example, if I need a cast of 30 performers, I work with 10 core members for two weeks and add 20 ensemble dancers for the last two weeks. This structure is more economical than paying all 30 performers for four weeks. You can also offer three levels of engagement, each with diminishing time and pay, which creates more flexibility in the budget and enables performers to commit to a project in line with their time constraints.

Determining performers' fees

When I first began making work that involved community dancers, it was common to work with unpaid volunteers as dancers who wanted the experience. My responsibility was (and still is) to give those participants an absolute gift, hopefully an enriching, transformative experience; otherwise, it would be exploitative. I was transparent about it and clear who was paid and who wasn't. However now it's a different time, and younger participants cannot afford to give up time without being paid. I now insist the performers are paid. It's a very complex issue.

Rosemary Lee

Performance fees are contingent on several factors. How many are needed? How many rehearsals are required? How many performances? Are you engaging experienced or inexperienced performers? Ideally, you will have adequate funds to pay separately for rehearsal and performance. No matter how much money is ultimately available, paying performers for their time is essential. The exception involves working with registered students pursuing an academic degree. The compensation for students can be either or both course credit and the opportunity to add professional experience to their educational portfolio/resume. However, these students should not have to pay for this experience. You should include in your planning budget money to cover any anticipated expenses—such as travel (bus, subway, gas) to and from rehearsals. You should never use students to subsidize your budget.

Avoid the temptation to let untrained, nonstudent performers work for nothing—for example, under the guise of community outreach. If you partner with a local community center/organization that provides free cultural and educational experiences, your performers may consciously and willingly volunteer to work with you. However, the right thing to do is to pay them something, especially if travel is involved. At a minimum, be mindful and willing to discuss compensation openly as you assemble your cast.

Pay disparity (performers and collaborators)

Unless all of your performers (musicians, actors, dancers, etc.) are unpaid registered students, pay disparities can result from creating a diverse team of performing artists. In the professional world, different economic models govern pay scales for musicians, actors, and dancers. In general, musicians may ask for more compensation and for less rehearsal time; dancers are historically underpaid; and actors fall somewhere between musicians and dancers. Actors and musicians also tend to be more unionized with rules that affect salary levels. While these disparities are prevalent in the field, I prefer to pay each collaborator based on workload and years of experience. I have also jettisoned some project components, like musicians performing live, when the fees not only were drastically higher than what I could pay my dancers but created a budgetary imbalance that prevented me from paying other performers fairly.

The same disparities affect other collaborating artists. The fee structure for established composers is far more developed and standardized than the fee structure for choreographers. Despite the inevitable discomfort associated with salary discussions, you should attempt to be as transparent, clear, and honest as possible with each person hired as you define roles and determine compensation. Discussing your expectations and creating letters or contracts that adhere to conversations during the hiring process are all part of maintaining a sense of clarity when establishing fees. Be mindful of the total number of hours you ask your team to work for the fees you are paying. One factor in assessing your fee structure's fairness is to divide the total number of hours by the compensation you are offering and compare the result to the minimum wage. Not all projects will meet the minimum wage standard, but your awareness can create an environment of sensitivity that affects your cast and crew.

Production Staff Fees/Salaries

PRODUCTION STAFF					
Stage Manager(s)					They are
Technical Crew (by department)					usually
Front of House Staff (box office, ushers, etc.)					paid at a
Production Assistants (might be broken out by department if appropriate)					daily rate.

Your production may need only one stage manager, or it may require several stage managers responsible for different sites that are a part of your overall project. Sometimes the technical director can double as the stage manager once the show is in production. The technical crew is responsible for hanging and focusing lights, installing sound and video equipment—anything that requires specific knowledge of technical production equipment. Production assistants can also serve as technical crew members depending on their experience. Fees for the production staff are determined by the number of days they will work. A stage manager is typically paid more than the technical crew, who are paid more than production assistants.

The front-of-house staff for a site-specific performance can be essential for creating a welcoming experience for the audience. If same-day tickets are sold, a front-of-house crew will ensure a seamless experience. Ushers are essential for handing out programs, helping people find the location to view the work, and acting as guides in a promenade performance. Filling these positions will depend on your site, your production size, and the resources available. When a festival is producing my work, the front-of-house staff is usually already in place and often not part of the working budget. It is also possible to find volunteers to help with the front-of-house needs, everything from box office to ushering.

Production Costs

PRODUCTION COSTS					
Site Rental/Permits					These costs
Support Space Rental (i.e., dressing rooms, portapotty)					are almost entirely
Catering Service					site- and
Transportation					location-
Rehearsal Space					dependent.
Audition Costs (ads, studio rental, etc.)					
Miscellaneous (cleaning supplies, batteries, etc.)					

Site-rental fees are generally uncommon, especially if you partner with an entity that manages or owns the location. If your work has corporate or commercial goals and support, the host site could ask for payment at its commercial/corporate rental rates. My production *Occupy* for the Yerba Buena Gardens was part of a free summer arts festival. However, if we had approached the gardens with a project wholly sponsored and initiated by Microsoft, Salesforce, or some other corporation, the rental fee could have been in the thousands of dollars. Sometimes, this fee is unavoidable. For *The Northfield Experience* we decided to pay a rental fee for the Grand Theater and Event Center. This commercial organization did not want to lose expected rental income during its high season for weddings and receptions. The producers decided that the site was central to the artistic vision and paid the fee.

A permit fee is common for many sites. Permitting fees are usually connected to state or city regulations and generally are not onerous. There can be fees for access to a site or even a fee to turn off municipal lights, as was the case in Milwaukee at the North Water Tower; the charge was under $100 to turn off two lights.

Renting support space (any essential space not available on site) is not common. However, if your site can't accommodate a required dressing room for your dancers, renting an adjacent space or tent is an option. Finding suitable storage space for costumes, props, sound, and lighting equipment could quickly become an expense added to the budget. When working at the decommissioned coal factory in Essen, Germany, we had to rent portable showers and toilets for rehearsals.

Catering might be necessary if you have to provide food or beverage for your performers and production team. For large numbers of performers and crew, you should plan to provide water, at a minimum. When long hours of rehearsal are required (e.g., technical rehearsals), or you have multiple performances in one day, or rehearsals are too far from civilization, meals are always appreciated—if your budget can afford them. Supplementing water with snacks is another way to communicate your support and care for your team.

Transportation costs include both expenses incurred for getting your performers to and from the site and any costs associated with transporting your audience. These costs can become significant when working on a project with multiple sites or when working with college students who may not have a car. *The Northfield Experience* incurred both of these costs. We had to rent buses to bring 200 student chorus members to a cemetery. The audience design also required audiences to take buses to different locations within the city in a prescribed manner. Transportation costs can range from paying subway fares to renting cars, vans, or buses. Do not let this expense come as a surprise (as it did for us in Northfield).

The rehearsal space budget line is for offsite rehearsals; there is a discussion of onsite and offsite rehearsal space in Chapter 12. It is advisable to request a backup space if weather is a factor or there is a danger the building's management could co-opt your indoor site. If rain begins unexpectedly during an outdoor rehearsal, moving the work indoors can save valuable time.

Audition funds are needed to support private or open/public auditions. Public auditions will require some form of marketing. It may be easier to post audition information through Facebook, Instagram, etc. However, reaching a more professional cohort could require targeted advertisements in specialized print and online publications. If a studio space is not available gratis, rental fees are usually higher for auditions than for rehearsals. Hiring an audition assistant to help with registering applicants or with conducting the audition is another possible expense.

Additional Production Costs

TECHNICAL COSTS					
Costume Construction/Rental					
Costume Maintenance and Cleaning					
Lighting Rental/Expendables					
Sound Recording					This is for playback.
Sound Equipment (sound system)					This is on-site (PA).
Communications (walkie-talkies or other)					
Video/Projection Rentals					
Sets/Props Elements					
Audience Support Elements					This could include chairs.

Transportation and Shipping					
Loss and Damage					Equipment breaks and gets lost. Make sure to account for contingencies.

Costume expenses depend on the number of performers and the length of the performance run. Will costumes be constructed, rented, or purchased? Custom-made clothing is usually more expensive than bought or rented clothing. Budgeting for costume maintenance (cleaning, repair, or replacement) is recommended if the costumes are worn for more than two days in addition to your technical and dress rehearsals. Asking performers to maintain their costumes is an option but adds more pressure to their role as performers and is usually not part of their compensation package. Collecting all costumes for maintenance reduces the possibility that they will be misplaced, lost, or damaged by the performers.

Lighting rental/expendables include all rental costs associated with lighting instruments, cabling, mixing boards, and any gel (color) needs (your expendables).

Sound requirements for performances can range from one speaker to an array of several speakers spread over a great distance. The need for sound for onsite rehearsals (or in a studio) is another essential item to consider. Audio playback for rehearsals can be challenging if you are working in a large outdoor space. Securing a portable yet powerful enough sound system requires research, and it is possible that purchasing it would be cheaper than renting it.

If your production staff must coordinate with each other over long distances or from different sites, you will need to budget for renting or purchasing two-way radios or other communication devices. This seemingly small aspect of your budget is something to consider carefully. Occasionally, when technical rehearsals begin,

I want to participate in the communication network. If I fail to mention this possibility in early planning meetings, and to include it in the budget, a headset will not be available without incurring additional expenses.

The use of digital projections has increased in popularity; some site projects rely almost exclusively on projections on ecological (rocks, trees, etc.) or urban (buildings) surfaces. The biannual BLINK festival in Cincinnati, Ohio, which showcases a variety of site-based light shows, comes to mind. The higher the lumens (projection power), the greater the cost of rental or purchase. Be aware that some long-term rentals may compete with the purchase price of a projection unit. If you plan to create many site projects, purchasing the equipment might be an investment that ultimately saves you money; you might even fund the purchase over time by renting it to future sites.

Visual elements not found on site are another common expense. The list of possible props can be endless. You might also want to create sets or backdrops, similar to those used for proscenium productions. These expenses depend on materials, design, and labor. I tend to use props sparingly, and those I do use are always inspired by the site. I integrated real books into the choreography for two of my site works, *Babel Index* (British Library) and *Open Book/Open House* (Humanities Building, Rice University, 2000). For both productions, I also designed custom-made books that contained lights to suggest the glow from a computer screen when opened. For *Mill Town*, set in a historic 19th-century mill factory, I incorporated large cylinder containers used to store cotton as props for an extended section of the work.

Audience-support elements refer to anything that enhances the audience experience: Will you need to rent chairs? Build a platform to place chairs on a flat or elevated surface? Create signage to aid navigation through the space? If these elements are not available at the host site, you must budget for them.

Transportation and shipping pertain to the transport of equipment needed for the production—whether you must rent a vehicle or use a commercial carrier.

A line item for loss and damage of equipment is rarely found in budgets, but you would be wise to consider this contingency. Keeping it on your budget template is one way to start a conversation about loss or damage with your collaborators.

Marketing Expenses

	MARKETING AND PROMOTION						
	Design (print and web)						
	Printing						
	Postage						
	Photography (for PR)						
	Press/Marketing Agent						
	Social Media Costs						
	Website Hosting and Maintenance						
	Paid Advertisements (online/print)						
	Marketing List Acquisition						
	Programs						

Marketing and promotion are essential to any project (and are discussed in Chapter 16). Even if the presenter/producer manages and pays for the project's marketing, effective marketing requires many steps, so consider which actions will be your responsibility and have budget implications. Some projects rely simply on word of mouth and spreading information through personal email lists and the social media accounts of everyone connected to the work. With larger projects, especially those connected to festivals, universities, and art centers, additional costs may be incurred, such as:

- Design services for any marketing materials, such as a website, posters, postcards, and programs.
- Printing for postcards, posters, programs, banners, signage, etc.
- Postage for mailed announcements, invitations, postcards, or brochures or fees for a commercial digital invitation service, such as e-vites, paperless posts, etc.
- Photography for publicity photos, posters, web pages published by press/marketing outlets. Consider paying an experienced photographer if you cannot find a qualified volunteer.
- Hiring a press/marketing agent is a luxury and this is sometimes handled by a person within an organization.
- Website hosting within your host organization is often possible, but some web presence is advised if you wish to host a preview of production photos, videos, etc.
- Social media costs are incurred if you hire someone to handle all the social media postings during your marketing period or decide to purchase ads on social media platforms.
- Programs handed out at performances (if desired) need to be created, designed, and printed.

Documentation Expenses

DOCUMENTATION						
Photography						This is very important!
Video Documentation (performance)						
Video Documentation (process)						
Video Editing						

Planning for documentation is essential (and is discussed at length in Chapter 17). Each of these four budget lines will ultimately help market your work, fund future work, and record the work for posterity and future reference. These benefits accrue both to you and your producing institutional partner.

It is possible to negotiate one fee for one videographer to document the creation process, performance, and final editing. Or you can hire a crew to capture the work and then hire an editor at a later date. The video and still photography fees depend on the number of days needed, how many cameras are recording, and the length of the final edited piece.

Administrative Expenses

	ADMINISTRATION						
	Office Space						
	Office Equipment (computers, desks, copier, etc.)						
	Office Supplies						
	Phone/Internet						
	Accounting						
	Legal						
	Insurance						This is very important!

This last category is listed if you submit a budget to a foundation or government funding agency (local, state, or national) for a project supported by a presenting organization or institution. These budget numbers are derived from an equation that (based on the length of your production schedule) takes a percentage of a presenter's yearly cost for each line item. For example, if the annual office supply expenditures are $600 and the proposed project will take a combined total of eight full weeks (two months), you will divide $600 by 12 (months): $50 (a month) for two months equals $100, which is the amount you would include in this budget.

Incorporating this number into your planning budget can make sense and help keep you and your presenter clear as to the actual costs of a project. All of the administrative costs might still be subsumed in a presenter's yearly operating budget. Still, some institutions like to record those costs in each project's specific budget for that year.

If you are self-producing and have limited funding sources, you only have to include the insurance budget line and ignore the other lines. Any work on public or private property poses a liability risk. Issues surrounding insurance are covered in Chapter 2.

At the bottom of your budget sheet, you should include a contingency line for unanticipated costs. If fundraising falls short, this line is often the first to be eliminated, but it is wise to include it initially. Typically, the contingency number is 5–15% of the total budget.

Last Thoughts

A planning budget intended for fundraising and planning purposes must and will reflect your priorities. If you want to get a clear picture of people's values, look at how they spend money. If you prioritize original music over original costumes, then your budget will include a fee for a composer and not for a costume designer—or perhaps just a fee for a costume coordinator, whose job would be simply to purchase or find costumes under your direction. The same is true of video documentation. You may be satisfied with only one camera instead of two or three covering your performances. All of these priorities will be reflected in the portion of the budget allocated to each.

Tailoring the budget to your specific funders (government, private foundations, individual donors, etc.) is advisable. You can accomplish this goal by creating multiple versions using the budget template presented in this chapter. A budget submitted to the National Endowment for the Arts, which requires very detailed accounting, will differ from one provided to a private donor who may only ask you to outline your needs in very broad categories.

A planning budget becomes a working budget when the fundraising window has closed and you and your partners have decided that the available funds are sufficient to support a workable version of your vision. At this point, everyone involved will operate under those budgetary conditions. Be patient, don't worry too much at this planning stage, but remember: details matter. Investing time in creating a reasonable, detailed planning budget will increase the likelihood of your producing a working budget that will sustain your team.

8
Fundraising for Your Artistic Plan

A Short Primer

> Fundraising. I don't want to remember fundraising [laughter].
>
> Noémie Lafrance

Raising money for artistic endeavors is not an artist's favorite use of time. Asking for money, no matter the reason, is fraught with trepidation, anxiety, tension—select any appropriate descriptor. Artists working in the nonprofit world within the for-profit universe must raise money to fund projects taking place in the public sphere. Creating budgets and asking for money are inevitable parts of the process of achieving your goals.

You probably work as a site artist because you believe that your creations have purpose and importance. Your primary motivation isn't to become rich or to collect good reviews but to contribute something meaningful to a community. Your *idea* or vision for a site is what will capture people's imagination, not your reputation or fame. Therefore, as a site artist, you must remember that your request for funds will be most effective if it is tied to people's connection to their community and history and to the story being told about their environment.

Fear Not

Creating big projects with large budgets is not a requirement. Starting small can be an instructive and less stressful first step in gaining experience and becoming comfortable asking for money. My career journey is not common or easily replicated or even recommended. My first professional engagement as a site artist was on the scale of Grand Central Terminal, my entrée into the site-specific world in a project could have gone catastrophically wrong. It is more common for artists to start with smaller projects before diving into large productions. Film directors often make a series of inexpensive short films (or commercials) before tackling a feature film. Composers write song cycles or several unrelated songs before attempting an entire opera or musical. Creating a small and more manageable site project, before embarking on a big-budget, large-scale creation, may be the more reasonable path.

As you gain experience, you will become more comfortable with the whole process and draw ever closer to realizing your larger artistic visions. With each passing project, asking for help, whether financial support or artistic guidance, will become easier. If asking for money or favors is difficult for you, find or hire a person you

On Site. Stephan Koplowitz, Oxford University Press. © Oxford University Press 2022. DOI: 10.1093/oso/9780197515235.003.0009

trust to help you with their time, knowledge, emotional support, and communication skills.

This chapter provides a short overview of fundraising avenues relevant to any artistic endeavor and specific to site projects.

> It's always useful to work with a partner. If an artist doesn't have a track record or a nonprofit of their own, it's important to figure out who can help produce the work.
>
> Martha Bowers

Four Phases of Fundraising (An Overview)

Research

Learn as much as you can about your site to better communicate your inspiration and artistic plan and to find potential connections for fundraising ideas. For example, are you working in an endangered site, perhaps an environmentally compromised outdoor area or a historic building threatened by neglect or demolition? Circumstances like these might provide opportunities for both funding and strategic partnerships.

Study the past fundraising successes of other artists and cultural institutions by reading the credit lines in printed programs or artists' websites to collect ideas for potential funding sources. Not all funding resources will be relevant, but identifying the names of culturally significant donors is a first step in eliminating all but the most pertinent sources for your specific project.

Talk to family members and your closest friends to learn whether they might have any artistically inclined connections. The goal is to expand your circle of friends and potential donors over time. While you must respect the desire of your family and friends desire to maintain their privacy and not disclose their connections, informing them of your project and need for backers might uncover valuable relationships, especially if your passion for your project inspires them to invest in your vision.

Prepare

Take the time to prepare your fundraising tools—written proposals, media, and printed matter—so that they effectively and persuasively make the case for funding and implementing your artistic plan. Based on your research, make sure that your materials align with your intended funders' values, interests, and mission.

> I have found that there are two main strategies for fundraising for site projects. One is to underscore its community accessibility, which opens up one avenue of funding. The other is to create quality documentation. Due to my research into the critical importance of location for dance film, I have prioritized documentation of my site work; this

has improved the overall image of my work and the success of my grant applications. The documentation actually funds the next project and then the next project and then the next project. Those are the two things that have made a big difference in terms of fundraising.

Melanie Kloetzel

Ask

Once you have found potential sources and have created the proper communication materials, do not hesitate to use them (Photo 8.1). Don't be shy about making your needs known; don't wait; don't lose your nerve; make the ask.

Cultivate and Acknowledge

As you raise money, it's important to continue cultivating new relationships (with individuals and institutions) and expressing your appreciation for current and past support you have received. If you say please, don't forget to say thanks. Take the time

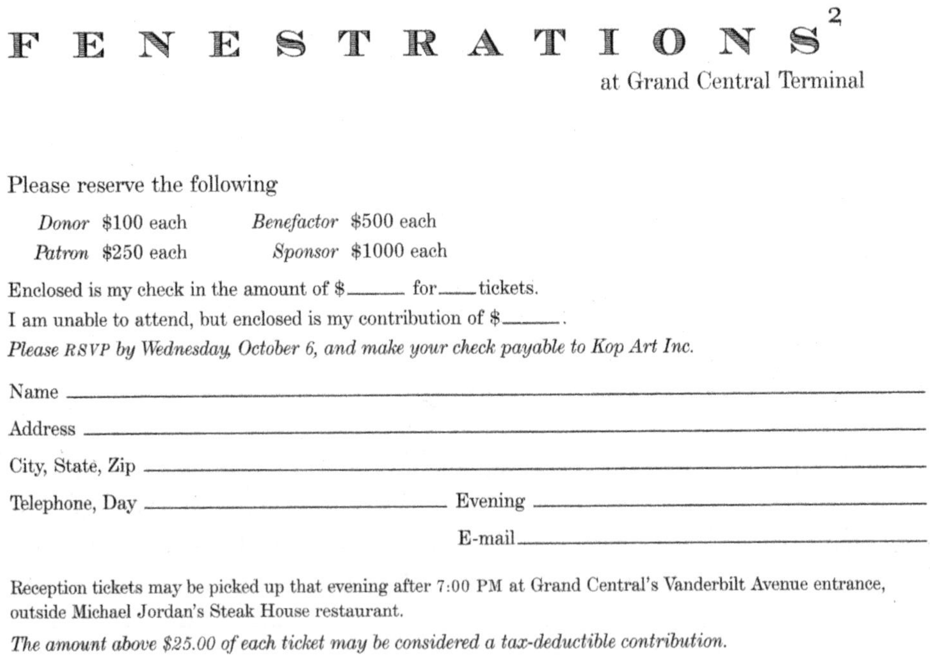

F E N E S T R A T I O N S²

at Grand Central Terminal

Please reserve the following

Donor $100 each   *Benefactor* $500 each
Patron $250 each   *Sponsor* $1000 each

Enclosed is my check in the amount of $_____ for____tickets.
I am unable to attend, but enclosed is my contribution of $_____.
Please RSVP by Wednesday, October 6, and make your check payable to Kop Art Inc.

Name _____

Address _____

City, State, Zip _____

Telephone, Day _____ Evening _____

E-mail_____

Reception tickets may be picked up that evening after 7:00 PM at Grand Central's Vanderbilt Avenue entrance, outside Michael Jordan's Steak House restaurant.
The amount above $25.00 of each ticket may be considered a tax-deductible contribution.

Photo 8.1 Return card for fundraising benefit at Grand Central Terminal in support of producing *Fenestrations*² (1999).
Photo courtesy Stephan Koplowitz.

to send periodic newsletters to your donor community alerting them to the status of ongoing projects and upcoming premieres.

Fundraising is about creative relationships. If you don't have a relationship with an individual, asking for money is probably not going to work. You must try to get that individual to understand and care about the importance of what you are doing. Fundraising takes tremendous patience because you have to work on developing relationships over time. Sometimes, I hear from people I haven't heard from in a year, and they ask me for money. I'm certainly not going to give if the only time I ever hear from them is when they're asking me for money. You would be surprised how often that happens.

Anne Hamburger

What Are Grantmaking Institutions Looking For? (An Overview)

I think it's easier to raise money for something that's exciting, actively engages community, and is different from just another event in the theater.

Laura Faure

A crucial step when approaching funding sources is to assure them that your project will align with their goals and interests. Prepare the following:

- *Statement of need*: Write a clear, concise description of your project and what specifically needs funding. This statement generally falls under the heading "Project Description" in many grant applications. Sometimes, specific needs are separated from the project narrative as a discrete paragraph or section in an application. Examples of particular needs could be funds for live or original music, documentation, or fees for performers and other collaborating artists.
- *Goals for the program/project*: What do you hope to accomplish? What is your short-term (current) vision and how does it fit your long-term goals and mission? If your artistic mission is to work with underserved populations, then make that clear.
- *Numbers served*: Who, and how many, will benefit from your project? Do not hesitate to include people who will experience the work through online documentation. Sometimes, it is also possible to include the artistic community that your work will engage, especially if a potential donor has a strong interest in that community. Be careful not to overstate these numbers.

Once you've secured a site, you have to be willing to spend at least half your time on the logistics, not the creation. But before that, understand you're just in a long line of people who want money, with many of them more established than you. One way

> to convince funders is to demonstrate that you're contributing to a community that people in the conventional theater can't reach.
>
> Elise Bernhardt

- *Disability and inclusion*: This is an area that has thanfully become a priority of many funders and should be addressed as part of any proposal. There is a discussion about disabilities, accessibility, and site work in Chapter 14.
- *Partnerships*: Are you creating or sustaining partnerships with other people, institutions, and communities through this project? What impact beyond the event itself will your project have? Will the project bring together a new set of community members, working cooperatively for the first time, or reunite them as a team?
- *Sustainability*: Does your project have the potential to plant seeds that could generate future projects or create value for you and your intended community? Will your project directly inspire new initiatives or generate income in some form? Will it expand access to the site or bring more attention to the site to help with its sustainability within the community?
- *Evaluation Plan*: What criteria will you use to measure the success of your project? How will you evaluate and measure the impact of your vision?

A useful guide for creating a proposal that addresses these requirements is George T. Doran's SMART acronym in the October 1981 issue of *Management Review*:

- *Specific*: Define and describe in clear language the project and vision.
- *Measurable*: Outline how you can measure the impact of the project.
- *Achievable*: Demonstrate that your vision is achievable given the resources at hand or requested.
- *Realistic*: Outline the reasons your project is realistic within the context of the greater community.
- *Timely*: Demonstrate the relevance of the work to current time and events.

Site Selection and Funding Challenges

> I think it is wise to think about your relationship to a project aside from the opportunity or because it sounds good or because you will get a grant. If it's driven by external forces outside of you and a community, then, it can be problematic.
>
> Amara Tabor-Smith

While I don't recommend that you select sites or projects solely because you can raise funds more easily for them, the relationship between fundraising and production is not easily severed. The fundraising potential of a site can become an important selling point to a presenter/producer. Indeed, some presenters do select projects based on their perceived potential for attracting donors. When Laura Faure, then director of the Bates Dance Festival, first approached me to create a site-specific project within the Lewiston/Auburn community, she was excited to share connections to community partners who could help provide budgetary support and access to sites. We spent two days researching the twin cities. Ultimately, Laura's ties to the community influenced my final choice of the Bates Mill Complex, a site rich in history that housed the Lewiston/Auburn Museum and was owned and developed by a long-time Bates Dance Festival donor. Without these prior connections, I might not have selected the historic mills at the Complex for *Mill Town*.

> Sometimes, what attracts donors is the site and who's already attached to it or the prestige that it has. Sometimes, it's your vision and passion that engage people in your idea. They get interested enough and want to jump on board if they're adventurous. Another huge selling point for funders, especially local funders, is that almost every one of our site works has engaged with diverse community members. Most funders value more impact, more reach into a community. Giving people in a community, nonprofessionals, a profound artistic experience that allows them to perform in a work and engage with major artists in the making of a piece is a huge selling point.
>
> Laura Faure

It can seem unfair if producers reject your proposed project because they perceive it as a funding challenge, but the fact is that institutions generally have only one funding cycle each year, each with a finite amount of available money, which limits the number of projects these institutions can fund. Presenters/producers want to collaborate on projects representing their artistic goals and make the best use of their administrative time. It is important to understand that everyone working in the arts (artists, presenters, producers, donors) brings unique contexts and challenges. Like you, presenters/producers have limited time and resources for fundraising. An outside producer may only want to work with a particular group of funders, all of whom have their own specific set of priorities. It is crucial to expand your awareness and sensitivity when negotiating with any outside entity. Ultimately, you may decide that self-producing is the best option to raise funds for a particular project. José Navarrete spoke to this very issue: "Have you thought about the concept of time and grant-making? Many grantors will dictate your creative process because they decide how much time you have to spend their money. We choose to take our time, but we need to present our request for time so that grantors understand that time is needed to build the rapport we want with a community or a site. It could be more than one year or two years."

Fundraising is a balancing act requiring you to consider many factors, some artistic and some more practical, some connected to the integrity of your vision and some related to fiscal realities. Ultimately, you will have to make choices and decisions based on considerations unique to each project. There is no formula, but as you gain more experience, you will find that your gut can be a good guide.

The Site in Relation to Fundraising

The specific relationship between your project and the site is a good starting place to identify potential funding sources. Perhaps your chosen venue is connected (by history, location, current use) to a contemporary social issue, or the site needs preservation or is part of an underserved community. Your artistic vision and plan might parallel the interests of individual donors, foundations, corporations, or government institutions.

Thorough research is the bedrock of any fundraising effort. Delving into the history and current use of your site will help uncover potential funding sources. Also, identifying additional partners (beyond the primary presenting organization) to help produce your project can expand your ability to find funding. When working on *Liquid Landscapes* (water-related sites) as part of my *TaskForce* project in Los Angeles, I created a partnership with Friends of the LA River to support one of the projects on that river. This partnership enabled us to secure tour buses and sell tickets to fund the transportation of our audience to four different river locations over six hours. Without this partnership, we never could have afforded to rent the buses, nor would we have had access to the organization's members who underwrote that production's cost.

> I learned very early that you had to convince people that a project would benefit them. Otherwise, they were like, "Why should we help you?" So it was always, how are we helping them? Normally, for corporations, it's sales or community engagement; for foundations, it would be visibility in a particular place.
>
> Elise Bernhardt

Where to Start? Expanding Your Circle

One way to approach fundraising is to think in terms of circles. You start with your own small circle of friends and family, making your fundraising needs known to them. There is a difference between informing your friends and family of your needs and asking them to contribute, and you should be clear about what you are asking so that they don't feel pressure if they are not inclined to offer monetary support. A good strategy is to begin by asking for advice, information, and introductions to others who will form a second circle. Your goal is to find like-minded people interested in the arts who have giving potential or skills that would support your efforts either in fundraising or with the production itself. The first circle is the circle that needs to be handled with special care and sensitivity because you don't want your relationships disrupted by your funding goals.

Your goal is to expand your connections to an ever-widening second circle that will support your vision. This cultivation takes time and happens over several projects. The effort and labor involved in this process, not to mention the competition for donors, make maintaining a consistent artistic practice very challenging.

The Power of Web Patrons (Crowdfunding)

As of this writing, the most ubiquitous form of fundraising for independent projects is through online solicitation: crowdfunding. Some of the more popular sites are Kickstarter, Indiegogo, GoFundMe, or Facebook. An advantage of crowdfunding is that the initial costs of creating your campaign can be low. Most platforms collect a percentage of the funds raised, and your only other expenses will be whatever time or funds you spend creating your written proposal and recorded video pitch. An internet search will help you identify which platforms are the most popular and help narrow your choice to a platform that fits your budget and goals. Crowdfunding has replaced, in many sectors, the older letter-writing campaigns. However, solicitation by mail is still practiced, it's just not as widespread.

Successful crowdfunding techniques can be researched by exploring and studying other online fundraising campaigns. As with all fundraising, clear written and oral articulation of a project is essential. Crowdfunding platforms are enhanced by a solid promotional video that makes a concise argument for a project's value and funding needs. Creating these materials takes time, but the internet's immediacy and reach can generate rapid results by leveraging social media's power. Researching other online funding campaigns will also spark ideas on how to shape the ask and determine the level of production needed for the video pitch. You'll discover that crowdfunding generally requires generating a list of perks associated with a particular donation level. These can range from a thank-you on social media ("for $10 or less") to being listed in the printed program or offering top donors a private tour of the site by the artist. The possibilities for offers are endless, but, ideally, they should reflect or be inspired by some aspect of your project, allowing for a greater sense of connection between donor philanthropy and your creative process.

Have a Party!? The Benefit of Benefits

> A benefit is not just about raising money but also about creating community and raising visibility. You get these fancy invitations into the hands of a lot of people who might not necessarily know anything about you. Benefits are not really about the money. It's really about the visibility.
>
> Elise Bernhardt

Before the internet, individual artists living in the analog world had two avenues for fundraising: a request letter, mailed to everyone within their social/community circle, or a benefit event/party (Photo 8.2). The costs of letters are time and postage, while a benefit is expensive and labor-intensive. However, benefits are an effective way to create community buy-in and support. Your circle of donors is expanded by having your friends invite their friends who invite their friends. A successful benefit is one

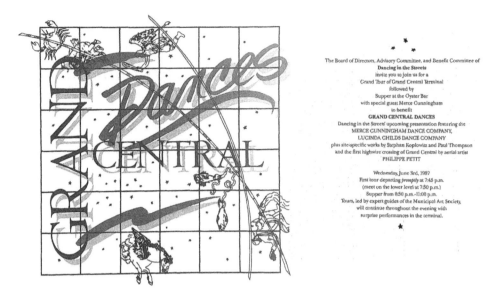

The Board of Directors, Advisory Committee, and Benefit Committee of
Dancing in the Streets
invite you to join us for a
Grand Tour of Grand Central Terminal
followed by
Supper at the Oyster Bar
with special guest Merce Cunningham
to benefit
GRAND CENTRAL DANCES
Dancing in the Streets' upcoming presentation featuring the
MERCE CUNNINGHAM DANCE COMPANY,
LUCINDA CHILDS DANCE COMPANY
plus site-specific works by Stephan Koplowitz and Paul Thompson
and the first highwire crossing of Grand Central by aerial artist
PHILIPPE PETIT

Wednesday, June 3rd, 1987
First tour departing *promptly* at 7:45 p.m.
(meet on the lower level at 7:30 p.m.)
Supper from 8:50 p.m.–11:00 p.m.
Tours, led by expert guides of the Municipal Art Society,
will continue throughout the evening with
surprise performances in the terminal.

Photo 8.2 Invitation for fundraising benefit for Dancing in the Streets at Grand Central Terminal, New York, NY, 1987.
Photo, courtesy Stephan Koplowitz.

method of expanding your circle more quickly, and benefits are an avenue to raise funds when other funding sources have been exhausted. The challenges of producing a benefit can be mitigated by someone willing to gift a celebrity's services, offer a unique venue, provide free catering (very rare), or underwrite the costs of the benefit.

Crowdfunding campaigns can also incorporate a benefit ticket as a donor perk, allowing your crowdfunding platform to work in tandem with selling tickets to the production. This strategy allows those who cannot attend the benefit or give at that level the opportunity to contribute and receive other privileges or simply to buy tickets.

The designs of a benefit event can be as varied as the art they support. You can invite donors to a preview of your project by hosting the event on the chosen site, or feature music by your composer, or creatively involve some of your performers (remember to compensate them for their time). Incorporating some aspect of your site, collaborative team, or vision of the work into your benefit's narrative can be powerful. The event should inspire and excite your invitees' interest in the work and provide an atmosphere of fun and inclusion—all in service of raising money and increasing attendance at performances.

When to hold a benefit

Scheduling a benefit is usually tied to the timing of your funding needs. If the event's purpose is to help raise money for the current project's budget, scheduling the benefit before the start of the production process is recommended. If the benefit is intended to complement an already funded project by securing needed additional funds for general operating expenses, the benefit can be scheduled during one of your dress rehearsals or at the premiere. Some organizations/artists are confident enough in the success of their benefit events to simply include projected benefit funds in the working budget no matter when the event is scheduled.

Where to hold a benefit?

If the performance is not ticketed and is free to the public, it might not be possible to use the site for a benefit event, and it may be necessary to locate an alternative space to host a private (ticketed) reception for your patrons. When my work returned to Grand Central Terminal in 1999, I created a benefit (to support my ongoing site work) and invited contributors to attend *Fenestrations*[2] free with the general public. We then gathered at a private location within walking distance of the terminal for an evening of drinks and light food. Staging a reception in Grand Central Terminal was not a possibility, or advisable given the acoustics and the crowds. However, other project sites have had the capacity to host a private event. My *Off the Walls* project at the Hudson River Museum (1996) began with a private evening premiere at a special ticketed price that included a reception with all participating artists (Photo 8.3).

The Off the Walls Benefit Committee

Invites you to

Off the Walls

See The Hudson River Museum come alive! Experience this astounding production commissioned by the Museum and created by nationally acclaimed choreographer Stephan Koplowitz.

Inspired by the Museum's art and architecture, it features many simultaneous dance, live music and theater performances throughout the Galleries, Glenview Mansion and The Andrus Planetarium.

Exclusive Benefit Performance
Saturday, November 16, 1996 8pm

Join Artistic Director/Choreographer Stephan Koplowitz and his ensemble of performers
for a "Cast Party"
Champagne Reception
to follow the Benefit Performance.

Tickets are $50 each

Info: 914/963-4550

At The Hudson River Museum of Westchester
511 Warburton Ave
Yonkers NY 10701-1899

Production sponsored by
Hastings Creative Arts Council with major support from Westchester Arts Council; Lila Wallace-Reader's Digest Arts Partners Program and an anonymous donor.

Cover © 1996 Claire Yaffa

Photo 8.3 Invitation for fundraising event at the Hudson River Museum for *Off the Walls* (1996), Yonkers, NY.
Photo courtesy Stephan Koplowitz.

In general, benefits are labor-intensive, presuppose the ability to sell a minimum number of tickets, and require an appropriate venue. A successful benefit brings many positive results and can help accelerate your reach into the community, supporting not only your current work but also subsequent work.

Finding and Applying for Grants

> We used to do big benefit fundraisers, but it was so much work for little return. I am much more comfortable and successful writing grants to foundations and government funders. It is still lots of work but more effective. It doesn't eat up the entire staff's time as with the benefit events, which took months of planning.
>
> Martha Bowers

Another conventional means of raising money in the nonprofit art world is to apply for grants. There are many books about this subject and online resources to help you find and identify which grants are most suited for your project. Internet searches can assist you, or you can subscribe to a grant information organization such as Candid (fconline.foundationcenter.org/). Talking to other artists and people in the field is another method of locating appropriate sources of funding. Approaching artists whose practice is related to your own or local arts institutions that have received outside funding for such projects can save time. Collecting funding information from the lists of donors and institutional funders included in the printed programs of local performances is another method for identifying possible sources. Inside the program you may find the names of foundations (public and private), government entities (national, state, or local), and businesses (large corporate or small local) that either give ongoing support or have specifically funded the work being presented.

Many funding sources will require a combination of a cover letter, a written proposal, and support materials, such as video work samples, photos, sound recordings, and letters of endorsement. They may also require you to answer specific questions with a strict word-count and other restrictions. Grant-making entities have their own funding cycles with strict funding deadlines. Taking the time to research these deadlines can sometimes influence the scheduling of your project. Often, presenters and producers will want sufficient lead-time to raise funds before fully committing to a project.

City, State, National Government Grants

Each of these grants will have its own set of application requirements. Your residency or length of residency in a particular city or state may preclude you from applying. Some grants are not available to individual, unaffiliated artists not connected to an institution or not part of a nonprofit corporation. Your resume may also need to demonstrate up to three recent years of professional (non-student) productions for you to qualify. Many government agencies that fund public art do not usually consider the performing arts in that funding category. These guidelines, especially the 1% for public art (which allocates 1% of publicly funded construction budgets for public art), exclude live performance and are reserved for permanent visual art projects—like murals and sculptures. Public art as defined by municipalities is slowly evolving (perhaps too slowly), but, as with all grants, carefully researching prerequisites will save you much time and energy.

> I think site-specific work brings great value. It takes something that usually happens in-doors and can create a collision of people and art, one that people didn't necessarily choose. I think we want that to be part of it, just the way public art is part of a city. We want public dance or performance to be part of a city. Why not? It has just as much right as a statue does. In terms of a city's vitality, it's central.
>
> Nancy Wozny

Public and Private Foundation Grants

What is the difference between a public and private foundation?

To quote the Council on Foundations: "Public foundations are grantmaking public charities that gain their funds from a variety of sources, which may include foundations, individuals, corporations, or public entities. Public foundations may engage in fundraising, and may seek broad public financial support" (cof.org).

To quote Foundation Source: "A private foundation is an independent legal entity set up for solely charitable purposes. Unlike a public charity, which relies on public fundraising to support its activities, the funding for a private foundation typically comes from a single individual, a family, or a corporation, which receives a tax deduction for donations" (foundationsource.com).

Regardless of which type of foundation you apply to, taking time to research the funder's mission and grant history will inform your actions and shape your application's focus.

Private Individuals

The best way to raise money from individuals is to ask them. That is a simple statement, but, so often, people avoid asking their friends or anyone else within their social orbit out of the understandable discomfort they associate with money and favors. This uneasiness is a key reason conventional benefit events and on-line crowdfunding-with-perks campaigns are preferred methods of approaching individuals. These two strategies allow your ask to appear transactional, removing the pressure of asking for an outright gift. Funds are donated in exchange for a fun party or a perk at a selected donor level. However, at times, the personal ask is necessary. If individuals with a large giving capacity have been identified, an ask might be the path to start your funding campaign: perhaps underwriting the costs of a benefit or making a lead donation to motivate other people within your circle.

Corporate Sponsorship

People frequently perceive corporate sponsorship as easier to acquire, only to discover otherwise. The perception is that for-profit companies have lots of extra money and should model generosity by supporting whatever benefits their community or society as a whole. The reality is that for-profit corporations are always aware of their bottom line; their annual profit matters, especially if their primary concern is their shareholders. Corporations make philanthropic decisions after careful consideration about their effect on the bottom line.

Within most large corporations are two departments that deal with sponsorship: the marketing department and the philanthropic/community relations department. Guess which group has the larger budget? The marketing department is most interested in exposure and branding—everything from producing television/media commercials to brokering marketing relationships with big national celebrities. It is common for pop stars to earn millions of dollars by allowing corporations (through their marketing department) to use their name. The corporate giving department is equally concerned with exposure. Still, it is not required to achieve the same level of exposure, so grants from this department need to be primarily tailored to the mission of the company's community engagement or social action priorities. The difference is that marketing budgets are tied directly to sales and profit margins while corporate philanthropy is aligned with public image and relations.

If your project has an apparent connection to a specific corporation through proximity, theme, or the cast's make-up, a request may be worth your time. Keep in mind that corporations are always looking for exposure in some form of publicity. If you can demonstrate that your project will attract a broad audience and will generate significant publicity, you may have the flexibility to approach both the marketing and philanthropic departments.

Some of my high-profile works (those in large metropolitan areas) have attracted, through personal connections, the support of two fashion companies that donated much-needed costumes. With a cast of 50 dancers staged in six locations around NYC, *The Grand Step Project* convinced both Tommy Hilfinger and New York & Company (owners at the time of Easy Spirit shoes) to make donations. Both companies were approached through personal connections. A board member of my nonprofit worked for Tommy Hilfinger, and a friend's colleague was the CEO of

New York & Company. It helps to have friends *near* people in high places, and that is a secret of success for any fundraising effort: research, network, and ask.

In-Kind Donations

In-kind gifts involve donating the goods and services themselves rather than the money needed to buy them. This category of giving is an excellent way to circumvent the need to raise cash for every line item in your budget. The search for in-kind donations is typically on artists' minds no matter where they may find themselves in the production process. Your planning budget will help identify your production needs, including those specific needs that may have in-kind donation potential. The search starts the moment you begin collaborating with a potential presenter, host site, or your circles of friends and donors.

In-Kind Services

I recommend that you not consider any artistic or core production roles as candidates for in-kind donations. Asking professional artists to donate their time without compensation should only be done under the most extreme circumstances. In some instances, you may be able to identify someone else to donate the funds to pay their fees. Focus instead on services that can be given without creating tensions or the perception of exploitation.

Security
This service is often a requirement when working in a building or outdoor space after hours. Many stakeholders will not feel comfortable having you and your performers working unsupervised or without an institutional representative in case of an emergency. Many of my past projects, especially those that have occurred in museums and public parks, have required funds to pay for staff members to work security after regular hours. If you have been granted permission to work on-site, the institutional stakeholder may be willing to pay for security or extra staff time: this is one direct way to seek a deeper, more invested relationship. How much further beyond simply providing access an organization is willing to go is a good indication of motivation and commitment to your project. I seek a site's maximum level of commitment not only because it helps with funding the project but because it brings extra value in the form of goodwill to everyone involved.

Marketing
This budget category entails several subcategories, some of which can be challenging—such as finding someone to donate the printing costs of posters,

postcards, or letters. However, a site may have its own in-house marketing department and be willing to help with design services and to write and distribute a press release on your behalf. Be aware that the release will be written from the host's point of view, and you may be limited in your ability to edit it to conform to your artistic or professional needs. Making a connection with an outside public relations/marketing firm could result in its working with you as part of its pro bono services. This opportunity is not common but possible if you are working in a city or a community where local businesses are interested in supporting and encouraging publicity around their town or region. My *Webbed Feats* (stephankoplowitz. com/webbedfeats, 1997) project was fortunate to be a pro-bono client of Connors Communications from 1996 to 1997 because Connie Connors, the director, was an ex-dancer and a significant player in the nascent creative digital economy in Manhattan.

If your host organization publishes a newsletter or has a website, do not hesitate to ask for the inclusion of your performances in any or all publications or mailings. You can also request permission to send one of your email or printed promotional letters to the host's mailing list.

Performance Guides/Docents/Front-of-House

For some site performances, you will need a front-of-house staff that welcomes audiences, handles tickets, and serves as performance guides. You can ask for volunteers from your circle of friends and donors or from the host organization. Volunteerism is common in nonprofit museums or concert venues where ushering duties are exchanged for free admission. Managing volunteers takes time and is only possible if your own paid staff or host partner assumes the responsibility.

Interns/Volunteers

The official and unwritten rules concerning engaging interns have changed from the days when interns were routinely treated as free labor with little respect for their rights or needs. The new perspective is that an unpaid intern should benefit the most from the relationship. Interns should not be asked to take on demanding jobs that paid professionals would usually do. Interns are there to learn and be exposed to new experiences while supporting your paid staff. Seeking interns or other volunteers is legitimate; just be aware that anyone volunteering is donating time and money by assuming any transportation costs to work on your project. So be considerate by understanding your interns' sacrifices: How long and costly is their commute? Will they miss any classes or other paid positions to work with you? How much time will be required to train them, answer their questions, and generally create a learning atmosphere? Are they replacing any paid staff positions? Is the person supervising them aware of their status and sensitive enough to their situation?

In-Kind Goods

In general, ask any production partners what access they have to any line-item needs in your budget that may have to be purchased or leased if they aren't donated.

Costumes

If you are working with a fashion company whose clothes and style harmonize with your vision and if your performance will attract a large audience and publicity, it is worth exploring the possibility of the company's providing the costumes. Elise Bernhardt, the producer of Grand Central Dances negotiated a collaboration with the Swiss watch company Swatch, known for creatively designed wristwatches. At that time, the company was attempting to expand into different leisure/athletic clothing lines, and I was invited to select from its catalog free clothing for my dancers. The marketing person at Swatch was thrilled to have a sponsorship banner placed in Grand Central Terminal, akin to a temporary billboard, to be seen by thousands of people during rehearsals and performances.

Space

Securing a site involves more than having access to the performance space. Unless you have negotiated complete access to an indoor site, having an alternative site for rehearsals when you cannot use the primary space is essential. Acquiring donated space is never easy, but it's worth the time and effort. If your use of the additional space does not entail additional costs, such as security, and does not displace rental income, the chances are greater that an individual or institution will want to help.

Technology

Technology encompasses any equipment that can support your artistic plan. If your production partner is an educational institution, asking to borrow the school's lighting, video cameras, video projectors, sound equipment can offset several budget lines. One of the advantages of working with a school, especially a college or university, is access to resources that support their educational mission. If you are invited to work with a college, your project is part of that mission.

Food and Drinks

The search for food and drink donations is usually motivated by having a benefit event or anticipating your cast and crew's needs during lengthy rehearsals. Food and drink are often costly. With the right connections, it is possible to find wine and specialty brewers delighted with the exposure they get by sponsoring your event (Photo 8.4). Your event's size may be less critical to a sponsor than your guest list. Outright gifts of prepared food are more difficult to acquire.

webbed feats

post party

to benefit the launch of webbedfeats.org and an ultimate performance in bryant park

co-chairs Betty Wasserman and Connie Connors invite you:

sponsored by

RUSSIAN VODKA

pseudo

600 broadway-6th floor

10-2am

dj odyssey

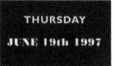

THURSDAY

JUNE 19th 1997

OPEN BAR!!!

$10 per person

performances by

gopoetry.com

video installation

No one under 21 admitted

Photo 8.4 Post-party invitation at the Pseudo loft, New York, NY to benefit the production of *Webbed Feats* (1997); all beverages listed were in-kind donations.
Photo, courtesy Stephan Koplowitz.

Last Thoughts

> Well, there was the time that I was visiting a corporate funder, and we were talking about them funding a project, and I broke with protocol and got down on my knees and put my hands together and said, "Please fund us!" It worked.
>
> Anne Hamburger

Despite the challenges of fundraising outlined in this chapter, the process is ultimately significant for the positive effect it has on your sense of self and self-confidence. The first time I initiated a fundraising event, a benefit connected to one of my early concert seasons in New York City, the gathering of the donors was gratifying on many levels. It not only generated much-needed funds but engendered emotions similar to attending one's own birthday celebration. In essence, it is an event that highlights your initiative and the birth of your vision or project, unites people for one cause, and creates a new social network. Receiving donations of any kind, at any level, is a powerful experience that communicates tangible support. It can serve as a reminder that your work has meaning and relevance in people's lives. Raising money can seem like a daunting task, but researching, writing, filming, and making the asks in a timely and appropriate manner will ensure more comfort with the process and, ultimately, success.

PART IV

CREATING/GENERATING CONTENT

9
Staging, Placing Your Work in a Site (One Method)

At this point in the process, you have completed site selection and site inventory and researched the design, history, current use, and the surrounding community. Your planning budget is now a working budget, and your fundraising efforts have succeeded in providing you the opportunity to start rehearsals. The subsequent chapters in this book will address many aspects of content creation and other production elements that affect your artistic plan and vision, beginning with a method designed to help you develop the narrative of your performance: *guiding the sight/site*. When creating a Category 1 site-specific work, which is uniquely inspired by the site, the site is the subject matter, possessing its unique design, history, current use, and community. The space is already full of meaning. Once you have developed your perspective on its meaning, you are ready to create an unfolding narrative inspired by the site's physical properties. You have two mutually supportive goals: deciding where the audience will focus their eyes, why one area should be seen before another; and moving the performers through the site in a manner that reveals your thematic concept. Simply stated, guiding the sight/site means managing the order in which you reveal the specific locations of a site--what aspect or area of the site you highlight first, second, third, etc. Your job is to take the audience on a tour of the site based on the theme, concept, and point of view of your artistic plan. The clearer your conceptual framework, the easier it will be to formulate your visual ideas when using this method.

Example 1: Fenestrations (One Site, One View)

When I conceived *Fenestrations*, my goal was to create a sense of grandeur and intimacy. How would I introduce this vast and intricate space to the audience? How would I organize the use of the space over time? Where, on what level, would I physically start the work? How exactly would I use these four levels to communicate a visual and temporal narrative? All of these questions are, with some variation, the same for each site-specific work. Guiding the sight/site is a method that helps you answer these questions.

Because of its two-dimensional nature (the audience in Grand Central faced a large, windowed, flat surface, much like a giant screen), *Fenestrations* provides a good illustration of how guiding the sight/site operates. When I started rehearsals for the work, I had already decided to focus on the theme of home given the

On Site. Stephan Koplowitz, Oxford University Press. © Oxford University Press 2022. DOI: 10.1093/oso/9780197515235.003.0010

Photo 9.1 The windows in Grand Central Terminal, Vanderbilt Ave., side, *Fenestrations*[2] (1999) by Stephan Koplowitz, New York, NY.
Photo © Tony Giovannetti.

terminal's function as a commuter train station and the large homeless population that inhabited the station in 1987. So I looked at the four stories of the windows as a two-dimensional representation of a home, as though we were looking inside a cut-out of a house (Photo 9.1).

I was working with space on a grand scale and, based on my site inventory, decided to fill the space with 36 dancers. There are four levels, each divided by three windows structured so that I could hide all the dancers in several locations on each level, thus allowing many options for the number of performers I could place on and off stage at any given moment. However, the performers could not move from one level (floor) to another but were confined to their assigned floor. The performance space is over 200 feet high and over 120 feet wide, an immense scale that was both an inspiration and a challenge.

To introduce the space and the concept, I had one performer ("dancer #1," Photo 9.2) walk from left to right across one window in the upper left corner of the façade (fourth level) and, when she had disappeared from view, had another performer ("dancer #2," Photo 9.2) enter from the left and walk across the third level middle window and disappear, followed by a performer ("dancer #3," Photo 9.2) appearing, again from the left, on the second level right window, and, finally, used dancers 4, 5, and 6 to complete the impression of one person walking through a home. I used this lone figure to emphasize the massive space and evoke an emotional response from the audience. The next image involved the figure being

Photo 9.2 The numbered arrows show the sequenced pathway of the individual dancers as they pass through the windows of Grand Central Terminal to give the illusion of a single person walking through the different levels in *Fenestrations*[2] (1999).
Photo © Stephan Koplowitz.

joined by another person and another until, at an early climatic moment, all 36 performers were revealed, which brought into focus the scale of the cast and the windows and suggested the mass of humanity populating this home. This reveal was such a surprise that it almost always elicited a burst of applause from the audience. This entire section of the work guided the viewers' focus to every point in the space of the windows and prepared them to experience new visual configurations with the cast of dancers.

After establishing the site's image as a house or home, I then proceeded to investigate other concepts (such as community and locomotion), using this method of guiding the sight/site. The method helped organize my thoughts and translate them visually into the space. Once I had my opening visual narrative, it was easier to create the work's subsequent movements.

Example 2: *Genesis Canyon* (Navigating Multiple Spaces)

Another example of guiding the sight/site is *Genesis Canyon*, created for the grand entrance hall at London's Natural History Museum. Instead of one space on which the audience can focus with one look, like the windows in Grand Central Terminal, the museum's entrance hall contains many different sub-locations that cannot be encompassed in a single glance (Photo 9.3). My site inventory resulted in three spaces on which I wanted the audience to focus at different times.

Photo 9.3 The Natural History Museum interior grand entrance, London, UK. Left to right: grand staircase; internal stone bridge; balconies that enclose the hall on three sides.
Photos Adobe Stock

The concept for *Genesis Canyon* was to create a narrative tied to the history of life, both evolution and human civilization. Given this concept, I decided that the audience would experience these three spaces in four discrete parts, in a specific order: the staircase, the stone bridge, the balconies, and then a return to the stairs. Each of these spaces represented a different part of the narrative timeline.

Genesis Canyon: Part One

Metaphorically, I had decided that the grand staircase at one end of the hall would represent the ocean, the sea where life began. I wanted to create the image of undulating water and a sense of multiple life forms emerging from the water. To achieve these effects, I did not want the audience to see steps; I did not want them to read the site as having steps. Thus, I began the performance with all 38 dancers lying down on the stairs, covering the length and width of these grand steps with a sea of bodies. In this case, my thematic intention determined my decision to reveal my entire cast at the start of the work. This opening tableau allowed for the creation of different images all connected to the concept of the beginning of life and the start of human evolution. I had performers rising and falling, vocalizing, making the sound of rain by tapping on the stone steps, etc. In time, the performers began to acquire the ability to move, first on all fours and then upright, creating different iconic formations that suggested early human rituals and ceremonies. The steps receded as steps and became wholly supportive of new images, much like a painting's canvas.

Genesis Canyon: Part Two

Maintaining the audience's singular focus on the steps-as-canvas lasted conceptually in the narrative until I wanted to suggest the Middle Ages. For that time period, I choreographed the dancers to appear, seemingly out of nowhere, on a pedestrian stone bridge located behind the audience as they faced the staircase. Guiding the sight/site required the audience to shift focus from the stairs and turn around to face the stone bridge. All of the dancers appeared on the bridge and performed a vocal and gestural sequence that evoked a visual sense of that period.

Genesis Canyon: Part Three

As the work continued and the narrative moved into the Renaissance, the performers moved from the bridge to the balconies on three sides of the entrance hall. The goal was to have the audience feel surrounded and immersed in the dancers' movements. Guiding the sight/site meant allowing the viewers to shift their focus all around, catching different repeatable movement phrases for 10 minutes and feeling a sense of the start of a new, more complex relationship to space and time associated with the Renaissance.

Genesis Canyon: Part Four

In the last section, which represented modern times, the performers returned to the stairs, gradually descending the staircase with movement that suggested they were falling forward through time accompanied by a score that abstractly suggested historical events. Once all of the performers returned to the steps, I wanted their relationship to these steps to contrast with what it had been in the first section. The dancers were no longer lying down (to cover the steps) but standing or sitting, creating tiers of human pixels that would pop up in different configurations during the last 10 minutes of the performance. The rate of movement and changes of levels were much faster and more intricate, capturing the complexity and quick pace of contemporary life. In this section, I wanted the audience to see the steps as steps.

Guiding the sight/site for *Genesis Canyon* was achieved in bold strokes, over vast spaces, requiring the audience to shift their focus with the introduction of each section.

Guiding the Sight/Site: Movement and Lighting

In both conventional theatrical productions and site creations, the two most common and effective ways of directing the audience's focus are movement and lighting. The movement of a performer attracts attention, for example, if other performers on the stage are stationary or if a performer moves in a different manner or direction from the others. Site artists generally rely on movement to attract audience focus, as illustrated by the choreographic narrative of *Genesis Canyon*. Shifts in audience attention were initiated by the appearance of dancers in a new location. Ideally, the narrative establishes the audience's journey through time and space (the site). It shapes their experience, which, in turn, results in an emotional response that is responsible for the meaning they derive from the work.

Audience attention can also be directed by lighting different objects or spaces at different times and intensities. However, stage lights are expensive to rent or to buy. As a result, the decision to use lights tends to depend, first, on whether they are essential for visibility—as was the case with *Fenestrations*, which was performed at night in very dim upper levels of the terminal—or, second, on the size of the budget. Once the decision has been made to use lights, site artists can employ them to support or underline the conceptual narrative they developed using the guiding sight/site technique. The narrative for *Fenestrations* was neither determined by nor dependent on the lighting design, but lights enhanced it. An additional benefit was that the lighting visually transformed the architectural elements of the site and heightened the performers' presence in a manner not possible during the daytime rehearsals.

Guiding the Sight/Site: Promenade Events

When creating an event that requires the audience to move and experience the art at different locations, the challenge becomes how to influence the audience's focus during those in-between moments when they are promenading from one site to another. There are two avenues to consider when faced with this decision:

- Do nothing; simply allow the audience to promenade and let their focus wander until they arrive at the next location.
- Attempt to guide their focus through a variety of different techniques.

The first avenue is often taken when the chosen site is filled with visually interesting details. The audience's journey needs no additional manipulation of focus because the site already offers a rich visual and/or aural experience that strengthens the whole event's immersive effect. It also allows the audience to walk while reflecting on the event that they just viewed in the prior location, the memory of which will influence their perspective of the site as they approach the next event. The distance between locations can provide another reason to opt to do nothing. You may want the audience to move from one location to another as quickly as possible without distractions. For really long distances, both budget and scale may simply make it impossible to affect audience focus as they move from location to location.

The second avenue can be approached in various ways, some requiring and others not requiring additional production elements (costing money). A low-cost method for attracting audience focus involves using several performance/event guides to lead audience groups to each location. These guides can be scripted and speak to their group as they move to the next location, thus keeping the focus on the words and information being shared. The script can take many forms: a real or imagined history or instructions to the audience to look at specific objects or details of the environment as they promenade. During *The Northfield Experience* project, audience members were taken on a tour that encompassed much of the city of Northfield, led by guides both on the bus and on foot. Considerable travel time separated the seven events experienced by each group. To maintain and direct the audience's focus, the guides gave small lectures on Northfield's history that often included information connected to each of the sites they were approaching. The goal for the two hours of *The Northfield Experience* was to ensure that the audiences felt part of an immersive event that held their attention.

Another method to affect focus is to place performers in the audience's path as they traverse from one point to another. This technique helps to create a human pathway that naturally guides an audience along a desired course. *Terratrium* (2003), commissioned by the Bates Dance Festival, took place immediately after a festival dance concert in the Schaeffer Theater. *Terratrium* was billed as an off-site grand finale to the concert program. I intended to guide the theater audience to the site and not lose their focus or desire to attend the finale. The site performance began by intercepting the audience as soon as they exited the theater: Three musicians performed outside the exit doors and, in pied-piper fashion, invited the audience to follow the music as they moved through an ensemble of dancers placed strategically along a 150-yard path leading directly to the entrance of Pettigrew Hall, where *Terratrium* was located.

This example highlights the use of sound as a means to attract focus. Audio, either live or recorded, can create a sense of continuity as audiences move from place to place. A guide's voice, live musicians, or recorded amplified sound can offer myriad possibilities for creative content, all in support of the overall artistic vision and design.

Another strategy for guiding an audience is the use of a mobile projector. Naka Dance Theater in their work *Race: Voices from the Tenderloin* (2010, Photo 9.4) used

Photo 9.4 Portable projection in *Race: Voices from the Tenderloin* (2016) by NAKA Dance Theater, San Francisco, CA.
Photo © Scott Tsuchitani, courtesy NAKA Dance Theater.

a mobile hand-held projector and invited the audience to follow a handheld screen that was continuing the narrative of the work as the audience walked from one live performance location to another.

Guiding the Sight/Site: Exhibition Structure

Some designs call for simultaneous events within one confined space, much like visual art placed within a gallery or museum. In this exhibition structure, an artist might not want to create a single pathway for the audience to move among the various events but to provide several possible paths. Audience movement results from your simply making each of the scattered events interesting so that the audience is motivated to visit as many as possible within the allotted timeframe. The second section of *Babel Index* at the British Library consisted of 14 discrete performances located throughout the space. The audience was given 20 minutes to wander and experience many or just a few of these mini-events. Several performances could be seen simultaneously, and the aim was to design each one to attract closer attention. Other smaller events were revealed as people wandered through the space. The overall feeling was that a living exhibition of human performance installations had been curated for the British Library.

Guiding the Sight/Site: Selective Memory

For some site projects, my design allows audiences to inhabit the performance space before the start of the event, let their focus wander about the space, and imaginatively anticipate what they are about to see. I want to give them a false sense of familiarity, a feeling that they think they know what will ensue. Then, when the performance unfolds with bodies, movement, sound, costumes, and light, I hope that the narrative I have developed using the technique of guiding the sight/site will provide an experience that is more intense and surprising than they had imagined.

For other projects, I keep the audience outside the performance areas, not allowing them much time to absorb the environment before the performance starts. This strategy builds palpable anticipation, much like an audience being told to wait in the theater lobby before the doors are opened or in their seats before the curtain is raised. A variation on this strategy is to bring an audience into the site through unconventional entrances—taking them through a side door or the back door, guiding their pathway into the space to create a new perception of that space. Your visual narrative may be achieved by not revealing, at least initially, the grandeur of the usual entryway.

Last Thoughts

Guiding the sight/site is a tool that allows you to organize how space is animated through the narrative's duration. The key to using this method effectively is to make decisions about how you want to reveal the site's visual components based on your conceptual goals. This method is wholly dependent on proper preparation, research, contemplation, ideation, and then execution. However, when using this method, it is useful to continually revisit the goals, to reassess whether the visual narrative remains in line with your conceptual framework and whether your content remains true to the site and your personal vision.

10
Site Content and Process

This chapter focuses on two types of content found in Category 1 and 2 site works and briefly describes a creative process for generating this content.

Physically dependent content is both inspired by the site and performed on the site. It engages the site's existing surfaces, structures, weight, volume, and size. The performance depends on the site. If the content were, somehow, removed from the site, performing it would require the recreation of the exact physical characteristics and dimensions of the site itself because the creation of physically dependent movement will often generate specific and unique physical techniques necessary for the proper performance of the created vocabulary.

I created *Kohler Körper* (1999) for a decommissioned coke (coal) factory in Essen, Germany. The third section took place in an area where hot coals were once dumped and cascaded down terra cotta tiles into bins to start the cooling process (Photo 10.1). This area was one long shaft (over 200 yards wide) with a 25-yard incline of approximately 45 degrees.

I decided to place the performers at the bottom of this shaft and created a physical narrative that involved having the dancers overcome gravity and attempt to traverse to the top of the site. All movement created for this ascent was in response to the terra cotta surface and the incline. Dancers had to learn how to execute movements while attempting to move uphill and how to allow gravity to occasionally pull them back down the incline. There were several variations of getting up and falling down, sliding, running, jumping, crawling, all in response to the physical properties on site. Performers had to rehearse on site to learn the nuances of these movements, often having to relearn simple actions in response to the specific architecture and gravitational pull.

Physically independent content is site-inspired creative material that does not rely on the physical properties of the actual site to be performed. This content includes all material—themes, metaphors, specific individual movements, and stage patterns—that you have created as a result of your knowledge, research, and impressions of the selected site. Although physically independent content can be performed on that site, it could also be performed at another location—on a stage, for example, against a visual projection of the original site without any physical recreation of the site.

You might, for example, want to create a piece inspired by the Eiffel Tower in Paris but not present the work at the actual tower. In today's connected digital world, you could conduct online research into the tower's architecture, its history, its current use, and its relationship to the surrounding community, all without visiting it. You could create a piece that does not require any of the performers or production

On Site. Stephan Koplowitz, Oxford University Press. © Oxford University Press 2022. DOI: 10.1093/oso/9780197515235.003.0011

Photo 10.1 Rehearsal, *Kokerei Projeck: Kohler Körper*, section 3 (1999) by Stephan Koplowitz, Essen, Germany.
Photo © Peter Brill.

elements to be in contact with the structure itself. You could then do one of two things: (1) You could stage the work in a conventional theater with a projected image of the tower as a backdrop. The audiences would experience it as a theatrical work inspired by the tower. (2) To make the work more relevant and to create a deeper connection to the site and structure, you could perform it at the actual tower, with the tower as background, giving it more of the feel of a site-specific work. These two options would result in very different audience experiences.

I am distinguishing these two types of content from each other not because the goal is to perform independent content elsewhere but because it's helpful to understand the ways an artist can think about content. While physically dependent content *must* be performed on site, physically independent content performed on site offers a more powerful, meaningful experience to an audience than performing it elsewhere.

My inclination is to make content that is a complex mixture of both modalities, emphasizing the physically dependent type. The more the content is physically attached to the site, the more visceral its impact on an audience. Watching bodies physically engage with the surfaces and volume of a particular site is the purest form of site work and leaves audiences with indelible images. Connecting content physically to a site is the unique hallmark of both site-specific and site-adaptive work. I have seen many site-specific works inspired by a site and staged on site, but because the creative material was not attached physically to the site, it appeared less intentional

and more arbitrary. Experience has taught me that an audience's emotional investment is directly proportional to the physical investment that the performers make
in the site. The choice to use physically dependent content creates an impact that
far exceeds the easier and safer choice of merely using the site as a backdrop for a
performance.

A Working Process for Creating Content

A good indicator of the extent to which movement will be physically dependent
or independent is your decision on where to hold rehearsals. The more unique the
physical elements, the more you will need to engage those elements physically in
rehearsal on site. If you can rehearse the work in an empty studio, the content is
most likely physically independent. Sometimes, there is a middle ground when, for
example, a site's physical elements can be reasonably replicated in a studio (an entrance, a balcony, a wall) in preparation for physically connecting your performers
to these elements in the actual site.

Deciding which type of content is best for your project depends on the selected
site and the approach you wish to take. You will probably discover that projects can
consist of a mixture of both physically independent and physically dependent content, sometimes within a short span of time. Physically independent material can be
as short as one phrase of movement or even one single movement/shape within a
longer phrase of physically dependent content; the reverse is also possible.

How does one begin the process of creating physically independent or physically
dependent content? The method I am suggesting occurs after all of the preproduction
research: site selection, site inventory, design elements, history, current use, and community. This preproduction period has generated thematic ideas and a sense of how
the work is structured from an audience perspective. The process of creating a narrative timeline through guiding the site/sight has also begun. Once this inquiry and work
period is complete, it is time to fill your compositional structure with artistic content.

Task-oriented approach

> I work almost purely with imagery. It's almost always an image that I give the performers.
> So I might say if the gesture is something like this [gestures], "Open your chest like a sun-
> flower opens to face the sun and moves with it through the day." To give them the right
> intention and quality for that they are doing, I use some kind of analogy, mostly from the
> natural world because our bodies respond instinctively. I don't tend to just demonstrate
> or go five-six-seven-eight; it's led by the intention and the image because that works for
> everyone. Metaphors transform our sense of movement and enliven us.
>
> Rosemary Lee

For performance-based work, I create content collaboratively with my cast. My methods are particular to my background and experience, and no two artists, no matter how they describe their collaborative process, will work exactly the same. The description of my process offers only a partial view that I share to provide insight into how the methods outlined in this book can be used.

Given that physical engagement with the site is an essential element, I want to organize a team of artists who possess qualities that will make them effective collaborators. I always tell performers interested in site work that there's no room for fear of dirt, of placing all parts of their body in water, grime, mud, grass, concrete, etc., as long as safety precautions are clearly established. I stress that we will physically engage the site. We will lie down, stand up, bounce off, jump over or under whatever is necessary to discover and create new visual images using movement that will elicit a sense of wonder and excitement.

In terms of past training, I look for technical proficiency that translates into physical confidence. I want to work with artists who have precise movement control in space and time. Rather than high leg extensions, triple turns, or extravagant leaps, I value a combination of fearlessness—a desire to explore space from head to toe, the courage to take informed risks—with a strong sense of presence, musicality, and a good memory. I also look for performers who can improvise, solve creative tasks/problems quickly, and communicate (teach) intelligently their discoveries to other performers who may later join our process. There is very little rote learning during this initial collaborative process.

> I build my choreography in collaboration with the performers. I give them assignments to come up with their own movement. I also create phrases within my established vocabulary. I create gestural language, and we work improvisationally with video. I give architectural tasks like, "You're confined in the space between these columns," or, "Make four six-count phrases circling around your tree that includes a turn, a jump, a level change, a psychological torment, and a hiccup."
>
> Mark Dendy

Core and ensemble cast

When working on a large scale with more than 15 or 20 performers, I divide the creation period into segments if time permits. Part one involves a core company of 5–10 people, selected with an emphasis on their creative and communication skills. I want to sketch/create as much of the overall content as possible with this smaller ensemble, typically for two weeks. If a work calls for a large unison or ensemble section, then one or two core members will represent five or more other performers. If one part needs 10 different duets, I may have all 10 duets created with only four people who will teach the material to incoming performers later in the rehearsal process. As mentioned in Chapter 7 (Planning Your Planning Budget), it is less expensive and easier to work more intimately with a smaller group. Sometimes, performers join just two days before a performance, depending on the size of the cast needed and the allotted rehearsal time. The closer to the performance a cast member joins, the more rote the learning process as the new members learn the movements developed by the earlier dancers. Performers are cast based on their audition and/or availability.

Early rehearsals

What are the big metaphors? What are the symbols? If trains are a theme, what can we do that will give you a sense of trains? They're linear, and they're lights in the dark moving across space. I will write lists of images that are associated with these metaphors. Or I will work with members of the community and see what material they can contribute, sometimes as simple as mothers dancing with baby carriages or kids on bikes.

Martha Bowers

One method to create physically dependent material is to explore how a body or a piece of visual art (such as a sculpture that will be connected to the site, not free-standing) can interact with the shape, volume, and surface of a site. To prepare for the first rehearsal, I select an area of the site to investigate and begin to visualize what I want to see (or hear). Sometimes, my images require clear and precise staging, choreography, or sound. At other times, a visual effect needs to be discovered through exploration on-site with performers. Early in the process, I use the site's physical properties to devise choreographic tasks for my performers to fulfill. These tasks are designed and inspired by the specifics of the site and the number of performers with whom I am currently rehearsing. At times, I give each person the same creative problem, asking each to work alone; other times, I assign a task to a group of two or more. Everything depends on the site and the physical challenges that it presents.

For example, if the site has a balcony with a railing (an architectural component I have encountered on several projects), I ask performers to create four different movements that involve holding onto the railing. I often preface a task by demonstrating my own interactions while challenging everyone to devise movements far more interesting than my generic demonstration. If I am consciously looking for physically dependent content, I direct my performers to make physical contact with the site and to make their creative decisions with contact in mind. I frequently emphasize the analogy of the site as a performing partner. Material generated from these tasks is selected, rejected, and edited for length, direction, timing, etc. Each rehearsal yields new content, and the path toward making both temporary or final decisions varies each day.

The Grand Step Project (Photo 10.2) started with a single dancer rolling down the stairs.

From the onset, the audience was confronted with a performer physically navigating the steps in a manner contrary to conventional walking. The body was horizontal (prone), not vertical, and the performer had to overcome the challenges of rolling on steps instead of a flat surface. The decision to have people rolling down steps (and,

Photo 10.2 *The Grand Step Project, Flight,* (2004) by Stephan Koplowitz, Cathedral of St. John the Divine, New York, NY.
Photo © Julie Lemberger.

subsequently, up the stairs) required a new technique for rolling that could only occur on the stairs. It was necessary to train each performer to roll down and up the steps without allowing the body to show the pull of gravity, which would typically cause a discontinuous bouncing as the body leaves each step's flat surface. I wanted performers to roll in a smooth manner—no bumps, nothing staccato, more legato in quality. To achieve this effect, we spent considerable time analyzing how the body would push and pull itself through space, what muscles needed to be activated, what other physical adjustments had to be made. We needed to develop a new physical technique to accomplish these movements. Physically dependent content poses these kinds of challenges.

The second section of *Occupy* at the Yerba Buena Gardens (San Francisco) took place among a collection of seven jagged rocks (Photo 10.3).

The challenge was to create a performance that did not merely use the rocks as a backdrop or frame. My goal was to connect the performers to the site to capture the theme of how spaces influence our bodies and pose challenges of accessibility. These rocks, jagged and asymmetrically spaced, were an apt visual metaphor, and I wanted to bring this concept to life through action (Photo 10.4). To this end, I assigned the performers several rehearsal tasks:

- Find four ways to place (drape) your body over a specific rock.
- Find three approaches to climb onto a rock.
- Find three ways to lean into a rock.

Photo 10.3 Butterfly Garden, Yerba Buena Gardens, San Francisco, CA.
Photo © Stephan Koplowitz.

Photo 10.4 *Occupy*, second section (2017) by Stephan Koplowitz, Yerba Buena Gardens, San Francisco, CA.
Photos © George Simiam.

• With a partner, create three scenarios of climbing and falling from a rock.

The goal was to exhaust many visual and movement possibilities before creating a narrative choreographic through-line. The results of these initial explorations generated more tasks and allowed me to begin to select, edit, and create movement phrases and pathways that became central to the final work.

One method that generated physically independent material came about during my work at London's Natural History Museum. For *Genesis Canyon*, having selected the theme of the history of life, I researched Charles Darwin and his writings. His travels and discoveries were part of the original motivation to build a Natural History Museum in London, separate from the British Museum. During my research, I was particularly inspired by his book *The Expression of the Emotions in Man and Animals*, in which Darwin explored connections between human emotions and their possible origins in animals and made an extensive catalog of emotions observed in both animals and humans. Based on this catalog, I created word chains that I gave to my performers, asking them to generate movement phrases based on each word string. I then edited and combined these to create new choreographic phrases that I wove into the fabric of the work. The site had inspired this entire process, yet this particular content was not dependent on the physical location for its creation or execution.

> Because of my interest in history, I use words that come out of historical sites and help to set up movement improvisation tasks. I might, for instance, get the dancers to think about their journey to the site. What was their pathway? I would ask them to draw a map of it, and then use this as a score for creating a movement phrase. They might do that with one part of their body and do something else with the story they may have written with another. When I was working on my project in Perth, I had the dancers write a haiku of how they arrived in Perth. One arrived from Sarajevo at the time of the Bosnian war, and she said, "arrived with fire and fury," and that word phrase became this movement phrase. So I'll work with narratives of the dancer's stories about their relationship to the place to generate dance material.
>
> Carol Brown

As content unfolds on any given project, I review the current progress, take inventory, and analyze the material to ascertain the balance between physically dependent and physically independent material. My motivations for this care taking are the challenge of delving as deeply as possible into a site's physicality and my bias toward physically dependent content.

> While assisting a site choreographer, I learned something about editing from the ruthlessness in his approach. It was useful, and it impacted my thinking about the creative process. It was inspiring to see the choreographer just be like, "Okay, I like this in isolation, but on the whole it doesn't work, so it's gone." Or, "We're going to cut two minutes out of that overture," or whatever it is. I like being exposed to that kind of lack

of preciousness. I think he was more ruthless for site work because there are too many vulnerable moments where you might lose the audience. It's because they're not captive, as in a proscenium theater where if they have a moment when their mind wanders, they are still in their seat and the piece brings them back later. There's something about site work where you're corralling their attention all the time, given the distractions in a real environment.

Sara Hook

Last thoughts

While teaching students site work, I notice that many beginning artists tend to create physically independent material, primarily because they are more familiar with that process from their experiences with conceptually based work for the stage. They are less familiar with physically dependent content, so they need to move outside their comfort zone and make a conscious effort to try something new. The rewards are worth the effort. The key for artists new to this process is to develop their skills incrementally, from small projects to larger ones—like carpenters or bricklayers. An awareness of what distinguishes physically independent from physically dependent content will influence your work process and creative decisions. As you engage with different sites and gain more experience, you will discover your own creative process and become increasingly confident in the power of physically dependent content to excite and move audiences.

11
Collaboration and Collaborative Elements

Introduction: A Short Primer on Collaboration

> Collaboration is all about relationships. I'm not a lone vision-maker. I feed on the creativity of the people that I'm with, and it's through our conversations, sitting on the porch talking about an idea, getting to know people's lives; it's about talking about what's important to us, what we're grieving, what we're looking forward to, what we're celebrating. It's in these conversations that the work I make is born. Even if an idea has sprung through me, it's through my collaborators that it comes to fruition.
>
> Amara Tabor-Smith

Finding your comfort level as a collaborative artist is part of the process of creating site-specific work. As with many performing arts projects, you often need to work with artists from other areas—composers, various designers, etc. Once a site is secured and a project conceived, selecting partners to realize your vision and structuring these collaborative relationships are the next natural steps. Four possible collaborative relationships are described here. You may find that you are most comfortable only working in one style or that different contexts require different relational structures. Hybrids are always possible.

> What I discovered about collaborative group work is that *everyone* has to be willing to put in the same amount of work.
>
> Melanie Kloetzel

One artistic director

In this dynamic, you are the lead artist responsible for creating and establishing the artistic vision, and all collaborators work in response to your direction to realize the work. You assign the creative tasks and make all final decisions concerning the appropriateness of each collaborator's contribution: text, choreography, performance, costumes, music, lighting, and set design—every artistic element of the project.

Equal partnership involving two collaborators

In this relationship, you and your collaborating partner share all the responsibilities of creating the artistic vision and together make decisions and assign tasks to any

On Site. Stephan Koplowitz, Oxford University Press. © Oxford University Press 2022. DOI: 10.1093/oso/9780197515235.003.0012

additional collaborating artists. The internal decision-making process depends on negotiations with your partner.

In the site-specific performance world, Sara Pearson and Patrik Widrig (PearsonWidrig Dance Theater), Olive Bieringa and Otto Ramstad (BodyCartography Project), Amara Tabor-Smith and Ellen Sebastien Chan (House/Full of Black Women), Debby Kajiyama and José Navarrete (NAKA Dance Theater), to name a few, have created collaborative partnerships with each person contributing different talents and sensibilities to their work. Each of these partnerships, in turn, collaborates with composers and designers who help realize their ultimate vision.

Cooperative with three or more collaborators

In this collaborative structure more than two people form a collaborative group, which creates the artistic concept, with each member of the collective contributing to its vision. No one person within the group takes the lead or credit above anyone else.

Independent

The independent collaborative structure allows each artist within the collaboration to work wholly independently of others, a relationship modeled most famously by Merce Cunningham and John Cage. In this model, each artist develops creative material separately. The only shared decisions might involve the length of the work (for time-based arts), how many performers (for costumes), and perhaps the size of the venue (for technical issues and possible set designs). The idea is that all of the elements are brought together during the week of technical rehearsals.

Variations

Each of these structures can have variations. For example, a solo artistic director might opt to begin a project with an equal partnership before taking on the role of final decision maker. One project can even contain all four structures. For example, one section of the work might have a solo artistic director while material for other parts is created by a collaborative group. Whatever the structure, it is essential that your lines of communication and areas of responsibility are clearly established from the beginning.

> My creative process is chaotic. When I say collaboration can be chaotic, what comes to mind is childbirth, the chaos of childbirth, breathe, push, surrender. There's a process to me that's not neat and tidy but is spontaneous and has friction, not dramatic friction but acting on creative impulses and knowing when something needs to change.
>
> Amara Tabor-Smith

Selecting a Collaborator

> I think it's a challenge to collaborate with friends. You have to know how to navigate that. For me, it's important because there are friendships I don't want to lose because of disagreements on budget or aesthetic decisions or whatever. It is true I have lost colleagues because a collaboration didn't work out or there wasn't a dialogue. What is most important for me is to be honest. I like to have things written down in advance. That's a tool, and I'm now more selective.
>
> nibia pastrana santiago

Research your potential collaborators' past achievements

Before your first meeting, do some research. Watch or listen to as many of their works as possible, and provide them with links to your own work. Regardless of their reputation or accomplishments, if their work and art-making approach are not compatible with your vision, collaboration will be fraught with danger. If you remain interested in working with artists whose past work does not connect to or complement your ideas, spend time describing your goals for the project to them, and ask specific questions that provide insight into their artistic approach. A composer who presents to you only past works featuring analog instruments may or may not be able to work with you if you are interested only in digital sound. Asking direct questions will help you determine what is possible.

In your initial meeting, also share the fee structure and the work schedule from start to final strike. Include specific dates of any deliverables—dates for an approved costume design or score, for example. As the collaboration progresses, do not be afraid to adhere to the agreements forged during your initial meetings. Do not allow deadlines to pass without clear, unforeseeable reasons.

> Having a timeline that is mutually agreed upon is helpful. "Can you work within this timeline?" "Yes, I can, but I'll need a week in advance for whatever." As long as things are agreed upon, that's the important thing. I can then plan out my time. If I'm a composer who is going to turn in something late, then I'll be the composer who doesn't get asked back to work with anyone. I think that it's a matter of responsibility on both sides when entering into a collaboration. I think the more experienced you are, the more you're able to say with certainty or confidence what you can agree to in terms of timelines and deadlines.
>
> John King

Explore artistic inspiration

Asking directly what motivates someone to work can be revealing. The responses can shed light on inspiration and current interests that can either disappoint or excite you. "I need the work" tells you one thing; "I have been exploring my fascination with 3-D sound" tells you something else. Try to formulate questions that explore the past experiences of any prospective collaborator: What qualities do they look for in an artistic director? What was their best/worst experience? Why?

> I don't think there has to be a shared aesthetic [with a collaborator], although I understand how that could pose some serious obstacles. But there has to be mutual respect and trust. There has to be strong communication. Like in all relationships, this takes time. The best collaborations for me happen when I've been able to spend time with someone and have broad conversations around what we believe in, our life experience, our priorities, even parenting—and how it all relates to our art-making.
>
> Joanna Haigood

Explore styles of working

> If someone says, "I want something that's kind of tranquil and serene," and then you go, "Well, does that mean that it's volume? Does that mean that it's something else?" Then you work it out; you get clear on what the word serene means because serene might mean different things for different people. As long as all the parties understand it, then you can move forward.
>
> John King

How you present your working process to candidates will depend on the collaborative structure you have chosen, and you need to ensure that any potential collaborator will work comfortably within that structure. Presenting specific challenges and asking questions about how someone might handle them can provide valuable insight: How comfortable are they with making revisions, especially more than once? Are they open to directorial suggestions about instrumentation or types of fabric? How will they respond to unanticipated crises? Articulating your expectations as precisely as possible will help you and your candidates determine whether you are a good match.

> Listening. So many people go into situations thinking they're right. I think this is the problem with our politics; this is a problem in families; this is the problem in relationships. I'm a practicing Buddhist, so one of the things we learn is active and mindful listening. So you're willing and open to changing your mind and your heart. Maybe *they* are right; perhaps that section *is* too long. Maybe I *could* start with that section first? Always consider and listen and not think you're right just because you're the lead artist. At the same time, when you know you're correct about something, you have to stand your ground; you have to have the strength of your conviction. You can't be a pushover, either.
>
> Mark Dendy

Four Areas of Artistic Collaboration

What follows is a discussion of methods and reasons to engage collaborators for four distinct artistic elements of a site-specific project: sound, costumes, media, and lights. Understanding their potential role in your work can add powerful dimensions to the experience of creation and performance.

Generating sound/aural content

The current state of audio technology offers many possibilities and opportunities for incorporating sound efficiently and cost-effectively outside of the conventional theater. As you consider this element, there are many factors to keep in mind: the relationship among sound, site, and content; its role or purpose in the production; the type of sound (existing ambient sounds, live or recorded sounds, vocal or instrumental sounds); budget issues. A productive collaborative relationship with either a composer or sound designer can make your artistic plan come to life.

A **composer** writes music. However, a score for site work often includes more than instrumental sounds, so a site composer is responsible for the arrangement of all sounds that will constitute the score for the performance: instrumental and found sounds; previously recorded audio, such as sound effects and spoken words; and newly created sounds using acoustic and digital technology, such as analog acoustic instruments, digital samplers, old-school synthesizers, etc.

A **sound designer** is an artist who selects the sound equipment best suited for a specific site, designs its placement, and calibrates the amplification (through sound mixing) to fit the acoustic properties of the space (indoor or outdoor).

Working with a composer

Collaborating with a composer for a site-specific project can be satisfying and exciting and can enhance the audience experience. You want to work with someone who can support your working process and the specifics of your project's creative needs.

Following are two scenarios to start a collaboration:

1. Your composer has previously created a score that is perfect for your site and artistic plan. Your next steps are to negotiate how the music or score is realized in the space (performed live, recorded, or a hybrid) and at what cost.

2. If you wish to commission an original score, two basic approaches are possible: You engage a composer and begin the collaboration. You spend time communicating to the composer your vision for the site. You immerse the composer in the place, ideally visiting the site together or, at least, conveying to the composer what you find inspirational about the site. You discuss your

thoughts about the kind of music or sound you wish to hear. On a contractually agreed date, the composer delivers a completed musical/sound score or shares some sketches of ideas. At that point, you either ask for revisions or accept the work. When the score is complete, you begin rehearsals using that score. Or you follow all the same initial steps (engaging a composer, site immersion, discussions), but the composer does not start writing until rehearsals are underway; the composer creates the score inspired by your narrative, timing, and compositional structure.

The process of creating an original score can have many variations. For example, a composer could start writing in response to your content and, later, compose a score for a section or portion that you have not yet begun to create, and then, later still, the composer could return to writing in response to your content. When creating an original score, your commissioned composer must be able to produce music within your unique timeline and aesthetic world(s). Site projects often have time-sensitive rehearsal periods. Your composer will have to quickly produce music/sound, perhaps using technology to aid in the process. Working with an artist who not only can create at a rapid pace but can arrange and produce the necessary score within your timeframe will mitigate pressure for everyone.

For some projects, you will need both a composer *and* a sound designer commissioned to support the composer and provide the best acoustic experience.

Working with performer-composers

Typically, composers compose, and musicians perform their compositions, much like choreographers who do not dance in their own works. However, with the advent of new sound technologies, more composers enjoy playing in real time on digital instruments or using analog devices in combination with various sound-processing machines. Finding artists who have an equal interest in performing and composing is far easier in today's contemporary music scene than ever before. There are even college music programs devoted to their training.

Commissioning a performer-composer can be advantageous on many levels. Performer-composers can compose quickly on their instrument(s); they are immersed in contemporary sound technology; and they offer the option of performing live in your work. I have worked with performer-composers for a variety of reasons, especially for projects that needed several different scores for multiple sites. Those with whom I worked in My *TaskForce* project in Los Angeles (Todd Reynolds), Idyllwild (Paul Chavez), and Plymouth, UK, (Hugh Nankivell) were composers who could also perform live and create through-composed works of recorded music.

Working with a sound designer

If live or recorded sound is part of your artistic plan, you need to consider the quality of the sound as it is broadcast into the acoustic space of your site. Working with amplified sound is a scalable proposition. A small, battery-powered Bluetooth speaker can suffice as the primary source for more intimate and smaller projects, while a large space may require an array of four to eight five-foot speakers. Regardless of size, you will have to consider technical factors to maximize the acoustic needs of your space. What equipment you will use, how that equipment will be calibrated, and where it will be placed are essential topics. You will determine if you need to engage a sound designer or can rely on your composer, stage manager, production director, or yourself to make these decisions. For smaller productions and spaces already equipped with necessary sound amplification, it may be easier to include as part of your production team personnel already on staff at the venue. Experienced technicians are often knowledgeable about a broad range of production elements. For large-scale works requiring sound to cover vast distances to reach large audiences, engaging a professional sound designer has benefits.

A sound designer can be engaged under two scenarios:

1. You hire a designer who creates a sound design for your production, generates a list of the necessary equipment, and calibrates the score and equipment to achieve maximum fidelity.
2. You first hire a sound rental company and explain your production goals. As part of the rental package, the company provides a trained technician who will oversee the equipment's placement and calibration.

Either way, your sound needs will be handled by someone whose specialty ensures that your audience's experience of space, equipment, and score is successful. A sound designer will work in close collaboration with you and your composer. Many decisions need to be made concerning how the sound will be broadcast. Some sound scores are made to be heard through one, two, four, or more channels. Sound equalization (balancing the treble and bass) is essential, especially if you are performing in the open air. A good sound designer can make a big difference in how your audience experiences your work.

During the production process for *Fenestrations* at New York's Grand Central Terminal, Rick Sirois, a sound designer who worked on site projects with Dancing in the Streets, shared an interesting fact about sound and large spaces. Rick asked me to deliver a mono mix of the recorded score for *Fenestrations*. Initially, I found this request puzzling, thinking that a stereo mix would offer a more sophisticated sound experience. But Rick explained that a mono mix, for which the entire audio information is replicated in all channels, allows audience members standing on one side of the terminal, far away from a second speaker, to hear the music's entire soundscape. A mono sound mix may seem counterintuitive, but it may be the most efficient way to ensure maximum and equal audience coverage when working with multi-speaker systems in large spaces.

When putting together a site-specific production, take the time to conceptualize how all the different production elements will work together. Sound, lights, costumes, staging, everything needs to synchronize with your vision.

The role of sound design

Some of the different ways sound can function in a site-specific production are outlined here. The list is not exhaustive but is shared to spark thought and inspiration.

Site and theme/concept

An essential role of sound is to reinforce or support the theme of the narrative. The creation of the score can come before or during rehearsals—or both. The process can begin during the research and conceptual phase and continue as the piece develops.

When I created *Union City* (1990) for the Great Hall of Washington DC's Union Station, 14 dancers performed on a high passageway behind the eight statues of Roman Legionnaires. The inspiration derived from the word *union* and the idea of bringing people together. I wanted the work to reflect aspects of United States history, including the divisive Civil War and the role the nation's capital played in saving the Union during that period. This site and theme fused with my interest in choral music, and *The Battle Hymn of the Republic* came almost instantly to mind, so I asked District of Columbia award-winning Eastern High Choir to sing it as part of the score for this work. Here was a rare instance in my process when a work of composed music inspired my choreography.

My commission for re-opening the New York Public Library for the Performing Arts at Lincoln Center, *(In)Formations*, was an occasion to celebrate the library, its mission, and its history. I commissioned composer Quentin Chiappetta to record interviews with several members of the current library staff. The conversations touched on topics connected to the library's vision and history. Chiappetta also selected audio samples from parts of the library's holdings in theater, music, and dance and mixed everything into his original musical composition. Given the specificity of the score, which included short musical interludes from famous Broadway productions, spoken words by eminent artists, and snippets of performances from radio transmissions, much of the choreography was created in response to the score or adapted to fit into the musical phrases. This work was an example of the musical score communicating as much site-specific content as the choreography.

Site and found sound

My research for *Play(as)* at the San Diego waterfront park compelled me to make an early decision about sound accompaniment. The performance site was a large fountain with four strong jets of water shooting continuously into its pool. The sound of these jets was loud and insistent and would dominate any composed sounds. So I decided, before the first rehearsal, to let the sound of water alone accompany the performance.

Working with the natural sounds of a site is one method to enhance a sense of immersion. However, it is also possible to integrate natural sounds with composed sounds, to harness those sounds through targeted recordings and repurpose them into a digital soundtrack. As noted in Chapter 4, composer John King created his score precisely in this fashion for our work in Spoleto, Italy, *Stabile/Mobile*. King spent time at the Alexander Calder sculpture and recorded the ambient sounds of the buses, cars, and trains that converged around the site and used the corten steel sculpture as a percussive instrument and recorded those sounds. All of these sounds were edited and incorporated into his score. During one of the performances, the recording of a bus pulling into the roundabout sounded so real that it gave the impression that the vehicle was actually in front of us, making it difficult to discern real life from the recording. Sound made site, life, and art blend in surprising ways.

The role of sound

Sound can play a visual role in a site production, affecting the perception of a site's size and scale, audience design, and audience focus.

Matching scale

When working in a large space or a space containing multiple sites (e.g., a museum, train station, small town), sometimes, my goal is to match the site's scale or expanse. One solution is to work with as many performers as possible. A chorus of 15 to 40 singers (or more) can not only serve to produce sound but, when placed strategically, create a visual impact that helps balance the ratio of performers to the scale of a site. The 90 singers of the Eastern High School Choir for the performance in Union Station were placed directly below the balcony of eight statues and 14 dancers (Photo 11.1). The chorus created a wall of humanity and voices that helped fill the space and match the grandeur of the architecture.

Creating ambiance

In other works, I have asked choruses to create an ambient soundscape to fill large spaces and extend the visual landscape. Two museum works, *Off the Walls* (Maine and New York), showcased multiple performances throughout the buildings' galleries and public areas. I collaborated with local high school choirs and their musical directors for both works, creating soundscapes by having the choruses sing continuously for 45 to 60 minutes from their known repertoire. We made one change: All words and syllables were replaced with only sounds (sometimes referred to as phonetization or a vocalise). At Gustavus Adolphus College, using two combined student choirs of 125 singers as part of *The Old New Thing* (2012), and at the North Shore Water Tower, *The Current Past* (2013) with Milwaukee's Bel Canto Chorus, we arranged the singing to be free of words and added new harmonics by dividing the choruses into two groups singing from the same score eight to 16 counts apart.

Photo 11.1 *Union City* (1990) by Stephan Koplowitz, in performance, Union Station, Washington, DC.
Photo ©Stephan Koplowitz.

Sound and visual focus

Live musicians can also direct an audience's focus. Placing musicians in strategic locations within a site can add another way to guide the sight/site from one area to another. New ideas for shifting focus and sound distribution can be inspired by the portability of a musical instrument or person's voice: a soprano, an accordion player, a marching brass ensemble, or even a laptop orchestra (which generates digital sound) with battery-powered speakers on wheels.

The Beginning was conceived to harness the power of singers and bring focus to a performance and served as the grand finale of *The Northfield Experience*, for which I had the opportunity to commission an original choral score from composer Justin Merritt. This was a three-part work, involving 220 singers (from three choruses selected from St. Olaf and Carleton Colleges) who performed specific choreography that framed the three sections, all taking place at the Northfield Cemetery. The singers were staged purposely to frame performance spaces and to lead audiences through the site. During each of the three sections, the chorus indicated where the performances occurred and how the audience navigated the site. *The Beginning* demonstrated the power of sight and sound to transport an audience into an alternate reality.

Working with live musicians and singers can be advantageous but challenging in terms of budget and added production complications. Keeping rehearsals with live musicians as short as possible by accessing an already known repertoire and working with entire ensembles can help with costs and scheduling. Given the budgetary challenge of transporting 220 singers, only one on-site rehearsal of *The Beginning* was possible for both singers and dancers together. I managed to work with the singers on campus only once before the dress rehearsal, hoping everything would come together. It was a risk worth taking.

Last thoughts

The introduction of sounds and music into any performance is a personal aesthetic choice. My prior training and experiences as a composer have greatly influenced my artistic path, eventually leading me to begin a career as a director/choreographer. Included in my studies was an immersion into the world of John Cage (Merce Cunningham's primary artistic partner) and the 20th-century notion that music can be the found sounds around us. From Cunningham, I learned the power of dance/movement when freed of its reliance on composed music. The merging of these two influences with site-specific creation allowed me to embrace the silence/ambiance of a site or to invent new scores to support my work. There are hundreds of variations to this relationship of place, sight, and sound. Take the time to consider the best combination for your vision and available resources. Music holds much power on our collective psyche, and it is an art form to revere—and to fear, if you ignore it.

Generating Costumes

Incorporating a formal costume design into your artistic plan depends on your production priorities. For some, costumes are last on a list of concerns, while for others they are at the very top. Regardless of your point of view or experience, you cannot ignore costumes for site projects because sometimes the performers' safety will depend on what they wear. Some sites contain physical challenges in their design or in the composition of performance surfaces.

As you decide on the role of costumes, consider the different types of costume artists and production personnel you might engage for a site project:

The **costume designer** designs costumes, collaborates with the director, and is in charge of the costume budget and hiring support personnel (costume coordinator/manager, fabricators, costume assistants who clean and repair, etc.). The designer is responsible for creating the look of all costumes; for communicating this look to the director using sketches, photographs, fabric swatches, or a combination of all three; and for working in tandem with other production team members (lighting designer, stage manager, etc.) as needed.

The **costume coordinator/manager** works with both the director and costume designer (if applicable), overseeing costume construction and purchase, managing fittings, and keeping track of the budget (if there is no costume designer). At times, the coordinator/manager is responsible for hiring support personnel.

A **costume assistant** can work in a variety of roles: costume construction (sewing, dyeing), fitting, and maintenance (repair and cleaning). The assistant reports to either the costume designer or manager.

One person can assume all of these roles and responsibilities.

Working with a costume designer

The costume design process can happen at any time in the production cycle as long as the creation of the costumes can be completed before the established deadline—often, the dress rehearsal or first performance. However, some site works demand earlier deadlines because the performers need more time to rehearse in costume—for example, if the artistic plan calls for historical dress or if the costumes have a specific function or design in relation to the environment (swimsuits or clothing that must be highly reflective or a particular color or cover all parts of the body, etc.).

In addition to making sure costume designers understand your work's narrative and concepts, you should encourage them to visit the site and attend rehearsals onsite. They need to know and understand the site's physical elements and how these might affect the performers and their movements in costume. The shared experience of attending rehearsals also allows you to build both your relationship with the designer and a common vocabulary based on the work.

Early in the conceptual or rehearsal stage, I ask a designer to create two or three quick sketches (Photo 11.2); these offer us the opportunity to compare ideas and to explore possible artistic directions. At this point, the idea is to avoid too much attachment to any one direction.

A sketch might take the form of a mood/idea board (Photo 11.3): a collage of images, photos, illustrations, color swatches collected from the web, books, magazines—anything that the designer feels captures some aspect of your artistic vision. The Pinterest website (pinterest.com) offers a useful tool for this exercise, but old-fashioned scissors and paste are fine, too.

Once you and your designer agree on a concept for costumes, you can ask for more thorough, detailed sketches and a mock-up of costumes to avoid any future misunderstandings.

Before contracting with a designer, make sure to discuss who will be responsible for costume construction and maintenance. Do not assume that all costume designers are interested in working beyond the design phase. When negotiating a fee, keep in mind that if a designer is only interested in design, then you will have to hire various assistants. Typically, designers have their own contacts and will discuss costs with you. Once you have agreed on a fee covering all these costs, it is essential to be clear that you expect the designer to manage the entire process for this fee.

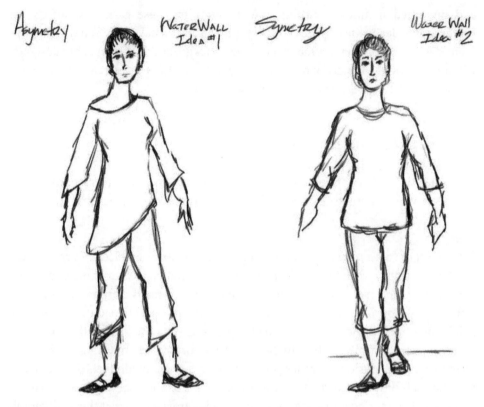

Photo 11.2 Initial sketches by Paige Wilson, costume designer for *Natural Acts in Artificial Water* (2012), Houston, TX.
Photo courtesy Paige Wilson.

Photo 11.3 Mood board created by Andrea M Gross, costume designer for *The Northfield Experience* (2018), Northfield, MN.
Photo courtesy Andrea M Gross.

Working with a costume coordinator/manager

You may have a clear idea for costumes and only require someone to procure or construct your design concept. For example, if your concept calls for 20 performers to wear simple black tops and bottoms, you could hire a costume coordinator willing and interested in finding, fitting, and maintaining these garments. Of course, bringing any idea to life requires creativity and a solid visual sense. You will find that many costume coordinators/managers have a background in design or are designers willing to work in a variety of roles. Your aim is to create a productive collaboration, so you must define these roles and establish clear goals.

The role of costumes: safety

Costumes play different roles in a site-specific production. Your first responsibility is to assess any site safety issues that might affect the welfare of the performers.

Feet

What level of foot protection will the performers require? Choices can range from bare feet to sturdy work boots. The site's surfaces will dictate your choices, but keep in mind that rehearsal footwear may be different from what is worn in performance. It may be appropriate for performers to wear their own sneakers during rehearsals and be fitted with a more specific shoe for performances. Make sure that you allow performers ample time to adjust to the fit and comfort of these new shoes before performance. Also, consider whether your performers can provide their own footwear for rehearsals or will need you to supply shoes for both rehearsals and performances. Some sites have surfaces that are so rugged (rocks, gravel, etc.) that they will rapidly degrade and ruin shoes during rehearsals. Asking performers to provide their own shoes for rehearsals may not be advisable or possible. This factor can have significant budget implications, so you need to consider it as you create your planning budget.

If all surfaces of a site consist of stone or concrete, allow performers to rehearse in protective footwear that will mitigate leg and foot injuries, such as shin splints, muscle exhaustion, and bruising. Performance wear may not require as much protection given each performance's relative brevity; you should discuss this issue with your designer and performers. Water-related sites offer an entirely different set of footwear challenges. Swimming pools, rivers, fountains, streams, all have different submerged surfaces and could require specialty footwear. One of my works performed in the Los Angeles River (*TaskForce*) required the purchase of heavy-duty water boots to protect performers from discarded, potentially injurious trash, such as cans or broken glass.

Skin

Protecting performers' other body parts from abrasive surfaces and weather-related elements (heat, cold, water, fire) is also essential. One extended section of *Horizon Time* (part of *Sullivant's Travels*, 2014) took place inside the new black box theater's lighting grid in Sullivant Hall at The Ohio State University (Photo 11.4). The grid's wire mesh was the performance surface for four dancers. During our initial rehearsals, it was apparent not only that the costumes had to provide full coverage of

Photo 11.4 *Horizon Time*, part of *Sullivant's Travels* (2014) by Stephan Koplowitz, Barnett Theater, The Ohio State University, Columbus, OH.
Photo ©Stephan Koplowitz.

arms, legs, and hands (with gloves), but that the fabric needed to be thick enough to protect all body parts in contact with the metal surface. Finding the right material to make these costumes required much trial and error.

Weather is another factor to consider. If excessive heat and sunlight or cold and wind threaten performers' safety, designing costumes to respond to these factors will be necessary. You will also need to ensure the fabrics themselves do not create the potential for dangerous entanglements with other performers or the site.

The role of costumes: capturing the concept

Once the practical safety factors have been addressed, you can consider how costumes will interact with the overall visual design and plan. The questions to answer focus on the relationships among the performers, the concept, and the work's narrative. These questions are pertinent to any performance project, whether for stage, film, or site: Who or what do your performers represent? Are they specific (real) people? Where do they come from? From what historical period? Are they an extension of a visual concept? Is this a work of abstraction in which the bodies are being manipulated purely for visual effect? Is this work a combination of reality and abstraction? Will you require a change of costume from one section to another? Are costume changes possible given the nature of the site or the length of the

Photo 11.5 Dancers on the mooring cells in the Mississippi River, *Solstice Falls on Fridays* (1985), choreography and costume design by Marylee Hardenbergh, Minneapolis, MN.
Photo ©James O. Phelps, courtesy Marylee Hardenbergh.

performance? Are the visual elements or the narrative dominant? Answering these questions early in your costume-conception process will help produce a design that addresses your performers' role within the context of the site. The costumes can enhance and extend your ability to communicate intention and theme.

Site artist Marylee Hardenbergh's work in and around rivers illustrates how performers can represent abstractions. An early work, *Solstice Falls on Fridays* (1985), placed 12 dancers on mooring cells on the Mississippi River, each dressed identically in red and blue costumes that augmented their visibility through color and the flow of the fabric (Photo 11.5). The performers' costumes highlighted the design of the round mooring cells through the use of color and shape. The excess fabric, suggesting wings, allowed the performers to occupy more volume within the cells' circular area, thus giving each solo performer a more impactful presence on each mooring. The path of these large mooring cells was reinforced by the line of color the costumes created.

Ann Carlson's *Night Light*, conceived as a site-specific installation that recreated archival photographs in the tradition of tableaux vivant, provides an example of performers who represented real people. Carlson was aiming to "create a collision between the historical moment and contemporary life" and to consider "what gets preserved in our memories, as well as, literally, what gets saved, conserved, and held onto as documents of historical truths" (Ann Carlson youtube.com channel). To achieve this effect, Carlson cast performers who resembled the figures in the

Photo 11.6 Examples of costumes for singers and dancers by Craig Givens, costume designer for *Genesis Canyon* (1996), Natural History Museum, London, UK.
Photo ©Tricia de Courcy Ling.

photographs and wanted the costumes to be as historically accurate and close to the originals as possible.

Genesis Canyon at London's Natural History Museum straddled both worlds of abstraction and historical reality. Performers were divided into two groups: an ensemble of 38 dancers and a group of three singers/actors (Sarah Jane Morris, Barnaby Stone, and Jonathan Stone, who also wrote the musical score). The concept was that the large ensemble would represent different visual themes during the four-part narrative. The three singers would represent tourists from the 1880s who were visiting the museum soon after its opening. Costume designer Craig Givens and I collaborated to highlight the difference between the two groups, giving the ensemble of dancers a less defined, more abstract look that allowed them to inhabit a variety of roles: mammals emerging from the ocean, early prehistoric humans, and, finally, contemporary people. The ensemble costumes were identical but were given a modern cut and designed with a texture and color that blended well with the architecture's color and surfaces (Photo 11.6). The singers were dressed as realistically as possible as Victorian tourists.

For *The Grand Step Project, Flight*, the costume concept was realistic and straightforward. I wanted the 50 dancers to portray urban office workers assembling (seemingly spontaneously) at New York City's grand, public staircases. The vision for the costumes was clear and specific; however, I needed a designer who could create a visual world of realistic office workers in clothes that ensured the dancers' safety navigating the stone steps and that offered a broad palette of design and color. Designer Kaibrina Sky Buck collected these costumes from retail, Goodwill, and Salvation Army stores and corporate donors. She had to make alterations, figure out a color scheme for the entire ensemble, and provide a balance of variety and similarity that would make the ensemble design seem random and coordinated at the same time.

The role of costumes: site and visibility

Aside from safety and aesthetic challenges, some sites may pose visibility problems. Are audience members positioned at a distance that will make the performers difficult to see? Are the surrounding surfaces a texture and color that potentially camouflage the human figure? The last section of *lines, tides, and shores* . . . (2013) for the Milwaukee Art Museum gardens placed the audience on a pedestrian bridge high above the site (Photo 11.7). Some performers danced as close to the audience as 30 yards while others were as far away as 100 yards. In previous sections, the audience-performer relationship was far more intimate; so I needed a costume design that would satisfy both perspectives. The designer (Lisa Christensen Quinn) and I decided to work with a colorful, bright palette of primary colors that heightened visibility from long distances and provided a sense of energy and variety in the more intimate sections.

Finding a color or colors that enhance visibility is a constant challenge in site work. There was a period when I used a lot of red in my costumes, because red is useful in creating an unmistakable silhouette for bodies placed in almost any environment, indoors or out, regardless of the surrounding textures and colors. For the 54 tailored costumes designed by Craig Givens for *Babel Index* at the British Library, I felt red brought a formal quality to the work, perhaps because of its associations

Photo 11.7 *lines, tides, and shores* . . . , section three (2013) by Stephan Koplowitz, Milwaukee Art Museum, Milwaukee, WI.
Photo ©Stephan Koplowitz.

Photo 11.8 *Kokerei Projekt: Kohler Körper,* overture and section one (1999) by Stephan Koplowitz, Essen, Germany.
Photo ©Peter Brill.

with royalty. The red would also make the human figure pop out against the marble, wood, and steel of the library spaces.

In Germany, for the *Kohler Körper*, performed in a repurposed coal energy factory, I wanted the level of grime and dirt to be reflected in the costumes. The designer, Bennie Vorhees, created a uniform similar to a factory worker's garment, but instead of the industrial colors of blue and grey, we chose white. The concept was that all 50 performers would begin the work with clean white uniforms, and as they progressed through the site and the performance, their clothes would reflect the accumulation of time, grime, and effort (Photo 11.8). This progression from white to the dark soot created a narrative that started with an image of very visible individuals and ended with an image of workers visually erased through their labor. This use of costumes encapsulated the overall theme of the human cost of coal and energy production.

Last thoughts

On one underfunded and self-produced site project, getting site permits, assembling a cast, finding the right music, etc., were so time-consuming that costumes became an unintended afterthought. As a result, I didn't hire a costume designer until the end of the production process. The result? The haste and pressure of costuming created unnecessary insecurity and tension among the cast and collaborative team. Early in rehearsals, performers usually ask, "What are we wearing?" If you can't answer confidently at some point, your authority as a director can be compromised. Additionally, the sooner costume issues are addressed, regardless of the budget size, the more likely you will discover creative and affordable solutions.

If you are a self-producing artist whose budget simply can't support costume design, the need for costumes doesn't just disappear. The performers have to wear something. You will likely have to make cost-effective decisions, which will be minimalist by nature and preclude hiring costume professionals. But you need to make that decision consciously, mindful of how it might affect the rest of the production. And you will still need to decide and tell your performers what they will be wearing, especially if the site raises safety issues. Costumes play functional and artistic roles in any production, and your costume plan can result in your performers feeling more confident and more artistically engaged in your work. Don't ignore this production element.

Incorporating Visual Elements and Media

Incorporating visual elements and media means using physical props, fabric, constructed sets, wearable sculpture, digital projections, or any visual element created for your production. Visual mediums have a long history of inclusion in theater, where set design and props are almost a given in most staged productions, from community centers to Broadway. In recent years, digital projection design has replaced set construction on several high-profile shows; it has even permeated classical music concerts, which are programming visual projections commissioned explicitly for each musical work. Visual media is ascendant given the rapid technological progress made each year in picture quality, ease of use, and cost.

Here are some collaborating artists who could be engaged in support of your work:

A **set designer** designs scenic elements in collaboration with you. These can take the form of entire painted backdrops, specific props to be used by performers, or visual installations placed within the site and performing area. A set designer would either construct the work or hire assistants.

If your production requires props—visual objects that are manipulated by performers or are part of a visual site installation—you may require a **prop master**, someone who finds and/or builds the props and ensures they are placed in the correct locations during the performance. This person could be employed by you or by another collaborative visual artist. Often, to control costs, the **stage manager** or a production assistant takes on this role.

A **media artist** is a generic term for anyone who uses technology—film, video, audio, the internet, interactive and mobile technology—to create works of art. The media artist's role in a site-specific project would be to realize your artistic plan, contribute conceptual ideas for the use of media, and engage other necessary artists and technicians (detailed later) for support and execution.

If your visual plan specifically requires video projection and no other forms of media, a **video** or **projection designer** (also referred to as a **video director**) would oversee and create a plan for both the content of the projections and their visibility in the space. Integrating film, motion graphics, or a live camera feed into the narrative is the primary responsibility of video directors/designers. They are also involved in selecting the type of hardware needed to fulfill a visual plan and oversee the placement and focusing of these projection elements. Increasingly, video projection is becoming part of lighting or set design as conventional lighting and set designers become more knowledgeable about all the instruments that create light, texture, and image.

Working with a media artist or video designer

Even if you are doing the conceptual work for any media components, you will likely need a media artist or projection designer to attend to the practical technical details. The surface on which an image is projected, its size, and duration will alter both the image and the site itself. It is not possible to take an image, moving or still, and simply throw it on a wall or other surface without specific calibration to optimize both the capacity of your projector and the image. Someone with technical expertise must coordinate the raw images with the site and available technology. Your collaboration with a media artist will require patience as you work on editing and processing such things as the imagery exposure and the aspect ratio (to sharpen the image) to fit the contours of the site's surfaces and textures. This creative collaborative process is akin to working with a sound designer, as discussed earlier.

The sooner you create the material you wish to project, the easier it will be to address any challenges that may appear. Rather than wait until dress rehearsal to see how projected images look in a space, I often ask my video designer to conduct a test with whatever instruments are available at the time. Sometimes, we merely hold a projector in our arms to throw the image onto the designated surfaces to discover anything that will spark new ideas or raise potential technical issues.

Projected elements, particularly moving images, can affect audience focus, which is both a good reason to use these elements and a warning. During your work sessions with a media artist/designer, be careful not to let enthusiasm for what is possible distract from what is necessary to keep the audience focus on the central narrative. Setting that boundary early in your discussions with your media artist (or any artistic collaborator) and maintaining it throughout your production are essential goals.

Working with visual and technological elements

When I started making site-specific work, I had a personal rule not to add to a site any foreign elements other than costumes, music, and lights. I aimed to keep the focus on the site in its natural state as much as possible. Of course, lights, sound, and costumes are significant additions to a site, but these additions were necessary to highlight the bodies, the human presence of performers. As time progressed and with new challenges, I began to see my early orthodoxy as a limiting factor rather than a virtue. I realized that other visual elements offered new possibilities for introducing novelty and reinforcing my thematic goals. So a new rule evolved to ensure that all creative decisions involving these visual elements were inspired by and connected to the site's design, history, or use. Not every project is suited to the addition of visual media. Any visual elements introduced should be organically and seamlessly a part of the fabric, texture, or design of the space and relate to the concepts and themes associated with the artistic vision for the site.

What follows are some examples of some of my past works that have incorporated visual components.

Visual elements: props and projections

My first departure from the avoidance of additional visual mediums was *Babel Index* for the British Library. The library only allowed access to its public spaces, forbidding entry to any of the stacks and interior research areas. This limitation, at first, was frustrating. Except for one area, the vast public spaces were devoid of any visual information that established the library as a library. The entryway with its vaulted view of three stories of balconies, the café area with its tables and chairs, the pristine white walls, all seemed closer to a modern hotel or hospital than a historically significant cultural institution devoted to books, information, and research. The publicity postcard (Photo 11.9) for *Babel Index* illustrates the generic quality of the space. If

Photo 11.9 Promotional post card for *Babel Index* (1998), produced by London's Dance Umbrella Festival.
Photo courtesy Stephan Koplowitz.

the words "British Library" were not included to identify the building, no one would know what the building housed. The dancers depicted could be dancing on hotel balconies.

During site visits and site inventory, I selected specific areas to accommodate performances and offer good sightlines for the audience. Still, I was dismayed by the lack of context the public spaces provided. I therefore felt the need to introduce visual components that would suggest a library. My decisions to use actual books as props handled by the performers and project images of text and objects from the British Library collection onto the white walls of the public spaces were successful solutions because they were organic to the site and narrative.

Just outside the library's entrance were 11 square concrete bollards (posts used to deter acts of terrorism, Photo 11.10), each large enough to accommodate a single standing person.

In the prelude for *Babel Index*, I placed on these bollards 11 performers, each holding a large book, fabricated to contain a small light that would illuminate their faces (Photo 11.11). These props suggested a library and captured the contemporary movement of text from pages in books to personal computer screens. Specifically, I played with the idea of illuminated manuscripts—the medieval texts adorned with illustrations and decorations, sometimes in gold and/or silver leaf. The British Library has one of the most celebrated collections of these books. The performers

Photo 11.10 Concrete bollards at the entrance of the British Library, London, UK.
Photo ©Stephan Koplowitz

Photo 11.11 *Babel Index*, prologue (1998), video stills from video documentation by Deborah May, British Library, London, UK.
Photo courtesy Stephan Koplowitz

opened and closed the prop books using various degrees of speed and motion for 20 minutes while audiences waited to enter the building.

The two public cafés were the performance spaces for part one. All of the tables and chairs were removed, and the audience viewed the performance looking down from three levels. The proximity of a large glass wall, containing the original book collection of King George III (known as the King's Collections) provided a visual library context, so I felt no need to incorporate additional props or media projections. However, the lighting design (by Simon Corder) transformed the floor to suggest a worn piece of parchment (Photo 11.12). Corder's lighting supported my intention to have the choreography depict a short history of the evolution of symbols and letters. Twenty-two dancers performed a series of maneuvers that created these graphic images and letters with their bodies.

In the second part, audience members were allowed to explore the entire remaining public spaces for 20 minutes and discover 11 different performances staged in these separate locations. In five of those areas, props were introduced. Three performances—a duet, trio, and quartet—used books passed from one person to another. Additionally, two quartets taking place in the generic corridors outside of each floor's elevators performed on a carpet of newspapers. Throughout the performance, the paper became tangled and torn, creating both a visual and soundscape.

In the third part, the audience stood at the bottom of the atrium entrance and looked up at the three balconies that faced outward. This part featured all 54

Photo 11.12 *Babel Index* section one (1998), video stills from video documentation by Deborah May, British Library, London, UK.
Photo courtesy Stephan Koplowitz.

Photo 11.13 *Babel Index,* section three (1998), video still from video documentation by Deborah May, British Library, London, UK.
Photo courtesy Stephan Koplowitz.

performers, each one carrying a book for the entire 15-minute finale. Additionally, media artist Markley Boyer projected photographs of different British Library artifacts (Photo 11.13) that he edited to fit within the balcony walls' narrow surfaces.

The visual elements introduced into the narrative of *Babel Index* were a natural outgrowth of the world the performers inhabited. The projections of the library's collection (seen in Photo 11.13, below each of the balcony railings) were like an x-ray of the building, illuminating and turning the library space inside out.

Visual elements: set design

My desire to embrace visual elements in site work gained more energy with my *TaskForce* project, which had three full iterations in Idyllwild, Los Angeles, and Plymouth, UK. The *TaskForce* structure called for creating a series of stand-alone site works within a short time (two to three weeks). For each project, I commissioned other artists to collaborate with me, giving each one a specific creative task inspired by the site. The results of their work became part of the performance and the site. Each of the three projects consisted of six to nine separate, stand-alone site-specific works, each at a different site, involving a different contributing artist from music, dance, theater, media, or visual art. Out of 21 different works, nine included commissioned work from a visual or media artist.

From *TaskForce*: Idyllwild:

For *Inspiration Point*, located outside Idyllwild overlooking the Coachella Valley, visual artists Judith Schonebaum and Hannah Ruskin (mother/daughter) were tasked as set designers to create a design/installation to blend with the already existing objects found in the space. Their design, seen in Photo 11.14, incorporated old reel-to-reel audio tape wrapped around the road barrier at the lookout point entrance. In addition, they added to the permanent signage found at the site.

From *TaskForce*: *Liquid Landscapes*, Los Angeles, CA:

For the first section of *Farmers Market* at the Original Farmers Market in Los Angeles, set designer and visual artist Roman Jaster created a mobile visual installation using the green wooden food carts (Photo 11.15) that have become almost a de facto logo for the market. The site-inspired performance took place among the food stalls and the market's pathways as a highly structured improvisation. Jaster's art-laden food carts were wheeled through the space as the performance unfolded, creating a visual disruption when least expected.

Two selected works from *TaskForce*: *Liquid Landscapes*, Plymouth, UK:

Photo 11.14 Visual installation by artists Judith Schonebaum and Hannah Ruskin for *TaskForce, Mapping Idyllwild* (2008), Inspiration Point, Idyllwild, CA.
Photo ©Stephan Koplowitz.

Photo 11.15 Visual installation by artist Roman Jaster for *TaskForce, Liquid Landscapes* (2008), Original Farmers Market, Los Angeles, CA.
Photo Scott Groller, courtesy CalArts.

For *Smeaton's Tower*, a work inspired by the tower on the Hoe of Plymouth (UK), I commissioned artist Ella Huhne, who specializes in fabric, to thread the tower with a large fabric instead of wrapping it. I wanted to break up the structure's linearity, to fracture its line and the expectation of seeing only straight lines. Huhne, working as a set designer whose task was to weave the fabric into the site's structure, spent much time finding material with the right texture, weight, durability, and color (Photo 11.16). She also designed the circuit as the fabric

Photo 11.16 Visual art installation by artist Ella Huhne for *TaskForce, Liquid Landscapes* (2009), Plymouth's Smeaton's Tower, Plymouth, UK.
Photo ©Stephan Koplowitz.

Photo 11.17 Visual art installation by artist Helen Snell for *TaskForce, Liquid Landscapes* (2009), Plymouth Landing, Plymouth, UK.
Photo ©Kevin Clifford.

was threaded through the top of the lighthouse tower. The result was that, even from afar, a viewer could see that something different was happening that invited closer inspection.

For the *Mayflower Steps* in Plymouth, the site from which the Plymouth pilgrims set sail for a new world, I gave my set designer, visual artist Helen Snell, the task of creating a design/installation of 200 paper boats. Snell's challenge was to create a basic boat design that was easily folded using a suitable paper size, weight, and color. I placed the boats in one long line that delineated the performance space along the Plymouth landing (Photo 11.17). When the performers reached the actual Plymouth steps, four large paper boats (made of reflective material) were launched into the water as part of the finale.

Visual elements: pre-recorded video mapping
Video mapping, or projector mapping, involves projecting images (of any kind) onto three-dimensional surfaces of varying sizes or dimensions. It is possible to transform everyday household objects and large-scale buildings into 3D projection surfaces, allowing the images to be viewed from different angles. Like many recent technological advancements, projector mapping is becoming more ubiquitous as software and hardware costs continue to fall. As of this writing, however, the process still requires software knowledge and the use of sophisticated projectors, all of which can add several thousand dollars to a project budget.

The ability to transform any building's exterior into a vibrant and kinetic projection surface creates new opportunities for adding visual information. It is now possible to alter a site by layering it with an entirely imaginative reality, as Photos 11.18 and 11.19 illustrate. Animated buildings can serve the same function as live

Photo 11.18 Waterfalls projected on the grounds surrounding the Chokseongnu Pavilion, (2017), Jinju, South Korea, by YMAP (Your Media Arts Project).
Photo courtesy HyungSu Kim.

Photo 11.19 Video projections by artist Luc Vanier for *The Current Past* (2013) at the North Point Water Tower, Milwaukee, WI.
Photo ©Stephan Koplowitz.

performers. And projected virtual performers can appear to be walking up or down a building or can look as though they are behind a virtual window. This technology is a form of augmented reality without the need for goggles or camera screen intermediaries.

For the performing arts, projection mapping allows the melding of images and performers in new formats and structures. Even independent of the performing arts, it has been used as an increasingly popular method of making buildings or entire neighborhoods come alive through kinetic visual imagery (e.g., Cincinnati's BLINK festival of light). In Milwaukee, for *The Current Past* (2013) at the North Point Water Tower, I used a combination of live and projection mapping on the top of the tower facade. In this work, I collaborated with dance/media artist Luc Vanier to insert live video inside a series of edited photographs based on the theme of water ecology. Projection mapping allowed me to animate the entire structure from the base, where 16 live dancers performed, to the top portion of the tower, which was our projection screen (Photo 11.19). Additionally, the use of live video created the effect of having dancers change size and location. Through technology, I felt I could balance the tall tower's visual scale with the real and virtual images of my narrative.

Of course, the decision to use projector mapping should be carefully considered. The ability to transform a building's surface into a projection screen offers both a creative opportunity and the potential danger of losing site-specific focus. What is your motivation for considering projected images? Will your images enhance or obliterate the design elements that drew you to the site in the first place? Ultimately, have the history, use, and community of the site inspired your projections? Do they support your original concept?

Visual elements: live video/image magnification

Like projector mapping, using a live video feed is becoming more common as the technology gets smaller and less expensive. It is now possible for anyone with a smartphone to broadcast live on the web at any time. Large music concerts (usually in the commercial world) use continuous live video to provide patrons with a closer view of the performance. Live feeds are becoming more sophisticated as performers mix live and prerecorded material to enhance the artistic experience. A term associated with concert live streaming is IMAG (image magnification), which can be an effective way to incorporate video projection into a site project. Live video is also used in various contexts for theatrical works to incorporate abstract design elements or give a different perspective of the stage space, both of which could apply to site productions.

On two occasions, I have used this method: for the water tower performance described earlier and at a pier in Chattanooga, Tennessee. For *Light Lines* (2005) at the Chattanooga waterfront pier, I incorporated my short film of site performances on historic city bridges followed by a continuous live IMAG feed magnifying details of the performance. Audience members were seated as far away as 200 yards, and the live video provided some semblance of detail and scale. The 10 × 10-foot projected

Photo 11.20 *Light Lines* (2005) by Stephan Koplowitz, waterfront pier, Chattanooga, TN. Photo ©Stephan Koplowitz.

image (seen in the lower-left corner of Photo 11.20) added an entirely new dimension to the work, merging digital and analog spaces in real time.

Visual elements: augmented and virtual reality

Technological advancements with smartphones have launched an entirely new location-based experience called augmented reality, which uses technology to project sounds, images, and text on the world we see. The most popular example of this technology is *Pokemon Go!*, a game that invites people to explore real sites with their smartphones or tablets (using GPS mapping technology in each device, Photo 11.21). The goal is to find and collect icons (that can only be seen when a camera phone is pointed at specific locations). Augmented reality is rapidly finding its way into many different areas of production, including retail experiences, advanced gaming, and the performing arts.

Augmented reality is different from virtual reality (VR), in which computer technology creates entire worlds and environments that can be explored through VR headsets. It is possible that, at some point, there will be a marriage of these two technologies allowing for a 3D experience to be explored in the real and virtual worlds simultaneously.

A popular use of augmented reality in specific sites is found in walking tours, many of which highlight historical aspects of a site. Like *[AR]T Walk* (2019), some have been purely artistic, created by Apple in partnership with the New Museum in New York City. Together, they commissioned Nick Cave, Nathalie Djurberg and

Photo 11.21 Examples of augmented reality being used on-site.
Photo Adobe Stock.

Hans Berg, Cao Fei, John Giorno, Carsten Höller, and Pipilotti Rist to create augmented reality artworks that could be viewed on a walking tour through Central
Park. The event served a dual purpose: promoting Apple products (iPads and
iPhones and earbuds) and showcasing the technology's novel use.

Last thoughts

I've had an interest in the convergence of visual technology and performance
since my college years. As my site work has evolved along with the democratiza-
tion of technology, I have become increasingly interested in exploring the creative
applications of all kinds of visual mediums to my site work. Each new generation of
artists will have their own relationship with visual media as technology continues
to evolve rapidly and plays an ever more essential role in the art world, especially in
site-specific projects.

Technology already enables creating digital/virtual space, and filmmakers have
been creating works on location and for locations for decades. It seems natural
to want to animate a space with as many different tools and resources as possible.
When working with any medium, the perennial danger is its potential to upstage
or distract from the central vision and theme of a work. As Canadian philosopher
Marshall McLuhan said, "The medium is the message": a medium's effect on society
is determined more by its characteristics than by its content. The latest iteration of
this dictum would be the smartphone, which has spawned an entirely new culture
of social interaction (Instagram) and new modes of transportation (Uber, Lyft), not
to mention a wholly new societal class of amateur photographers and filmmakers
(YouTube). As with any other collaborative art, making conscious and informed
choices when incorporating visual mediums is the best course of action. And unlike the continuing grand social experiments that currently lack adequate anticipation or controls (the effect of computers in education, the impact of social media

on psychological health and the political process, etc.), artists can experiment and remove anything that damages their artistic vision.

Designing Lights

Lighting design for site-specific productions is *necessary* under two conditions: if your performance is outdoors at night and there is no artificial light available, or if the performance is indoors and the available light is not sufficient to satisfy aesthetic and/or public safety concerns. Lighting design is *possible* only if your budget can cover the costs. Some site projects may offer a choice. The site may have sufficient daylight or existing artificial lighting, but it might also have the capacity for you to create a lighting design that would enhance your artistic vision. So, weighing the advantages and disadvantages of working with lights is a place to start.

Lighting is often the main ingredient in creating what people call "the magic of theater"—all of the special effects that any conventional theater can bestow on a work. The myriad of available lighting techniques applied to site work can seem even more magical. Lights can transform details and aspects of a space and a body in motion to create a sense of novelty, surprise, and atmosphere. The click of a switch can alter the mood of a space. Lights can also support the staging and narrative of the work, and as mentioned in Chapter 9 (Staging, Placing Your Work in a Site), lighting is a tool for *guiding the sight/site*, which helps direct audience focus as the action unfolds. Augmenting whatever natural illumination is available at a site (depending on the time of day) provides a higher level of control over the visual aspects of your work. Choosing to perform on-site at night, possibly during off-hours, gives an audience an entirely different experience than if the work happens during normal hours amid regular public activity. An evening performance can make audiences feel that they are part of an exclusive event that offers an entirely new perspective on a familiar site.

It is possible to work with lighting, even on a small budget. Many sites contain in-house lighting or, like some outdoor urban sites, have permanent lights in place for public safety. Sometimes, all that is needed is the addition of a few select lights strategically placed.

Here is a list of artists and personnel you might engage:

A **lighting designer** collaborates with the director, choreographer, costumer, media artist or video director, and composer to design lighting that creates visibility, atmosphere, and mood and helps guide audience focus—always mindful of performer and audience safety and budget limitations.

A **lighting electrician** is responsible for realizing the lighting designer's lighting plan (the light plot) by hanging and focusing instruments and connecting electrical cables.

A **lighting assistant** supports the lighting electrician or lighting designer by providing extra labor as needed to hang and focus lights and, if trained, can also assume the role of **light board operator**, executing the lighting designer's light cues.

Sometimes the **technical director** (the person in charge of all technical needs—see Chapter 5, Staffing Key Production Roles) will assume the role of lighting designer, which can save time and money.

Engaging and working with a lighting designer

Lighting is a powerful medium. If your project requires lighting other than just a general wash of ambient light, I recommend working with an experienced professional who knows how to hang, focus, and navigate the technical requirements of your location. The artistry lighting designers bring to a project adds to your work's overall impact and has the potential to open previously unforeseen perspectives on your work.

All professional lighting designers understand the angles needed to cover a performance space, have a strong background in lighting technology, and have a thorough knowledge of color, texture, and reflective surfaces in relation to illumination. Lighting designers who have architectural experience or a background outside conventional theater can be particularly valuable in large-scale site work. However, regardless of past experience, the priority is to engage someone who communicates well, understands your vision for the project, and can think creatively within a small or large budget. If I am seriously considering incorporating lighting into a site project, I seek the counsel of either a technical director or lighting designer to help ascertain the feasibility and projected costs.

Your initial discussions with lighting designers are similar to conversations with costume designers: What is the theme of the work? Is the period historical or contemporary? Does the performance evoke a specific time of day? Do the lights suggest a natural light source (the sun rising or setting, a lamp shining through an unseen window) or carry a thematic meaning? Most importantly, what is the relationship between the light and the site's design, history, and current use? Grounding your collaborators thoroughly in your vision of the site will ensure that their contributions will be both their best ideas and the ones most suited to your needs.

Lighting contingencies and needs

When starting to design lighting for a site project, the first step is to determine the locations of power sources and the amperage available. Identifying the **Authority Having Jurisdiction** (AHJ) is first on your production timeline. The AHJ is the organization, office, or individual responsible for approving layout drawings to ensure that equipment, installation, and procedures conform to local code. Depending on the municipality in which the site is located, you may need to speak with local fire officials, a planning board, or a building superintendent—someone with AHJ authority. Whom to contact depends entirely on location. This person or entity will make it legally possible to hook into power, add power, and hang lights.

Power

Once you have established the AHJ, your next priority is to determine how your lighting instruments, sound equipment, and other technological needs get plugged in with safe and adequate power. The most cost-effective scenario is using the existing power found at your site, whether in a building or an outdoor space. Bringing electrical power to a site can be expensive, so it is best to exhaust all other possibilities before renting equipment.

If power has to be brought in, renting generators is a common practice, and selecting the type of generator and its location within the site are important decisions. The sound a generator creates is another consideration. Generally, the more expensive the generator, the less noise it will emit when operated. Fortunately, technological advances have resulted in producing several choices for quiet generators, depending on your budget. Additionally, the combination of new powerful battery technology and light-emitting diode (LED) instruments, which require 80% less energy and can be housed in smaller cases, offer new options at less cost. Bringing lights to remote geographical sites is possible with less effort than ever.

Lighting instruments

Repurposing lighting instruments that are already on-site can be less costly and maintain the look of the site by avoiding the introduction of lights that clash with a site's architecture. Depending on location and regulations, it may be possible to refocus available light fixtures, change the light bulbs, and/or add color gels. All of these methods require permission and your guarantee that these changes will not result in damage.

Renting a lighting package (instruments, cables, gels, dimming boards, etc.) will incur costs. These rental costs for hardware are only the first part of a lighting budget, which must also cover costs for labor, transportation, and, possibly, extra power. It is surprising how quickly lighting expenditures can mount, so plan carefully to ensure that your budget can cover the total cost.

Masking

Despite the aesthetic and thematic contributions light can bring to a site project, the instruments and cables necessary to create lighting effects can also be aesthetically intrusive. If the site contains no existing places for hanging instruments, you will have to decide where you can place lighting trees and cables and assess their aesthetic impact on audience sightlines. These are issues you must discuss with your lighting designer well before installation, especially if you are concerned about altering the site's character or historical feel. Creating an effective masking plan for installation can be a significant challenge for your lighting team.

Masking may also be needed to avoid shining light into your audience's eyes. If your performance is outdoors in a populated area, you may find that you have to consider the effects of your lights on neighbors who are not part of the audience. The last thing you want is to have to deal with complaints late in the production process during technical rehearsals. Designing the most efficient installation of lights to maximize the comfort and safety of all is as important a goal as satisfying your visibility and thematic aspirations.

The role of lighting

The fundamental role of any lighting is to make things visible. Once that threshold has been crossed, you can consider more artistic lighting uses: creating atmosphere, mood, time of day, theme, audience focus, etc. Lighting can emphasize the physical, architectural properties of a site, giving them a role in shaping an audience's emotional response. Light, shadow, and color elicit feelings, so I have often used lighting to transform physical areas to create a mood and focus the attention of an audience on some aspect of the site as they await the entrance of the performers. Lighting designers enjoy these opportunities to showcase their artistry in a manner that is unconnected to performers and harnesses the properties of pure light. However, it's important to remember that this use of lighting should always serve the conceptual goals of the work itself.

Simon Corder, the lighting designer for *Babel Index* at the British Library, illuminated inside the large entry hall several lighting landscapes that made the space look larger and created a mood to heighten the experience of stepping into a new world. Tony Giovannetti worked similarly in Grand Central Terminal, focusing large pools of light onto the terminal floor at different locations and times as a prelude, each hour before our performances of *Fenestrations*[2] (Photo 11.22). These pools of light served as a subtle way to announce that something unusual was happening in the terminal. Some members of the public walked through the light, thinking it was perhaps natural light and not noticing anything different; others stopped and tried to find the source. The outline of the light carved a space within the expanse of the terminal floor and, for an hour, became visible in other locations.

Existing lighting sources

Sites come with two primary sources of light: natural daylight from the sun and/or various artificial sources. For indoor projects, the existing lighting is whatever fixed lighting is found and operating at the time of your performance and whatever might be coming through windows. For some projects, you may want to keep all of the artificial light on to avoid the cost of renting more. If you prefer to create your own lighting design, especially if you intend to use media projections, you may need to

Photo 11.22 Pre-show lighting, by lighting designer Tony Giovannetti for *Fenestrations²* (1999), Grand Central Terminal, New York, NY.
Photo ©Tony Giovannetti.

request permission to turn off the artificial sources, in which case you will need to explore that option early in your planning.

During *Fenestrations²*, the newly restored Grand Central Terminal was much brighter than it had been for the original project. New lighting had been installed, and all of the grime of the past 100 years had been washed away. The terminal was a far more naturally reflective space. Unfortunately, we could not convince the station's superintendent to dim or turn off enough lights to give our performances as much lighting contrast as we had achieved almost 20 years earlier. This brighter atmosphere altered the dramatic effect of the work. *Fenestrations* was conceived initially as a more contemplative work, which touched on the concept of home and belonging. In this new light, the new version had a more celebratory feeling that emphasized the design qualities of the bodies in motion rather than of the themes initially embedded in the work.

In Milwaukee, for *The Current Past*, sited in the middle of a traffic roundabout, convincing the city to turn off a few of the street lamps that were impeding the audience's view of the images projected on the lighted water tower required lengthy negotiations. Ultimately, we were granted the permits, which helped create a more vivid picture of the illuminated tower.

Relying solely on natural sunlight for site work is a common choice, especially during daytime and outdoors. Working outdoors in daylight can be anxiety-inducing, mainly because illumination varies with the weather. Rain or dark clouds will inevitably alter the mood of your work. Additionally, if you rehearse in an open, sunny site where your performers cast interesting shadows, you may be tempted to incorporate those shadows into your work. Don't. Clouds will likely spoil your plans. Playing with light and shadows can be fun, but you should do so only when you can control your light source. Site artists typically consider the usual weather and available light when selecting an outdoor performance date and time. Knowing the times of sunrise and sunset can help determine what role natural lighting can play in your design. I have scheduled performances precisely to coincide with twilight with the hope (not the guarantee) of capturing those lighting elements. Remember that the time of a sunset does not translate into instant darkness; there is, on average, between 70 and 100 minutes of light before complete darkness, depending on the season and geographic location (the further north, the longer it takes to achieve darkness after sunset). Making site visits during the time of day or night you are planning a performance will help you visualize your plans, though you'll have to consider the date, as well.

Two site/light projects

Both versions of *Fenestrations* are examples of works that, given their evening performances, were entirely dependent on artificial lighting to be seen and experienced (Photo 11.23). Lighting designer Tony Giovannetti placed lights on each of the four glass floors at the set of three windows and was able to have independent control over each of these twelve areas.

Once I had finished the staging and choreography, Giovannetti started to write lighting cues based on the movement narrative. His lighting added to the choreographed movement another layer of energy and momentum not felt when the work was in rehearsal during the daylight hours. The lighting also fully supported the concept of spirituality reflected in the image of the stained-glass windows and captured in the *Fenestrations*' musical score.

Photo 11.23 *Fenestrations*[2] (1999) video stills from video documentation by Alex Rappaport, Grand Central Terminal, New York, NY.
Photo courtesy Stephan Koplowitz.

Photo 11.24 Wexner Center for the Arts under construction (left photo) and *Phantom Fenestrations* by Stephan Koplowitz (1988), Columbus, OH.
Photo courtesy Stephan Koplowitz.

A year after working in Grand Central Terminal in 1987, Giovannetti and I collaborated on another light and movement work at the then-under-construction Wexner Center for the Arts in Columbus, Ohio. This project was Giovannetti's conception: a site performance using choreographed shadows of bodies projected from the inside of a building (Photo 11.24). The effect was achieved by placing and focusing large klieg lights inside the Wexner Center's shell and placing, also inside the building's shell, four scaffolds large and high enough to accommodate one or two bodies. The shadows were projected onto the massive glass façade of the building. Giovannetti's concept was to use the entire building as a lightbox. I called the work *Phantom Fenestrations* (1988). It included three ironworkers who walked in slow-motion silhouette along the large iron lattice in front of the building's glass wall while the human shadows danced behind them.

Last thoughts

Like visual media, lighting that feels organic to the site and supports your artistic plans offers significant benefits: more control of mood, atmosphere, and audience focus and the opportunity to transform an audience's experience of a site with which they are familiar only during daylight hours. Lighting's powerful presence and potential expense demand thoughtful planning with your collaborators and technical team. Still, the rewards are worth the effort.

PART V
CREATIVE AND PRODUCTION CHALLENGES

12
Rehearsal Process

Your ability to generate content depends on collaborating effectively, meaning fairly and forthrightly, with partnering artists, especially your performers. This section will discuss some techniques for making your on-site and off-site rehearsal process as creative and productive as possible.

> There is the aspect of getting the performers to buy into the project, which is always there no matter the type of project. There's a phase where they're open to what's going on, but then there's the other phase when they ask, "Is this going to work? Will all this work yield something I'm proud of?" This is definitely part of every process that I've ever been in. The challenge is to navigate that moment. I have observed directors do several helpful things—letting performers in on the artistic plans, letting them hear the music early on, showing them the architectural mapping, asking them to participate in research tasks, endorsing their input and opinions.
>
> Sara Hook

How Much Time?

Determining the amount of rehearsal time needed is not an exact science. Some projects are constrained either by budget or by the date of the opening. Funds can determine if there is enough money to rehearse longer than a certain number of days or hours with a particular number of performers. Site access might be limited to as little as a couple of weeks. It's important to discuss these issues early in the process of negotiating with site stakeholders. Your sense of the time you will need for any given project will determine if a particular site's accessibility is appropriate for you.

Time On-Site/Off-Site

Once the rehearsal period has been established, you will need to know the exact dates and times you will have access to the site. What will be the ratio of on-site to off-site rehearsals? For some projects, it is possible to replicate a site in a studio or some other ample space removed from the actual site, allowing you to create and sketch material shielded from the distractions of a potentially noisy, cold, busy site. During the creation of *Fenestrations* (both versions), I was able to replicate the four

On Site. Stephan Koplowitz, Oxford University Press. © Oxford University Press 2022. DOI: 10.1093/oso/9780197515235.003.0013

levels of catwalks inside the windows of Grand Central Terminal in a large gymnasium (Photo 12.1) and a rehearsal studio. For *Fenestrations 3.0* (1991), created for the windows, again with catwalks, at the 30th Street Station in Philadelphia, I rehearsed in a public park (Photo 12.1) and studio.

Working off-site can be more comfortable for the performers, providing ready access to bathrooms and other amenities as needed. If your site is outdoors, your indoor rehearsals shield everyone from the interruptions of rain or the annoyances of a hot sun or strong winds. Working off-site can simply make rehearsals run more quickly and smoothly. Working in Grand Central Terminal created such a vast distance between me and the dancers that we had to communicate via walkie-talkie in 1987 and cell phones in 1999. Both methods required that information from me be relayed from one contact person to everyone else. This method of giving directions and corrections effectively transformed what would have been a one-hour rehearsal in a studio, where I could simply speak and be heard instantly, into a two-hour rehearsal on-site.

Some sites are so unique that their design cannot be replicated in a studio or at another location. In those instances, you will need as much access to the site as possible—if not complete access. Early in *The Grand Step Project*, I created some of the staging and movement phrases in a studio with my core company of dancers. It was a way of having them start to kinesthetically memorize material on a flat surface without negotiating the difficulties of the stone steps. Once these phrases were in their bodies, it was easier to adapt the learned material to the steps, making adjustments as needed. This method was most effective for all movement phrases that required an upright and standing position, but the characteristics of the actual site still demanded that we spend much more time on the steps than in a studio.

Too much time off-site can sometimes be harmful. The starting point for rehearsals of *Babel Index* for the British Museum was the section inspired by the evolution of writing. I had hoped to rehearse it in the café area, where the work was to

Photo 12.1 *Fenestrations²* (1999) rehearsals in the Packer Collegiate Institute gymnasium, Brooklyn, NY, and outdoor rehearsal for *Fenestration 3.0* (1991), Philadelphia, PA.
Photo courtesy Stephan Koplowitz

be seen from two to three stories above the floor. Unfortunately, the British Library administration denied access during the first week for three days. Although I knew this would be a problem, I had no choice but to carry on in a studio. I spent three full days creating material for that section and, on the fourth day, brought my cast to the library café (with all the tables removed). As I watched the work unfold from the proper vantage point, I realized that I had miscalculated. I had to discard more than two thirds of all the new material created in the studio; it felt almost like starting over. The anxiety of this experience reinforced my belief in the need to negotiate a proper balance between on-site and off-site rehearsals.

If negotiations are not necessary, if I am free to rehearse on-site as needed, I have developed a balanced general schedule: begin with a ratio of two days off-site to one day on-site for the first week, and then slowly increase the number of days on-site, culminating with only on-site rehearsals the last two weeks before the premiere. After a certain point in the process, off-site work is less and less productive regardless of the site's design. Performers need to get accustomed to the actual site: the physical characteristics, sightlines, changes in weather and light, the public's presence, etc.

As mentioned earlier in a discussion of budgets (Chapter 7, Planning Your Planning Budget), if you are working outdoors, I recommend always having indoor studio space available in case of inclement weather. This option will prevent your losing an entire day to unforeseen circumstances. You will also have to decide what time of day to hold rehearsals. Temperature, visibility, and the comfort of the performers are factors to consider. If, for example, your performances are scheduled during the day in a hot climate, you may want to hold many of your early rehearsals during the evening when it's cooler. However, you still must have enough rehearsals during the heat of actual performance time to ensure that your performers are acclimated.

Rehearsing with the Urban Public

The ratio of on-site to off-site rehearsals does not always depend on access to a site. It may be advisable to work off-site even if the site is available. Distractions are serious factors to consider, especially if they are likely to compete for your performers' attention. At times, we have hundreds of people walking by or stopping to watch our rehearsals. Although this sort of publicity can be beneficial, especially in generating interest that builds a potential audience, you must also anticipate its drawbacks. When I was rehearsing on the steps of St. John the Divine for *The Grand Step Project* on a weekend, it seemed as though every 15 minutes a newly married couple would appear on the steps to get photos taken with the church as a backdrop. It was always difficult for *us* to resist watching these site-specific performances.

Inquisitive passersby will often approach you, perhaps interrupting your focus during rehearsal to ask questions. Their curiosity is natural and can be fine if you can control the interactions and maintain a continuous flow of your rehearsals. The first step is to create a handout that succinctly explains what you are doing and includes the performance dates. The handout serves as a quick way to answer most if not all of their questions, which usually start with "what are you doing?" or "why are you doing that?" This document can either be a formal printed marketing piece or a neatly photocopied fact sheet with all pertinent information. Depending on the project, I have used both. I usually encourage whoever is producing my work (if I am not self-producing) to print a promotional postcard as early as possible to have something more polished to hand out. Examples of these handouts can be seen in Chapter 16 (Promoting and Marketing the Work).

The other strategy for avoiding interruptions is to hire a production assistant who handles public interactions, answers questions, and hands out these materials. The production assistant also helps ensure that the public does not wander into your workspace and serves as a buffer during critical moments when you need to keep people away from a specific rehearsal location. This strategy can be difficult when working in densely trafficked urban sites. The public does not like interruptions to their daily routine. If you are working on a site that serves as an access point (entrance or exit), you should create an alternative route for people or block access only at short intervals that will not overly try people's patience. I faced this challenge when working on various grand public staircases that served as entrances to the New York Public Library and a municipal court building in the Bronx. In each case, we created a side access point that allowed people to come and go while we occupied the rest of the space. This arrangement would have been impossible to accomplish without the help of a production assistant.

An unanticipated challenge arose in Houston, Texas, during our rehearsals in Waterwall Park. The first section of the performance took place against the ground-floor windows of a tall skyscraper, the Williams Tower. Behind those windows were bank employees, and our weekday rehearsals became a major annoyance to those employees, who were distracted by performers leaning and climbing on the windows of their offices. One week before our premiere, we were told that we could not rehearse that portion of the work during business hours. The problem was that we had no way of rescheduling our rehearsals to accommodate this new challenge. The solution was to rehearse the work out of order at the tower after the bank had closed. This schedule was not ideal, but we managed. It underscored that some contingencies manifest without warning no matter how much you prepare.

Preproduction planning can help you reduce delays by establishing lines of communication. In Houston, as soon as the bank voiced its unhappiness over our distracting the employees, we knew exactly with whom we needed to speak. Before starting rehearsals, ensure that everyone who manages a site has your rehearsal schedule and signs off on your plans. If possible, include the dates when you plan to introduce sound so that you can discuss any concerns about volume as a potential source of distraction. You may have to limit either the volume or the time of day that you can use sound. These issues are best addressed before you start your rehearsal period, but flexibility is required, no matter when unforeseen problems arise.

If you are working on a site that is part of a large institution or your site covers considerable acreage, your presence may be challenged by security guards or even the public, unaware that you have been given permission. If you were issued a permit, keep that permit (or a copy) physically with you at all times. If your consent to use the site comes from a managing agent, have an official letter of approval with you. Make sure that you have the phone numbers of all of the important people you would need to contact if your presence is challenged or some emergency arises. Your goal is to ensure that you maximize rehearsal time, so the more quickly you anticipate and resolve issues, the better.

Another approach to working with urban audiences is to allow for a sharing of the public space during rehearsals and performances. Debby Kajiyama of NAKA Dance Theater described her experiences with a recent project:

> Rehearsals versus performance, got really blurred while working on *RACE: Stories from the Tenderloin*. We rehearsed and performed all in public spaces around the Tenderloin in San Francisco. Sometimes, I couldn't tell which gathering was a rehearsal and which was a performance. Rehearsals suddenly became performances just because we were in public spaces and got an audience. Performances became rehearsals because we weren't positive that key performers would be able to show up and what improvised content might arise. Actually, it was more that the line between real life and performance was blurred. The project was based on people's stories, and there were several times someone would stand up and deliver an emphatic, impromptu monologue about their life that stunned all of us, cast and audience included. Those were electric moments; somehow, the audience knew that it was no longer a performance for the stage or street corner. It was a time for one's life to be witnessed.

The unpredictability of rehearsing in public is an element that can bring inspiration, joy, and unwelcome surprises, all dependent on factors such as your intent, how you structure a rehearsal, and your awareness of your surroundings and community. Rehearsing in public demands that you anticipate and prepare for any unwanted reactions or contingencies that may interrupt your work.

Concentrated Rehearsal Periods

Some projects require that you create everything in a short, concentrated period. If you are working outside of your home base, you will need to carefully plan and negotiate the number of weeks and times you'll want access to the site. Creation periods for projects outside my home base, such as *TaskForce*, can be as short as one week and as many as four. The rehearsal period for the Bates Dance Festival (*Mill Town*) was four weeks. Projects like these put considerable pressure on preproduction preparation for both you and the producer.

Working from your home base, which eliminates travel expenses and increases your availability, can potentially relieve some of that pressure by allowing you more flexibility when negotiating time and access. Creating *The Grand Step Project* in my home city of New York enabled me to work three to four times a week over a 10-week period, which would not have been possible if I had had to travel to another city.

Longer Timeframes and Phased Rehearsals

A discussion in the previous chapters on budgets (Chapter 6) and the working process (Chapter 7) outlined a strategy for working with a large ensemble of performers that would support a creative process and allow for some cost savings. This strategy pertains to projects with 15 or more performers. Some of my large-scale works have required between 18 and 78 performers, and this method of working over a more extended period has reduced the stress and pressure that can arise when creating for a big group and helped control costs. The basic premise is to start small and build in size. For a typical project, especially one created away from a home base, I divide rehearsals into two work periods separated by a gap period.

Period one: I create a **core company** of 3–12 performers, depending on the final cast and budget size. These performers are selected for their ability to work creatively and are experienced enough to teach other cast members as the process moves forward.

In general, I try to allot at least one full week (six days) of rehearsal (minimum of six hours a day, preferably eight hours) and, for larger projects, two weeks (10–11 days of rehearsal). The goal is to work as quickly as possible to create either seed material for a specific section or a first draft of an entire section. If 20 people will perform in a section and I am working with 10 during the core company rehearsal period, I double up and have one person represent two. I also take the time to create the appropriate individual material for each of the final performers, teaching one person the movement for two people. The more content generated during the initial core company sessions, the faster and easier the process becomes when more performers join the production. Additionally, working creatively with a large group becomes easier after establishing and testing methods and tasks with the smaller core company.

At the end of this first rehearsal period, I arrange for a private showing and make a video recording of all the material we created. I invite all the significant and interested stakeholders connected to the project: the producers and staff, including whoever is in charge of marketing; all collaborators; and, if appropriate, selected journalists who are interested in writing a preview. This showing aims to allow everyone to see the current status of the project, communicate a sense of the work's vision, and get feedback from each stakeholder. If your creative sessions have generated material in which you are confident, this showing can be a huge morale booster and help motivate everyone involved to support the project. Conversely, if you have some doubts about your work, getting fresh eyes on the material can give you a new perspective that will result in creative discoveries and unique solutions. Having video documentation of the content serves as a record of the creative material to aid in recall by performers (if needed) later in the process. It also allows further study and provides the composer, costumer, and others something tangible to look at during the gap period.

Gap period: This period is anywhere from one to three months. It allows collaborators to prepare for the second creation/rehearsal period before performance. It also allows more time to hire performers if needed and resolve any new issues or challenges that arose during the first session. It gives you a chance to gain distance and perspective on your work and make revisions to your plan if needed. It offers producers the opportunity to market the work armed with more detail from the first rehearsal period. Typically, publicity photos are shot during the first phase, and the gap provides time for marketing materials to be printed and disseminated. It is a pause that refreshes everyone involved.

Period two: The length of this period depends on the size of the production. One week (which includes technical and dress rehearsals) would be the shortest, but you could need as many as five weeks (as I did for my work at the British Library).

The **ensemble performers** constitute the group who join at this juncture. After the core company rehearsals, if you are assembling a large cast (more than 25), you can either bring the entire ensemble into the process at the beginning of the second period or divide the remaining ensemble performers into two or three groups that you phase in as needed. Each group is paid a different fee determined by the amount of time they work. The more performers who join late in the process, the less the cost. An additional benefit of this phased approach is that performers can choose how much time they want to be engaged in the project, thus increasing your potential talent pool. Be careful not to be too economical when adding ensemble performers; they need sufficient time to learn the material thoroughly.

Weather is Always a Challenge

No matter how you structure your rehearsal periods, planning an outdoor project will require you to prepare for unexpected weather. While you can always try your best to schedule a performance to reduce the likelihood of rain or cold, sometimes inclement weather is unavoidable. Most of the locals living in Plymouth, UK, derided my month-long rehearsal and performance schedule for *TaskForce*. "You realize," they said, "you'll be working mostly in the rain?" My only response was to say that we would do the best we could under the circumstances.

It's always wise to schedule enough rehearsals to offset days of rain and to have indoor rehearsal space available. Another strategy is to create, if possible, a performance schedule that includes one or two rain days. Make sure your cast knows in advance what sort of bad weather (how much rain, how cold) will trigger your decision to cancel or postpone a rehearsal or performance. There are two reasons for such disruption: either the performers are at risk of injury because water or cold makes the performing surfaces slick and unmanageable, or the sound and/or lighting equipment won't function in these conditions. If neither of these circumstances applies to your work, you are free to state in your marketing materials that performances will occur rain or shine. If you can shield lighting or sound equipment from adverse weather conditions, you can sometimes avoid cancelations. However, protecting microphones can be impossible, in which case you will have to make a decision. In Milwaukee at the Northpoint Watertower location, we had a full chorus singing into four microphones. Rain started to fall, and, given that the lighting equipment was covered and protected and the mics were not, we decided to continue with the performance but without an amplified chorus—a better decision than canceling the entire event.

You may wonder why I have not mentioned the effect of inclement weather on the audience. Generally, the audience is not at risk of injury if the ground is wet. If they are motivated to attend a performance in the rain, all they need to bring is proper clothing or an umbrella or both. The worst that can happen to an audience in the rain is getting wet. Weather conditions affecting audience safety (lightning, very high winds, etc.) also apply to the performers.

Last Thoughts

Given the vagaries of weather and other variables that affect the amount of rehearsal time needed for any given production, I strongly recommend that you not begin any site-specific project without first negotiating access to the site and securing an off-site rehearsal location. This strategy will enable you to start work with a clear rehearsal plan that allows for the maximum amount of distraction-free and productive creation. Devising a rehearsal schedule that balances the needs of site stakeholders and your artistic plan with the physical safety and fair compensation of your performers requires time and careful thought. Sharing a draft of this schedule with *everyone* involved in the production before rehearsals begin will prevent surprises and miscommunication and support everyone's commitment and investment.

The method of dividing your rehearsals into three periods and phasing in the additional cast members when working with large ensembles is a classic example of tackling a large project by breaking it down into smaller parts. When the work finally comes together during the last week of rehearsals, the aim and the result are often a recognition that the whole is far greater than the parts.

13
Rehearsal Safety

Maintaining a safe environment during your rehearsals and performances is essential, and the recent Covid-19 pandemic made health and safety prime issues. The coronavirus brought the performing arts to a standstill while people researched and created new protocols to permit safer social interaction. As a leading resource for all aspects of safety for public events, the Event Safety Alliance publishes a comprehensive guide for general event safety and the reopening of venues (eventsafetyalliance. org). This chapter will cover the many other essential safety challenges typically affecting site projects.

Proper safety promotes productivity and an efficient use of rehearsal time. Safety has special significance for site-specific works given the myriad of potential sites and the range of environmental and design challenges they present.

The focus on safety begins with the permitting and permissions process discussed in Chapter 2. Be prepared to answer questions about liability, safety, insurance, and your plans for the site. Site stakeholders will want to know if your artistic plan will put performers and/or audience members at risk of physical harm. No one wants to invite a lawsuit.

Safety—Not Just Physical

Site-specific works, like other performance works, can pose emotional challenges for the performers and audiences. If your work requires any form of nudity (and has been approved by the site's stakeholders), you must discuss with performers before engaging their services the details of what you envision. In addition, the dramatic content of some works can trigger emotional stress like that described by Joanna Haigood: "In the case of *Invisible Wings*, acting out the violence of slavery was traumatizing for many of us. It required a lot time in the process to deal with the complexity of the emotions we were experiencing. There were many difficult and painful moments, but it was also healing. It was life-changing. I think it is important for everyone in this country to reflect and engage with this history and with racism, but it has to be in a safe situation. Otherwise, it can do more harm than good."

Just as you would post warnings about using strobe lights or artificial smoke, you should consider posting notices for audiences if there is content that could possibly elicit uncomfortable emotional responses.

On Site. Stephan Koplowitz, Oxford University Press. © Oxford University Press 2022. DOI: 10.1093/oso/9780197515235.003.0014

Perspectives on Production Safety

You might think that safety issues ought to be self-evident and obvious, but imagining all contingencies, from several angles and perspectives, ensures that nothing is overlooked. Consider safety from the standpoint of your producers/site stakeholders, collaborators, performers, production technicians, staff, and audience members. Each of these constituents will have safety concerns applicable to everyone else and unique to their role in the project.

Producers/Stakeholders

Producers and the site's stakeholders care about potential liability resulting from an accident. It is paramount that you show them that you have both insurance and any permits required and have taken all necessary precautions. Getting their approval for your project depends on your meeting these obligations, regardless of how excited they may be about your artistic plans. Your responsibility is to clearly and honestly communicate how you plan to keep your company, crew members, and audiences safe.

In addition to their concern for people's safety, stakeholders will also want to ensure the safety of the site. For example, if you are working in a museum, they will want to know that you have considered the potential impact of both the performers and audience on the museum's collection or the building itself. What precautions will you put in place? Are you adequately insured for any damage?

Do not attend meetings with this constituency without having thought through the topics of safety and insurance. I also often convey in these meetings that I have engaged experienced, professional dancers, actors, and singers trained in body control techniques. At my initial meetings with these stakeholders, I ask about their specific safety concerns and address them in such a way that they feel confident that they can trust me. For example, when negotiating at Waterwall Park in Houston for *Natural Acts in Artificial Water* with the park's water engineer, I requested that performers be allowed to climb inside the fountain up to a ledge 15-feet high. But I emphasized that they would simply stand and sway side to side without engaging in movement that could potentially be injurious.

All of my work in the UK had to pass through the Health and Safety Executive, equivalent to Occupational Safety and Health Administration (OSHA) in the United States, which maintains safety standards for workplace environments. A Health and Safety representative came to interview me and conduct a site visit on a few occasions. In the third section of *Genesis Canyon*, all of the performers stood behind the stone balcony railings enclosing the second level inside the entrance hall of London's Natural History Museum (Photo 13.1). I asked Health and Safety if

Photo 13.1 Balcony section, *Genesis Canyon* (1996) by Stephan Koplowitz, Natural History Museum, London, UK.
Photo © Tricia de Courcy Ling.

I could position a small platform underneath each area where performers would be stationed to increase their height and allow more of their upper body to be seen from below. Request denied. I compensated through the choreography and accepted that less of the upper torso would be visible.

Honesty and clarity should rule your exchanges with any official connected to safety or health regulations and/or permits. If these officials require changes, such as not letting a performer stand at a certain height or too close to a ledge, it is best to agree and make accommodations to preserve an amicable relationship. The last things you want are more restrictions or outright denial of access. If their request truly ruins your artistic goal, you can certainly try to negotiate. You may have to enlist another stakeholder as an ally, but always work to maintain a good working relationship with officials.

Collaborators

All artists partnering on the project will want to know that their working conditions are safe—that they will not be associated with an unsafe production. Like the producers, these team members will ask questions about site accessibility and exposure to environmental dangers that may affect them. Special consideration should be given to those responsible for the project's key elements, such as composers providing live music curious how sound will be safely reproduced or costume designers wanting to know what safety issues they need to address in their designs.

Production Technicians/Staff

The safety issues of the support staff and technicians are similar to those for collaborators. The same safety procedures followed in a conventional theater regarding the handling of lights and other technologies apply to site work. However, the potential for danger can be magnified by weather conditions. Electricity and moisture (even a heavy dew) can be lethal combinations; high winds can topple light or speaker towers; excessive heat can damage sound and lighting equipment. Ultimately, site work is very different from indoor theater and requires particular caution. If you have hired technicians who are new to working in a certain environment or have no prior site-specific experience, you must communicate clearly and thoroughly about those differences. Any new contingencies specific to your site, no matter how much experience your crew has, deserve ample attention. Accidents can happen when you make assumptions about dangers you think should be obvious to everyone. Site-specific creation is about breaking old habits in order to work successfully in new spaces. Talk about safety as though the site conditions are new to everyone.

Audience

Audience safety must be addressed early in any production process. Here are some of the factors to consider:

- If you are working indoors, ensure you have not blocked emergency exits or dimmed lights that allow people to see where the exits are located.
- During promenade performances, ensure that the audience pathways are free of obstacles (debris, cables, or terrain) that could cause injury or impede access.
- Regardless of whether you are working indoors or outdoors, be certain you have planned for physical distancing and masking protocols that may apply. You must maintain them throughout the performance, especially during any movement from one location to another.
- Provide masks, hand sanitizers, touchless ticketing or programs, and limited use of bathrooms as needed.
- All technical equipment and power cables need to be correctly installed and secured and present no danger to the audience (and crew); focus especially on cables laid across either performing or audience access areas.
- If you are using strobe lights or fog machines, provide warnings in the program, on a carefully placed sign, or in an announcement before the performance.

- If the site is in a remote area, it is your responsibility to communicate to the audience the safest path or means of transportation to and from that location. Consider the time of day (and available light), especially if your performance begins in daylight and ends during the night.
- In your marketing material, include as many safety suggestions as possible: the need to wear appropriate clothing and shoes if there will be contact with water or rough terrain; accessibility issues (discussed in more detail in the next chapter) if your site will not be accessible by wheelchair or to anyone who cannot stand or walk for an extended period; any expectations that your audience will move (promenade) during the performance.

In general, consider the audience experience if the weather takes an unexpected turn, and decide what you might need to communicate or provide to ensure your audience's safety and happiness in those circumstances. For example, you might want to provide free water and/or folding hand-fans if you anticipate hot weather or inexpensive plastic ponchos if rain is expected.

If your site will not accommodate toilets, that, too, needs to be noted in your promotional materials, and you must provide in your program clear instructions for how audience members can access bathrooms. The decision to provide toilets has budget implications and needs to be made when creating your working budget.

Performers

The list of safety considerations for your performers is also extensive and depends on the site itself. What follows are a series of topics that you will or may need to address.

Physical distancing and masking

There are many different health and safety protocols to follow. During the first year of the Covid-19 pandemic, some performing ensembles (and film groups) quarantined together, forming a "bubble" with strict rules about isolating from anyone outside of their cohort. This strategy allows close physical contact without masks for rehearsals and performances. However, it may not be possible for some productions, in which case all performers would have to wear a mask. A site's capacity to support distancing requirements between performers will determine whether a project is viable or must be abandoned.

Bathrooms/changing rooms

Bathrooms are necessary and not always easy to locate. Distance can create problems, regardless of whether you are in a city or a remote rural area. Interrupting rehearsals for bathroom breaks is inevitable, but if your cast must travel long distances to restrooms during these breaks, rehearsal time is diminished, and you add a level of danger in travel. Clean and safe places to change clothing in private are necessary when performers need to travel directly from a rehearsal to another job or appointment, so these, too, are best located nearby.

Shoes

The previous chapter on costumes (Chapter 11, Collaboration and Collaborative Elements) discussed the importance of shoes as the starting point for site-specific costume design. You must discuss shoes with your costume designer after conducting a site inventory, with a particular emphasis on surfaces and textures and their impact on bodies. Performers will often rehearse in footwear that offers the most protection and safety (usually sneakers with strong support) and, for performances, wear shoes that maintain safety but do not always have to provide the same level of support, given that performances are shorter than rehearsals.

Clothing

As with shoes, your cast must wear clothes that allow for comfort and protection against whatever adverse conditions (sun, rain, mosquitos, rough terrain, etc.) the site presents during rehearsals and performances. If the site will cause excessive wear and tear on clothing, remind performers to wear rugged, inexpensive clothing.

> The biggest thing is Lyme disease.
>
> Jennifer Monson

Nourishment/Location

If a site is too far from sources of food and water, your cast and crew may have to bring their own, or you may have to provide them—at least water. Keeping your cast adequately fed and hydrated, no matter the season or location, is an important safety issue. Location can also affect rehearsal time. Sometimes, performers must travel 45 minutes or more to return home, meet other commitments, and eat between your rehearsal and these other commitments. It's easy to imagine how these contingencies might affect rehearsal time. Plan for them as you create your rehearsal schedule and decide whether you need to include food and/or water in your budget.

Weather

You must always be aware of weather forecasts and understand the effect of weather conditions on performance surfaces; if performers risk injury navigating slippery surfaces, you will have to cancel rehearsals. Excessive cold or heat or high winds are all reasons to cancel or reschedule outdoor rehearsals and move them indoors if possible. It is helpful to have a clear idea what degree of inclement weather will trigger a change of rehearsal venue or cancel/postpone work. How much rain? How low does the temperature have to be? How many minutes would you rehearse in a cold environment or one with excessive heat?

> There's an organization called the Event Safety Alliance, which didn't exist until 2012, which is a great resource. I'm also always concerned about weather in outdoor events,

and when I was working at Lincoln Center, outdoors on the plaza, there was a safety officer who subscribed to a weather service that will give you specific real-time forecasts for your exact GPS coordinates and keep you up to date, minute by minute. It is invaluable for safety issues.

Tony Giovannetti

Urban Grime

Working in a city with surfaces subjected to both heavy and varied use creates many challenges: Wild urban creatures (pigeons, squirrels) and domesticated and stray animals create dirt and leave excrement; people leave chewing gum and discard all sorts of trash. The best approach is to bring a set of your own cleaning supplies: a broom, brushes, paper towels, whatever is appropriate for the particular mess that you must clean up. The production assistants who worked on *The Grand Step Project* in New York City always arrived early to a rehearsal at one of our public staircases to sweep, scrape, and brush the steps and clear them of debris of all types. Site-specific performers are known for their tolerance for dirt and grime, but it never hurts to help reduce the amount that your cast has to endure.

Every site has safety challenges. At Bethesda Terrace [in Central Park, New York], we were sitting on the stairs with a megaphone calling out to the dancers, giving directions like, "run, freeze, collapse, crawl." But they're not dancing full-out, and finally we walk up and ask about what the problem was. They said, "Look at the floor." It was full rat turds and used needles and condoms. So we learned to come two hours early with big brooms to clear the floor every time. You have to be willing to troubleshoot like that, never knowing what might arise.

Sara Pearson and Patrik Widrig

Rehearsal Protocols

There are many protocols [around rigging], and we're constantly reassessing them. Monitoring performers' safety is a huge responsibility and can be extremely stressful. That said, I place a lot of trust in the riggers we work with. They are experienced and work at the highest industry standard. They are the lead in engineering and also weigh in on the preparedness of dancers. I give them power to say, "Nope, this dancer is not ready." It's important that we are all in agreement and nothing moves until then.

Joanna Haigood

This last topic is perhaps the most important. It is vital that, from the moment your creation/rehearsal process begins, you communicate to your performers your ground rules about rehearsal and personal safety. The crux of your conversations should revolve around this one maxim: If performers are asked to do something in a rehearsal that makes them uncomfortable or unsafe physically or emotionally, they are encouraged and expected to speak up immediately, usually to the director or an assistant director.

When I was working on *Babel Index* in London, the first section involved an intricate series of phrases of quick directional changes. One dropped beat or ill-timed movement would send some part of one person's body slamming into another person. My rehearsal director Sara Hook and I noticed that many of our dancers were developing serious bruises requiring medical aid. We realized that they were not speaking up or asking questions. The next day, we explained that we wanted people to stop rehearsals if they were uncertain how to execute a movement without potentially hurting themselves or another person. In essence, everyone must take responsibility for safety, and the director's job is to create a working environment that welcomes questions and discussion.

> We almost drowned a performer. I asked her to run out into the water as though a boat was leaving. She was wearing this period costume that, when it got wet, got really heavy. She started yelling, "I'm drowning." We quickly saved her, of course. But during *Safe Harbor*, we ended up getting a certified scuba diver in a wet suit who was there at the ready to jump in to make sure no one did drown.
>
> Martha Bowers

A Rehearsal Safety/Comfort Check List

> It's important to remind dancers about self-care when they're working on concrete and to stop now and then even if it's just for a few minutes. Have them lie down and put their legs up. It's worth the five or ten minutes. It also reminds them that they need to be doing it on their own. I always remind them of RICE (rest, ice, compression, and elevation) and tell them not to get too crazy in between rehearsals.
>
> Mark Dendy

The following is a list of items to consider acquiring depending on your project's duration, timing, and location.

- *Physical distancing and masking protocols:* Distancing protocols will depend on your location and community directives. Inform your cast in writing before rehearsals begin what procedures you will follow. Will you provide masks and hand sanitizer, take each person's temperature, keep performers six feet apart? Will you regularly sterilize parts of the spaces you use?
- *First-aid kit:* You should always have a first-aid kit containing the basics, including a few cold packs (the chemical kind) in case of acute sprains or other serious injuries that might cause swelling.
- *Ice:* If possible, bring real ice, packed in plastic bags in a cooler.

- *Umbrellas*: If you are aware that you may work in rain or excessive sunlight and heat, umbrellas can provide temporary relief and protect equipment (Photo 13.2).
- *Towels*: If you are working on a site with a mixture of dirt and water, towels can come in handy to keep body parts dry and clean and shoes free of debris.
- *Blanket or drop cloth*: If you are in a remote area or an urban environment that is dirty or not near a changing room, a drop cloth or large blanket can provide a place for the cast to place personal items or a place to sit or lie down without getting dirty.
- *Mobile phone charger*: Make sure that you have backup power for your phone. Safety often depends on the ability to communicate quickly and reliably.
- *Production assistant*: Engage someone to assist with your rehearsals, especially if you are working either with a large cast or in a remote area where security for your ensemble's belongings is not available. An assistant can help in case of injury by providing an extra pair of hands, transportation to a medical facility, etc.

Photo 13.2 Beach umbrella, provided by *TaskForce* performer Alexandria Yalj (pictured), used for sun and heat protection when shooting site-specific *TaskForce* film *Chinatown: Watermark* (2008) Big Tujunga Wash Bridge, Sylmar, CA.
Photo © Stephan Koplowitz.

Last Thoughts

Ensuring that everyone knows at the start of a project how you will address safety and security issues during rehearsals and performances benefits everyone involved. When starting a project, always discuss with your cast all aspects of safety and your plans for addressing them. I learned the hard way in the UK how important it is to be transparent and available to one's cast to maintain a safe environment. Reiterating your willingness to listen and explain instructions is advised, no matter how precise your initial conversations were. One cannot overcompensate when it comes to creating a safe environment. Site-specific work offers the excitement of working outside the comforts of conventional performance spaces, but it should not engender fear of injury for participants or audiences.

14
Creating for Physically Integrated Casts and Accessibility

Accessibility: A Personal Journey

Prior to working with AXIS Dance Company, a prestigious ensemble of dancers with and without physical disabilities, during the creation of *Occupy* at the Yerba Buena Gardens in San Francisco in 2017, my experience with wheelchair-accessible site projects was limited, and my understanding of the challenges and rewards of this work was, in retrospect, clearly deficient. It was not until I was immersed in the process of creating a production for AXIS with a physically integrated cast of dancers that I realized just how unaware I had been of the needs of disabled audiences and performers.

My exposure to issues regarding accessibility and working with integrated casts began in the 1990s when I encountered the work of Candoco, a physically integrated dance company in the UK. Then in 2003, I met a few members of AXIS Dance and Judith Smith, its artistic director (now emerita), while we were all working at the Bates Dance Festival. After that meeting at Bates, Smith expressed an interest in working with me on a site-specific project. We kept in touch for the next 11 years, Smith periodically reminding me that she was still thinking about a potential project.

Then, in 2014, she called to invite me to fly to the Bay Area for a full day of site research and conversation. The goal was to identify a mutually acceptable site, that would be suitable for me and would meet the goals of AXIS Dance, to create a work that animated a public space and fully engaged the company in the creation process. Smith had prepared a list of potential sites both in Oakland (which she preferred, as it is the home base of AXIS Dance) and in San Francisco.

> I like to use the terms disabled and nondisabled rather than abled and disabled. It shifts the paradigm because I don't feel disabled people are not able. I also don't use the term "wheelchair-bound" or "confined to." I prefer to use "dancer in a chair." I mean, we are not bound to the chair.
>
> Judith Smith

Site Selection

The cliché—if you want to get to know someone, walk a mile in her shoes—could not have been more apt (despite the irony). Smith, who has been living with a spinal cord

On Site. Stephan Koplowitz, Oxford University Press. © Oxford University Press 2022. DOI: 10.1093/oso/9780197515235.003.0015

injury since age 17, picked me up that morning at Oakland International Airport in her specially modified minivan. We scouted sites, driving many miles and taking several side trips on the BART metro system. Throughout the day I noticed all the intricacies involved in negotiating these forms of transportation in a wheelchair: the discrete actions needed to get in and out of a vehicle as driver or passenger and the challenges of using public transportation. The level of physical strength and the endurance needed to make these journeys were revelations. With each visit, I increasingly experienced the site from Smith's perspective. Often, I was appalled at how accessibility was clearly either an afterthought or just nonexistent. For example, several elevators in the BART stations were not working or were filthy, unsanitary, and located in areas that required considerable effort to access.

During our travels, I realized that my orientation toward site inventory was changing. I was collecting new details about accessibility and audience design. We visited the Oakland Museum of California and, given that the building was constructed (in 1969) before the American Disabilities Act (ADA, 1990), discovered that many locations in the museum could not be reached by wheelchair. The museum was compliant (retroactively) with the ADA guidelines, but wheelchair access had not been considered in the original design, so some of the hallways and access points to galleries were cramped. Additionally, there was no way to move from one level to another except by using the small, retrofitted elevator. This site's condition was particularly disappointing because Smith had wanted to partner with the museum, given its proximity to her home base.

Our day ended with a visit to the Yerba Buena Gardens, created on the Moscone Convention Center's roof in downtown San Francisco, next to the Yerba Buena Center for the Arts. This had been the location of a previous site-based performance by AXIS, part of the Yerba Buena Gardens Festival. The designers' of the park (which was completed in 1998 in compliance with the ADA) had made accessibility a priority, both functionally and aesthetically. Our visit to the gardens that day was an antidote to a frustrating series of visits to sites that were not accessible enough or too small for the intended audience or not artistically interesting. We couldn't have found a better partner. My experience with Smith that day helped me discover my failure to fully consider accessibility in all my prior work. At the gardens, my education on accessibility was just beginning.

Creative Process

> I like to see material that is built in a way that movement is being translated both from a nondisabled body to a disabled body and from a disabled body to a nondisabled body. I use the word and idea of translation very specifically rather than the word adaptation. Adaptation suggests that disabled people are just trying to learn nondisabled movement and mimic it as closely as they can.
>
> Judith Smith

Once permissions were secured, the process of making *Occupy* took both a conventional and unconventional route. Although I tried to follow my usual site inventory method, I also considered factors that would affect a cast of disabled and nondisabled performers. For the first time, I found it challenging to conduct site inventory objectively without considering the likely interactions between the landscape and the performers' bodies. This would be my first creation for this mixture of performers, and I wanted to meet the high artistic standards of AXIS. Prior to this commission, I never considered my performers' physical range of motion; I took it for granted and observed the physical characteristics of chosen sites only through the lens of my experiences with the performers with whom I had always worked. In this new context, I discovered a need to look through new lenses provided by performers in and out of wheelchairs.

This discovery influenced my conceptual direction. While my previous site work focused on finding harmony between bodies and architecture/design, I began to develop an interest in new themes about how space affects all people depending on their individual range of motion. I started to think about the use and design of public spaces: how these influence our daily emotional life (Is there enough green, accessible space within a city?); our politics (Is free assembly in public encouraged?); and access to our community (Do public spaces encourage community gatherings and activities?). I realized that because of their needs, disabled people can find public spaces inhospitable and unwelcoming.

I have written in previous chapters about exploring human proportion in space, creating a scale and balance between a site and performers. My work with a new range of physicalities in the Yerba Buena Gardens added a new dimension to this exploration. An integrated cast creates greater variety in how bodies occupy space. A performer in a wheelchair has a different body mass and center of gravity from a standing performer; each will have a different visual impact and will move through space in their own unique manner.

My new perspective inspired the selection of six spaces around the park, ranging from small and intimate to expansive. Instead of seeking a balance among design, architecture, and people, I wanted to take the opposite direction—to investigate what happens when too many bodies are placed within a space. I wanted to create a tension between our current concerns around public spaces (design, size, proportion, accessibility, sustainability) and their effects on our daily life.

Additionally, contemporary urban architectural design, known for its sensitivity to the human experience in terms of usability, scale, and engagement, can seem less impressive if economic factors result in people losing their personal/domestic space as it becomes increasingly unaffordable as a result of urban overcrowding. The creation of the Yerba Buena development area necessitated the demolition of low-income housing, which was the beginning of a trend that has made San Francisco such an expensive city. Thus, my artistic concept was to put too many people in one place and let the energy of that imbalance generate content for *Occupy*. During rehearsals, my performers and I explored how the crowded locations I chose affected their movements.

Before these rehearsals began, I knew I needed to understand how to work with a physically integrated cast. To support my education and reduce the anxiety caused by my inexperience, I asked AXIS Dance Company if it would allow for a two-day work session before the start of formal rehearsals. These extra days would be an orientation session for me—providing me an opportunity to ask basic questions, experiment with rehearsal methods, and generally become more accustomed to creating content for performers with their range of abilities.

One specific and basic need was to investigate the possibilities of movement for dancers using a wheelchair, both in solo phrases and in concert with other bodies. So I asked performers many "is this possible?" questions and began to build my own vocabulary of possibilities. To learn more, I tested some of my task-oriented methods. For example, I drew the dimensions of the garden sites on a studio floor and experimented with creative tasks to discover movement specific to those dimensions. I was particularly curious to see how a group of dancers, some in wheelchairs and some not, could move within the confines of one space (which was ultimately part of Section 4, Photo 14.1). I wanted to discover how the performers moved and how the space would frame them in action.

Photo 14.1 Butterfly Garden, Yerba Buena Gardens, site for *Occupy*, section 4 (2017), San Francisco, CA.
Photo © Stephan Koplowitz.

I gave these movement tasks to each performer individually because I needed to see each dancer's unique solution to the task. I was not interested in translating one person's movement into the body of another person. As with any creative process, one activity inspired a new idea or course of action. I found myself happily working and creating with these new dancers and, with each passing moment, feeling supported and more confident in the process. Even after the first day of this rehearsal period, I told Smith how transformative and informative I was finding the whole experience of working with AXIS. She chuckled and said that it seemed AXIS was becoming a school for physically *nondisabled* choreographers and artists. She noted that my response to this experience was no different from that of many other artists when they worked with the company for the first time.

Designing the Production

> I am very cautious about attending site or installation work, and why is that? Because more often than not, nothing has been considered around how somebody in a wheelchair is going to navigate the path of travel or have decent sightlines. I'm pretty skeptical about going to site work for the most part unless I know where it is and what's going to be happening because, so often, my experience is just watching a sea of butts in front of me.
>
> Judith Smith

As my work progressed with the ensemble of AXIS dancers, I also began to consider audience design from a new perspective, to imagine how someone in a wheelchair would navigate the six locations for the promenade production that I had conceived. Each space would need to accommodate not just a sizable audience but a mixture of those who would be sitting and standing.

We created a ticket reservation system to prepare for each new audience (a challenge previously discussed in Chapter 3, Designing the Event, Structuring the Audience). We asked registrants if they had any special accessibility needs, which enabled us to anticipate those needs as we prepared for each performance. We knew how many chairs to place in each of the six sites, and we reserved areas for people who would be in their own chairs. As a result, *Occupy* required a thorough walk-through by the production team during production week to balance comfort with the aesthetic aim of how the work should be seen. However, many of my initial instructions and audience placements were upended because *Occupy* proved to be so popular. Our audiences increased with each performance, and as a result, we were compelled to expand the audience viewing areas and create new sightlines for the work (Photo 14.2). Turning people away from a public space was not possible in this urban park. So, for the finale, I designed two viewing "fronts" despite having made the work initially for just one.

Photo 14.2 *Occupy*, section 6, (20017) by Stephan Koplowitz, Yerba Buena Gardens, San Francisco, CA.
Photo © George Simian.

Creative/Rehearsal Process

The creation of *Occupy* was similar to the creation of my other works and, at the same time, quite different. Movement had to be performed by different bodies, some of whom used wheelchairs. At first, the process seemed slow, but it quickly became second nature as we became a collaborative ensemble, comfortable exchanging ideas and providing feedback. Often, because I was dealing with such a range of movement approaches, I found it difficult to communicate or demonstrate the visual image in my head. This difficulty stemmed as much from my own inexperience working with disabled performers as from the inherent challenge of making any site-specific content. Discovering what movement works conceptually and what works actually from the point of view of the performers is always a process of trial-and-error, a reality that becomes clearer as the range of performers' abilities increases. The less specifically I had prepared my instructions for this range, the slower the process and the more frequent the need to find multiple solutions for a task.

At times, the dancers in wheelchairs questioned the choreography if they felt their roles might be perceived as an afterthought or were not fully integrated into the narrative flow. We invariably had productive discussions. One significant challenge arose in Section 3 of *Occupy* when it was impossible to use wheelchairs because of the rocky and cramped terrain. My solution was to have the wheelchair-using dancers carried by other performers to different places during the performance. Someone suggested that this solution objectified these performers by treating them like backpacks. The observation was spot on, though I certainly hadn't intended such an image. The revised solution expanded the notion of carrying to include non-wheelchair-using performers, as well. My intention in Section 3 (Photo 14.3) was to create a mini-community that tried to occupy one particular rock but was ultimately thwarted because the rock was too small; our solution was a more successful clarification of this visual idea.

Photo 14.3 *Occupy*, section 3 (2017) by Stephan Koplowitz, Yerba Buena Gardens, San Francisco, CA.
Photo © George Simian.

Given that many cast members were inexperienced with site-specific work and I was inexperienced with choreographing for physically integrated performers, we all gained new perspectives on performance and creation. Maintaining an open mind and listening to your collaborators is always important in any production, but those skills become even more significant in this context.

Here are some practical issues to keep in mind when working with a physically integrated cast (or any production):

1. Ensure that, before every rehearsal, you provide a proper physical warm-up that is appropriate for all cast members. Warm-ups are always required, but whoever leads them must meet the needs of all physical abilities in the cast, even allowing time for individuals to address their individual warm-up needs as part of the warm-up period.

2. Provide time for water, food, and bathroom breaks adequate for the different needs of the performers. Dancers with disabilities must meet their needs for rest and bathroom breaks on different schedules and sometimes require more frequent breaks.

3. If you are working outdoors, investigate how the different surfaces will affect the movement of wheelchairs. Grass, dirt, gravel, etc., all have their particular challenges that need to be incorporated into your choreography. Grass is particularly difficult and needs to be considered if unison phrasing is required or long distances need to be traversed. Working on Section 5 in *Occupy* required performing on grass and

concrete. The performers' varying mobility altered the timing within that section, which contained a series of still moments requiring everyone to start and stop simultaneously. The performers whose wheelchairs moved over grass needed a little more time to fulfill their movement sequence and find stillness.

4. Understand that wheelchairs come in different models with various capacities for movement. When choreographing, you will need to accommodate differences in their weight and design, especially, again, in unison passages.

5. Engage a costume designer who is sensitive to everyone's physicality and who can effectively create clothing that is both functional and flattering. Creating clothing that can easily be put on and taken off by disabled performers and that takes into consideration their physical position in a chair is important.

6. Allow time for feedback and discussion, and be sensitive to how all performers perceive themselves and might be perceived by an audience.

A Second Work

Later that same year (2017), I was commissioned to create a work for a physically integrated performance cast by Arts Spark Texas (Celia Hughes, executive director, and Silva Laukkanen, director of integrated dance). They asked me to work with members of one of their programs, the Body Shift Collective in Austin, Texas. I conducted a week-long site-specific residency resulting in a public performance. I had a little more confidence starting work with Body Shift after my experience with AXIS, but the Body Shift community of performers was markedly different. AXIS is a professional integrated dance company; all of the performers have had some technical training regardless of their background. Body Shift works with interested members of the greater Austin community, all of whom have varying levels of training in dance and improvisation.

Working on any project with performers with different levels of experience, especially in a short rehearsal/creation period, requires an extra level of sensitivity and planning. Performers in a mixed cast always need ample time to digest and memorize material, factors that can influence site selection. Often, smaller sites that require covering less ground are preferable. The site I ultimately chose for Body Shift was a small pocket park (a mini-park, usually created on one parcel of land) located on the grounds of an old power station. I selected it for its small size and its design—one level that provided easy access for performers and audience. Its name, Sparky Pocket Park, reflected its history and inspired the name of my work: *Sparky Park Project A site-inspired ritual for a pocket park* (Photo 14.4).

The performance was designed in three sections: an opening circular ritual movement piece for the entire cast of 15, followed by a 30-minute section during which the audience could wander around the less-than-one-acre park and watch seven different simultaneous mini-performances. The third and final section involved all performers, who interacted with a special public art work (a wall) that surrounded the new modern power tower.

Photo 14.4 Sparky Pocket Park and *Sparky Park Project* (2017) by Stephan Koplowitz, Austin TX. Photo © Stephan Koplowitz.

Body Shift had engaged (without audition) performers who represented a far greater range of physical abilities and wheelchair capabilities. These circumstances further emphasized the importance of taking sufficient time to get to know performers individually, their relationship to their chairs, and the functional range of these devices on different terrains. This knowledge is essential for determining the amount of rehearsal time required for movement creation and retention. Physically integrated site work is both site-specific and performer-specific: both affect your physical approach to the performance.

Last Thoughts

To artists working with integrated casts, I advise do your research. There's so much online and so many things that you can listen to and look at now. Also, I think a good strategy for choreographers new to integrated performance groups is to bring them in early to workshop with the dancers, to get familiar with the company. Basically, take your time, there's going to be a learning curve.

Judith Smith

I would like to work more often with physically integrated casts for site-specific productions because public performance, public art, gains more power when it reflects the general population. Inclusivity provides a more immersive experience. Public site work is about many things, including accessibility, and what better way to communicate that concept than with a cast that reflects all parts of our community and society.

PART VI
MORE CHALLENGES (THEY NEVER END)

15
Working with a Set Budget after Fundraising

Chapter 7 (Planning Your Planning Budget) discussed creating a budget for both planning and fundraising purposes. This chapter assumes that those activities are complete and that you are now in possession of a final budget with a fixed amount of money. There are several paths forward:

Scenario #1: You have raised 100% of your fundraising goal.
Action: Congratulate everyone involved, and get to work.
Scenario #2: You have raised 75% of your goal.
Action: Congratulations are still in order; begin to reassess and reallocate each budget line to match your new total.
Scenario #3: You have raised 50% of your budgetary goal.
Action: Do not despair; raising money is and has always been a challenge in the arts. By delving deeply into each budget line, you can assess whether the project remains viable or can be revised to fit a new budget. Another course of action is to delay the project and extend the fundraising timeline. Typically, given grant deadlines, a decision to continue the process translates into a one-year delay unless you pursue individual donors, corporations, or foundations with shorter grant periods. For any grants you received during your initial fundraising effort, your decision to delay your project's start may require negotiating with your funding sources to extend the grants into another grant period. Some funding institutions can be flexible, while others are stricter. Be sure to explain the extenuating circumstances; funding institutions want to help, but they also want to maintain a sense of fairness and consistency for all grantees.

No matter what level of fundraising has been achieved, once work on your production begins, unforeseen contingencies will arise, forcing you to make strategic revisions to the budget. This chapter describes ways to make your budget more responsive to your financial reality before and during the production process.

> I'm constantly shuffling the budget during production, pretty much on a daily basis. We budget for contingencies as things inevitably come up that you don't expect. Budgeting is harder to predict in certain circumstances when you are away from the known theater environment. I'm always assessing and reassessing budgets right to the last day.
>
> Joanna Haigood

On Site. Stephan Koplowitz, Oxford University Press. © Oxford University Press 2022. DOI: 10.1093/oso/9780197515235.003.0016

Closing a Budget Gap: Strategies Prior to Production

Identify goods or labor that could be donated or be procured at a discount

Finding discounts can be time-consuming. Even using the internet to locate less expensive vendors or wholesalers can take more time than any savings might justify; that assessment will depend on your artistic/production priorities, especially if lower cost results in a loss of quantity or quality.

The following list suggests possible goods and services for which you can seek donations.

Material goods

Costumes: You might get lucky and find a clothing company willing to donate all your costumes; or you might enlist volunteers to sew costumes, leaving fabric as the only expense. If your project is associated with an educational institution, the theater or dance department may have clothing that fits your vision. Looking for inexpensive clothes at thrift stores is another possibility. Thrift shop clothes may still need alterations but, if appropriate, can result in meaningful savings. Or you could decide not to spend anything on costumes and ask your performers to wear something from their own closet. I do not recommend this option.

Rehearsal space: As long as rehearsing on-site incurs no extra costs, negotiating as much time as possible to rehearse on the site will reduce the need to rent an additional space. Ask whether your site contains any alternate spaces large enough to conduct rehearsals. I rehearsed in a large unused exhibition hall in London's Natural History Museum (*Genesis Canyon*) when the Great Hall was unavailable. Sometimes, a large conference room on-site can suffice for some activities. An unused gymnasium at a local school or an empty warehouse owned by a local business can also be worth investigating. If you have the time to research possibilities, significant savings are possible.

Technical equipment, lights, video, sound: I have only used donated technical equipment when educational institutions were the commissioning body. Most colleges own lights, sound, and digital video equipment. However, even within an educational environment, access to technology can be difficult. Each academic department has its own needs and requests for equipment. If your project is housed at a university, a good strategy is to work with as many different academic departments as possible to expand your potential resources for equipment.

Food: Many catering/food companies will be hesitant to provide free food but may be willing to provide prepared food at cost, resulting in a substantial discount. During *Stabile/Mobile* in Spoleto, Italy, the host producer negotiated significant discounts with local restaurants, which helped feed my performers during rehearsals.

Labor

Internships: Even if an educational institution does not commission your project, you can contact nearby colleges or universities and ask if they are interested in allowing their students to intern as production assistants, rehearsal assistants, social-marketing assistants, photographers, or videographers. Students often seek opportunities to add professional experiences to their resumes. Be sure to adhere to all the regulations affecting interns' hours, benefits, and pay.

Volunteers: Often, volunteers are recruited to help with many front-of-house activities: program-folding, distribution, ticket sales, audience control, and guidance. Some host institutions have an already identified pool of volunteers; others will post notices to recruit them. Remember that all volunteers will need proper training.

Pro bono professional work: For a limited time, a lawyer, accountant, or marketing professional could be willing to donate some hours of pro bono work to support your project. Establishing new relationships can take time, so you should seek pro bono work as early in the process as possible. Keep in mind that the more specific and prescribed your request for time and labor, the more likely you will get a quick response. If your host institution is a nonprofit, you might find an appropriate professional volunteer on the board of directors, or someone on the board may have an outside contact willing to help you. The more contacts you and your host organization have, the greater your chances of securing pro bono services.

Eliminate budget lines or reduce amounts

> It's happened to me that I've run out of money. I just reduce. I modify; I make it smaller; I work with fewer collaborators. Unfortunately, I once had to let a dramaturg go. I often start projects before I have full funding, so I'm moving ahead and have to modify as I go. But for me, the end product isn't the goal. It's the process, the research; that's my practice, and often I need to start that process before all funding has been found.
>
> Jennifer Monson

If your artistic plan requires media (projections), live music, or a large ensemble of performers, consider working with less. Perhaps you can replace live music with recorded sound; perhaps you can use a smaller cast. You can make these decisions only if the reductions and revisions will not (in your estimation) damage or alter the artistic vision beyond repair.

Another strategy for reducing the budget is to trim your fee and the fees paid to other artistic collaborators. This strategy has risks because some of your collaborating artists might be unwilling (or less enthusiastic) to work for less money, in which case you would need to find appropriate replacements without offering compensation that is exploitative for both yourself and other artists. Tensions can arise if you and your producing partner disagree about this strategy. Therefore, you should discuss this eventuality with the executive producer before the fundraising period is complete. Additionally, when negotiating fees with other collaborators before final budget allocations, remind them that the fee will depend on fundraising and that an amount will be confirmed at a specific date. If you think it appropriate, ask artists if they are open to further negotiations, but be prepared for artists to tell you that their fee is nonnegotiable.

The bottom line

Having these discussions about various potential budgetary challenges *before* creative work has begun will mitigate the inevitable sense of loss you will feel if, later, you have to make compromises or sacrifices in a project to which you are emotionally attached. Anticipating problems will also enable you to rethink, even reconceive, the entire project without fear of being accused of miscommunication or broken promises. If you decide to reconceive a project, remember that you can still adhere to your initial core inspiration for working on the selected site and to a rigorous site-specific approach. However, if a delay or a revision of plans is not possible, it may be best to abandon this project or put it on indefinite hold.

Closing a Budget Gap: During Production

> I've been in the middle of a production and realized that I needed more dancers than I could afford. When that happens, I either don't pay myself, or I'll ask my board for help. If you realize you need more money, you either go into debt for a while or ask for help.
>
> Debra Loewen

Some budget lines, such as costumes or labor, are just estimates of cost and need. During some productions, expenditures are lower than anticipated, resulting in a surplus. As a producing partner, you need to be able to transfer any line surpluses to other priorities, so negotiating with your commissioning organization for this authority is essential for keeping the project on track.

Unforeseen budget contingencies

During a production, there may be unanticipated expenses precipitated by extreme weather, labor strikes, crime, terrorism, pandemic, loss of key personnel, shortages of materials, unforeseen price increases—the possibilities are, unfortunately, endless. As a result, your budget should contain a line for contingencies (usually anywhere from 5–10% of the total budget). However, be wary of reallocating contingency funds too quickly when faced with an initial budget gap. Hoping that no further unforeseen expenses will arise is always a gamble.

I have worked on a few projects during which budget shortfalls occurred and, in one instance, almost resulted in preventing video documentation. *Babel Index* (1998), commissioned by the Dance Umbrella Festival with the British Library, did not receive final approval until a month before rehearsals were to begin. Several grants were denied or underfunded, and last-minute fundraising efforts were proving difficult. Dance Umbrella Festival, very motivated to bring the work to fruition, decided to move forward with only a small margin of budgetary safety. As a result, two weeks before the premiere, we learned that we didn't have the funds to hire a videographer and crew to document the work properly. A few days later, the architect of the newly opened British Library, Sir Colin St. John Wilson, came to watch a rehearsal at the library on which he had spent decades of his life working. It was the first time in my career that I had interacted with an architect of a building that I was animating. After the two-hour rehearsal, Wilson was thoroughly engaged and enthusiastically told us that he intended to invite all his friends to see the work; he looked forward to having the video document in the years to come. When I explained that we didn't have the funds for proper documentation, he said this was a serious matter and that he would make phone calls that evening to secure the funds. He seemed very confident. The next morning, the Dance Umbrella Festival received a phone call saying that a check was being issued to cover the documentation costs.

Not all budget gap dramas secure such happy endings. Some producers when faced with these challenges close to a premiere have been forced to borrow from other parts of their institution at potentially great cost to the institution's future activities. These sorts of experiences are the primary reason many commissioning entities are careful when undertaking large art projects.

Maintaining a Smooth Fiscal Process

This section outlines some standard fiscal issues and practices that need to be clarified before starting a production.

Decide who is authorized to write the checks

Creating a sound process and clear lines of communication concerning how money is allocated, spent, and accounted for will forestall tension and misunderstanding within your team and with a host organization. If you are self-producing, you will be in charge of all fiscal matters. You should inform all other personnel of your policies and procedures for project expenditures and maintaining the budget. If you are working with an executive producer, be sure to discuss the commissioning organization's policies and procedures before starting the production period to avoid misunderstandings and any financial missteps.

Most importantly, if working with a partnering institution, make sure both of you agree on who will be authorized to pay the bills. Some organizations want to write you a check for a large portion of the project's budget, making you responsible for writing checks and accounting for expenditures. Unless you already have a book-keeper or an accountant, you should try to negotiate for the host organization to take on the payment and accounting tasks, with only your fee and reimbursed expenses paid directly to you. If you must assume the role of primary fiscal agent, you should include in the working budget a line-item for either hiring help or paying yourself a fee for taking on this job of, essentially, business manager for the project. Make sure you also build into your plans enough time to fulfill these tasks.

Decide which members of your team are authorized to do the purchasing

Do the collaborative artists who need to secure materials use their credit cards or cash to make purchases and then submit an invoice with receipts for reimbursement? Or does the commissioning entity make all purchases directly? This decision usually also applies to travel, accommodations, etc. An alternative policy is to advance authorized purchasers a check or petty cash, which is then reconciled when they submit receipts for whatever they purchased from the advanced funds.

The most common practice that I have encountered when working with a host organization is that purchases are made and invoices and receipts are submitted to a business manager. Each organization has its own policies, and the sooner you discuss these issues, the easier for all involved. As with any project or job, the longer you delay submitting receipts and invoices, the more difficult it will be to get reimbursed. Make sure that everyone on your team understands these policies and procedures.

Decide who is responsible for keeping accurate records and receipts

Whoever is responsible for submitting final reports to funding sources is normally responsible for keeping all financial records accurate and up-to-date. This includes safeguarding all submitted receipts. An accountant is not needed at this juncture, simply a person with good bookkeeping skills. Ultimately, the final report will contain an assessment of the project, including information about how money was spent. This report is discussed in more detail in Chapter 18 (Assessment).

Last Thoughts

Your ability to navigate funding challenges depends on how much direct control you have over the funding process and how a budget is allocated and spent. Creating a strong partnership with your commissioning entity or, if self-producing, being realistic about what is possible, whom to approach for funds, and what your final budget can accomplish will allow you to make decisions more easily and rationally.

16
Promoting and Marketing the Work

Marketing strategies for artistic works could fill an entire book. This chapter will outline some methods and strategies that you can use to attract audiences and critics and to publicize your vision and project. For you to use these strategies, you must ensure that your initial negotiations with the commissioning organizations (if applicable) result in your having a clear and specific role in creating and disseminating all marketing materials. You must also agree on how you will be credited in these materials.

Words and Images

To properly market any event, you must create two essential collections from which to produce marketing tools such as press releases, postcards, posters, websites, social media postings, advertisements, event programs, etc.

1. *A collection of precise, carefully considered words and well-crafted phrases and sentences that describe the project*: The process of developing these begins early in the project so that you can explain it to commissioning organizations, to licensing bodies, and, later, to potential funders and collaborators. As the project develops and moves toward the premiere, you will find that you can sharpen your descriptive language, making it increasingly specific as you develop the right title and explanatory text and include collaborating artists' names. If your commissioning partners are leading the marketing campaign, provide them with your own words describing the project before any materials are created to ensure that the messaging captures your voice in content and style. You don't want the message to be written by someone trying to interpret your vision.

Finding appropriate words to describe your vision can start with answering these questions:

What was the inspiration for the work—for example, a personal story or formal thematic concepts?
Does the work connect to any previous projects?
What do you believe are the site's most compelling characteristics?
What are some of the challenges in making this work?
What do you hope to achieve or communicate by creating this work?

On Site. Stephan Koplowitz, Oxford University Press. © Oxford University Press 2022. DOI: 10.1093/oso/9780197515235.003.0017

2. *A collection of images (videos and stills) that will engage people and effectively reinforce the descriptive text*: Creating these images yourself will ensure that they represent, as much as possible, the work itself. Although developing these publicity materials is a challenge, the earlier you can work on them (either before or soon after the start of rehearsals), the more manageable the task becomes.

Title strategies

Some commissioning organizations will require that you give your work a title before you feel ready—while the piece is still developing in early rehearsals. Unless you know, at the outset, exactly the title you want to use, you should be prepared to begin a marketing campaign with a working title that can be used for marketing and as a placeholder for the final title. For example, in Germany, we started marketing the work with the title *Kokerei-Projek* (the name of the site, Kokerei, and the word project). By the time of the premiere, I had settled on the name *Kokerei-Projek. Khole Körper* (*Coal Bodies*). In contrast, *The Grand Step Project* was the title that I used for marketing from beginning to end. However, this project consisted of two major sections: a performance by a chorus and then a choral dance on the steps. Ultimately, I gave the dance section its own title (*Flight*).

Image strategies

Start collecting images early. You can begin by taking photos of the site itself. It may not be necessary or desirable to create photographic images staged with performers, given your project's concept. Only expend the effort if you can reasonably approximate your artistic intentions. Unique pictures of the empty site, without performers, especially if the site is relatively unknown, can be useful for promoting the work from the outset. You can highlight specific locations that will be important to ideas you plan to present verbally in video or print. You can also shoot photos with performers on site—either members of your cast or other willing participants—to create images that mirror or approximate an image that you envision for the completed work. Staging these photos communicates the concept of humans interacting with the site. I have directed these sorts of publicity photos with performers at different points during the rehearsal process. The earliest shoots are always the most challenging—when there are no costumes, only a few available performers, and little created content. Fortunately, inspiration tends to arrive: In the absence of costumes, you can use color as the unifying factor and emphasize the human form instead of costumes. You can describe the look you want and ask the performers to wear something from their closets. Photographing a few dancers from interesting angles on-site can create the feeling of a larger ensemble. For obvious reasons, you should be present at publicity shoots. If that's not possible, be sure to give clear and specific instructions to whoever will be in charge and, if appropriate, ask to attend via video conferencing so that you can guide the shoot.

If photography alone isn't sufficient, another strategy is to stage a video interview during which you explain your concept, intercut with whatever site images you have created. A staged interview is simply a conversation between you and the primary commissioner or a key collaborator. Whatever the context, the goal is to have an exchange of ideas and information. The edited video can become a valuable marketing tool to explain to potential audiences what to expect and to excite their interest. These videos can also be used for a crowdsourced fundraising campaign.

Four Examples: Publicity Photos

Genesis Canyon

Despite my absence from this photo shoot at London's Natural History Museum, I was pleased with the image because it captured the site in a complimentary manner, placed the dancers in a location that was central to the performance, and gave a sense of kinetic energy by blurring the performers (Photo 16.1). However, another image taken during that same shoot became a source of frustration, especially because it was submitted to a magazine for a feature story without my approval. In my absence, a performer was mistakenly photographed in a physical position and location not part of the artistic plan. From that moment on, however, I wrote into my contracts that I must be present for publicity photo shoots and have a voice in selecting images for publicity: lesson learned.

Photo 16.1 Publicity postcard with photo by Chris Nash for *Genesis Canyon* (1996), produced by London's Dance Umbrella Festival.
Photo courtesy Stephan Koplowitz.

The Grand Step Project

This project had the added challenge of a large cast (50) and six different grand staircases located in three boroughs of New York City. On our first day of rehearsal, I decided to take the 10 performers of the core company to three of the staircases. I staged several photographs at each location to create a composite image that combined photos of performers with images of all six of the selected grand staircases. Using the same performers in several images created a sense of a large cast. The postcard emphasizes the multiplicity of sites and performers and highlights the two primary elements: the public staircases and people (Photo 16.2).

Water Sight, Milwaukee

The two publicity photos in the postcard (Photo 16.3) were taken during rehearsals with the core performers at the University of Wisconsin, Milwaukee. The project used two sites, one for daytime performance and the other for night. Because a nighttime publicity shoot was not possible, the water tower's photo was edited to suggest nighttime.

Social Media

At the time of writing this book, some of the most visited social media sites include Facebook, Instagram, Twitter, LinkedIn, TikTok, Tumblr, and Pinterest. Within a few years, new sites will emerge while others fade away. What will remain constant is our ability to share information virtually no matter what platform we use. Employed correctly, social media is a fast and low-cost method for raising awareness of your project. Sites like Facebook/Instagram can host live streaming and archiving. They allow people to express interest in attending, post comments on the project, make a reservation, or buy a ticket.

Designating someone on the production team or hiring a specific person to handle social media marketing can save you time. Whoever manages the work must have comfort and facility with the mechanics of the medium and a clear understanding of the most effective content and posting schedule needed for each platform. Additionally, encouraging all cast and production team members to post (with guidance) within their network expands your marketing reach. I prefer to control shared images (both moving and still) that are taken from rehearsals. However, if you want your cast and production team to post to their network, you must allow room for their own creativity and spontaneity. At some point, you have to trust that, with guidance, everyone will create and post appropriately. The goal is to imbue your

DANCING IN THE STREETS PRESENTS

THE GRAND STEP PROJECT
by Stephan Koplowitz

June 15 – 28, 2004

dancing
in the STReeTs

Photo 16.2 Publicity image for poster and postcard for *The Grand Step Project* (2004), produced by Dancing in the Streets.
Photo courtesy Stephan Koplowitz.

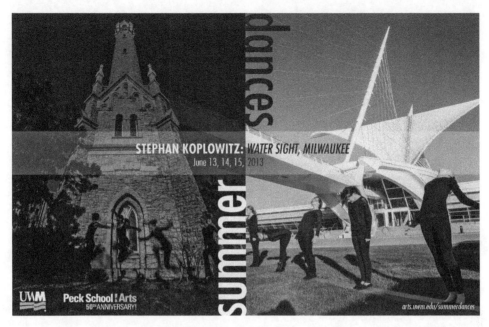

Photo 16.3 Publicity postcard for *Summer Dances, Water Sight, Milwaukee* (2013), produced by University of Wisconsin Milwaukee Department of Dance.
Photo courtesy Stephan Koplowitz.

project with a sense of camaraderie that generates messages that feel honest and enthusiastic.

Website

Will you create a centralized website to drive all interest to the same place or modify an existing site? You may have to purchase an appropriate domain. It may be cost-effective to simply add a page to an existing website, either your own or that of your commissioning partner. The advantage of having a dedicated webpage is that all of your social, print, and broadcast media can point people to the same location. A website can be the repository for all kinds of information, images, and video and link to any social media sites that share information.

A website can help extend the length of a printed performance program, which is usually limited to a certain number of pages. A note in the program can direct your audience to the main website, which can include the biographies of all participants (not just the top collaborators). A QR code in the program allows anyone with a smartphone to view the extended program on the website—at the performance or at home after attending the production (see Photo 16.4).

Stephan Koplowitz: TaskForce
Natural Acts in Artificial Water
A site-specific promenade performance in six sections
for the Gerald D. Hines Waterwall Park

Concept, Direction and Choreography: Stephan Koplowitz
Rehearsal Director: Teresa Chapman
Core Company Performers:
Shanon Adams, Christopher Cardenas, Rebekah Chappel,
Alexandra DiNunzio, Kristen Frankiewicz, Catalina Molnari,
Kara Newton, Lindsey Sarah Thompson, Toni Valle
Special thanks to the Core Company Performers for their important creative contributions to this work.

Extended Company Performers:
Jessica Capistran, Roberta Cortes, Erica Henderson,
Mallory Horn, Sean Keil, Sarah Leung, Tina Shariffskul,
Robin Worley (understudy)

Music: Space City Gamelan
Aaron Hermes, Musical Director
Araceli Camacho-McMahan, Rashida Hagakore, Yvonne Kendall,
Ashdin Medhora, Danny Mauer, Brittany Rohrman

Costume Design: Paige Wilson
Assistant Costume Design: James McDaniel

Project Coordination: Josh Davis
Stage Managers: Elizabeth Pelz, Bryan Wallace

Video Documentation: Andrew Ford
Photo Documentation: Ed Schipul

Stephan Koplowitz would like to thank:
DiverseWorks Artistic Director Sixto Wagan for his vision, the invitation to make this work and for his collaboration in the creation of this project and the entire staff at DiverseWorks for their support; Della Mizera and John Breeding of Uptown Houston for their warm welcome and partnership; Karen Farber of the Mitchell Center for the Arts; Michael Parsons and Richard Flores, our water engineers; the University of Houston's School of Theater and Dance; David Sheingold for his intelligent consultancy and advice, Karen Stokes for her friendship and important advice; Steven Lavine, President of CalArts, and Lisa Barr TAC Producer for their support of TaskForce; and to my collaborative team of artists and performers, thank you for your hard work, dedication and focus during this intensive and exciting process.

Choreographer Stephan Koplowitz has designed the performance to respond to all areas of the Gerald D. Hines Waterwall Park. To best view the performance, we ask the audience to follow our ushers as a group through the six sections of the work.

BACK STORY: *Natural Acts in Artificial Water* is part of Stephan Koplowitz, national/international initiative TaskForce, a site-art dance touring company that works on a project to project basis which began in Idyllwild, Los Angeles CA (2008) and Plymouth, UK (2009). The performance in Houston marks a new evolution of the project *TaskForce: United (States)* which engages local artists, performers and institutions to create original site works across the United States. TaskForce is a process oriented performance laboratory that draws inspiration from the architecture, history, culture, and ecology of a specific site, city or region, all connected by a common theme. To date, the common theme Koplowitz has chosen for his TaskForce projects is water. Since its inception, TaskForce has created more than 20 distinct site-specific works and has collaborated with over 30 different artists in music, theater, visual art and media. In Houston, over the past six months, Mr. Koplowitz developed the concept and structure of the performance and conducted pre-production research with the producing partners. Though the ideas have been gestating for a while, in keeping with the TaskForce model, this Houston based company of sixteen dancers underwent nine days of intensive rehearsals to develop this weekend's performances.

PRINCIPAL COLLABORATORS

Stephan Koplowitz is an internationally renowned director, choreographer, and media artist known for his site-specific, multi-media works created for architecturally significant sites. He has won numerous awards for his work including an Alpert Award in the Arts (2004), a Guggenheim Fellowship in Choreography (2003), a New York Dance and Performance Award "Bessie" (2000), and six National Endowment for the Arts Choreography Fellowships (1988–97). His work has been produced across the United States and internationally, and in the past twenty-five years he has created 62 works and been awarded 42 commissions. Currently based in Los Angeles, Koplowitz is on faculty and is Dean of The Sharon Disney Lund School of Dance at the California Institute of the Arts. In October, 2000, Koplowitz premiered *Open Book/Open House* with 50 dancers for the new Humanities Building at Rice University, Houston. In 2007, he created *Isaea)*, a site-specific work for Boston's Institute for Contemporary Art (ICA). Commissioner by Summer Stages Dance and the ICA, it was named one of the Top Ten Dance Productions of 2007 by the Boston Globe. In May 2012, Koplowitz premiered four new site-specific performance events commissioned for the 150th anniversary of the founding of Gustavus Adolphus College, outside of Minneapolis, MN. This summer, he has been invited to the prestigious La Mama/Umbria Summer Institute to teach directing and conduct a residency/workshop on site specificity as part of the Spoleto Festival).
For more info: koplowitzprojects.com or youtube.com/lanycart

Space City Gamelan features modern and contemporary compositions performed on Indonesian instruments. This bell-chime orchestra is one of the only privately operated gamelans in the United States. Self-described as "psychotropic jungle lullaby trance," this band will leave you wanting to stay in the dream world they weave with their sound.

Teresa Chapman is Associate Professor at the University of Houston where she teaches dance technique, aesthetics, and pedagogy. As a performer, she dances for Karen Stokes Dance and has been seen in works by many other Houston-based choreographers. She has also performed with artists in Santa Barbara, San Francisco, Los Angeles, Washington DC, and New York. In addition, Teresa is an independent choreographer. She received her MFA in Dance from California State University, Long Beach.

Paige A. Wilson is Assistant Professor of Costume Design and Technology at the University of Houston School of Theatre and Dance. She received her MFA in Theatre from the University of Houston and her BFA in Dance at the University of Louisiana at Lafayette.

Support for Stephan Koplowitz: TaskForce - Natural Acts in Artificial Water is provided by the Transatlantic Arts Consortium (TAC), a collaboration between CalArts, The Dartington Hall Trust, and Idy8wild Arts: Modern B&B; Uptown Houston; and DiverseWorks Underwriters and Major Donors including: The National Endowment for the Arts, Houston Endowment, The City of Houston through the Houston Arts Alliance, Texas Commission on the Arts, The Brown Foundation and the Cullen Trust for the Performing Arts.

ABOUT DIVERSEWORKS ARTSPACE
Known for its groundbreaking artistic and educational programs, DiverseWorks is one of the premiere contemporary arts centers in the United States. DiverseWorks has been a hub for the presentation of daring and innovative work, a commissioner of major artistic projects across disciplines, and an advocate for artists worldwide. Founded by artists for artists, DiverseWorks continues its commitment to bold artistic exploration, creative risk-taking, and building audiences for contemporary art.

For more info, videos and bios of our dancers, visit DiverseWorks.org or scan:

www.diverseworks.org

INSIGHT OUT
A Weekend Festival of Media and Live Performance

May 19 - 8 pm
Scoot-In
Sesquicentennial Park
400 Texas Ave.
Houstonians can walk, ride their bikes or mopeds, carpool, take the bus or drive to this unique drive-in film event. Presented by Aurora Picture Show and curated by Bart Weiss of the Dallas Video Festival.

May 20 - noon and 3 pm
Seven in the Third
Project Row Houses
2505 – 2521 Holman St.
Composer Travis Weller provides a site-specific score that's spread across seven of Houston's historic Project Row Houses. Presented by the Cynthia Woods Mitchell Center for the Arts.

Photo 16.4 Program for *Natural Acts in Artificial Water* (2012), produced by Diverseworks. Photo courtesy Stephan Koplowitz.

On Line Publications and Blogs and Bloggers

Despite the paucity of conventional journalists writing for print publications, several experienced art critics are writing for online (only) publications or their own blogs. Other writers with no professional credentials except for a love of the arts write blogs that have earned a sizable readership. All of these writers offer you marketing potential and are worth contacting about writing stories that feature your project before the premiere. You can also invite them to attend and write a review of the work. You can contact them in any number of ways: perhaps an email query with a press release attached, or a phone call from your publicist/marketing director, who might have a working relationship already established. You may want to create your own blog or have an official project blogger who narrates a running commentary of the work as it unfolds. This blog could be one feature of a website; new blog entries could also be tagged on social media.

IRL (In Real Life) Marketing

On-site rehearsals as marketing: postcards and flyers

As mentioned in an earlier chapter, rehearsing in public attracts attention. It can create interactions with people, some of whom will be curious enough to want to ask questions—providing you with an opportunity to spread the word about your project, one person at a time. To capitalize on these moments, I create an information

F E N E S T R A T I O N S²

Celebrating the restoration and reopening of **Grand Central Terminal**.

Director/Choreographer Stephan Koplowitz

has been commissioned by the Metropolitan Transportation Authority to create an enhanced version of his acclaimed 1987 site-specific work, FENESTRATIONS, now for an ensemble of **72 dancers** utilizing *both sets* of the large windows at opposite ends of the terminal. FENESTRATIONS² evokes the splendor of these Beaux Arts windows within the grandeur of one of the nation's great public spaces. This event is part of the MTA's **"Grand Central In-Motion"**, a festival of music, dance and food.

Thursday through Sunday, October 14, 15, 16, 17, 1999.

FENESTRATIONS² will be performed at 7pm, 8pm and 9pm in the main terminal.

Lighting Design by Tony Giovannetti, Musical Score by Jack Freudenheim & Stephan Koplowitz

Performed by Sarah Adams, Rebecca Alson-Milkman, Natasha Aretha, Malin Bostrom, Alex Boucher, Erica Bowen, Kimberly Cadden, Nuttakom Chamyen, Isabel Chen, Christine Conklin, Donna Costello, Julie Crosby, Francisco Rider Da Silva, Kieber De Freitas, Dereka Deleveaux, Amy De Long, Stephanie Dixon, Jennifer Edwards, Lenore, Eggleston, David Fletcher, Yuu Fujita, Kathaleen Gibson, Leslie Guth, Hristoula Haraka, Essence Harris, Kyra Himmelbaum, Daniela Hoff, Jessica Howe, Sara Joel, Andrea Johnston, Heidi Kinney, Mandy Kirschner, Vicky Kolovou, Gabriele Kroos, Susan Lamberth, Andrea Lieske, Naomi Luppescu, Solomon Matea, Harry Mavromichalis, Brendan McCall, Sally-Anne McConnell, Wakana Meguro, Carolin Micklitz, David Miller, Michaela Miller, Saeko Miyake, Hiroshi Miyamoto, Claudia Munhoz, Noriko Nagamoto, Johan Parlagutan, Jennifer Perfilio, Jule Jo Ramirez, Romy Reading, Jennifer Risch, Rebecca Robinson, Mata Sakka Rikaki, Amanda Schneider, Kathy Shamoun, Eva Silverstein, Amber Smith, Sasha Soreff, Jennie Sussman, Dean Sweeney, Yasko Takeno, Akito Takimoto, Makeda Thomas, Jennifer Torriero, Danielle Tinsley, Jennifer Uzzi, Hugo Vilardell, Jennifer Walker, Lisa Wright. **Rehearsal Directors: Alexandra Beller and Jessie Miles**

FREE EVENT   FREE EVENT   FREE EVENT

photo:Jonathan Atkins

Photo 16.5 Rehearsal flyer for *Fenestrations²* (1999), presented by the Metropolitan Transit Authority in association with Jones, Lange, LaSalle.
Photo courtesy Stephan Koplowitz.

sheet or postcard that describes the project and contains the performance dates, ticket availability, website, etc. When I first started this strategy in 1999 for the very public Grand Central Terminal project, I photocopied an 8 1/2 × 11 sheet of paper filled with relevant information (Photo 16.5). Aside from the most pertinent details, I decided to list all 72 performers for the simple reason that, in addition to crediting their work, the list might motivate people to see if they knew someone in the cast. The flyers had a somewhat homemade feeling, as they were created in a basic word processing application and photocopied, but they were an inexpensive and quick solution.

In later years, budget permitting, more polished printed materials were created, like the small business cards for the Milwaukee site project that contained a QR code to send people to a website (Photo 16.6).

For *Sullivant's Travels*, we printed cards to look like trading/collectible cards (Photo 16.7).

The idea for both of these promotional tools was to give people something inexpensive and small enough to stick in a pocket, and perhaps on a refrigerator. You can also provide these printed postcards, flyers, or business-sized cards to all production

Photo 16.6 Small publicity card for *Summer Dances, Water Sight, Milwaukee*, produced by University of Wisconsin Milwaukee Department of Dance, card measures 3.5 × 2 inches.
Photo courtesy Stephan Koplowitz.

Photo 16.7 Front and back of "baseball card" promotional material for *Sullivant's Travels* (2014), produced by The Ohio State University Department of Dance and College of Arts and Sciences.
Photo courtesy Stephan Koplowitz.

personnel so that they, too, can distribute them any time on- or off-site. And, of course, you can mail postcards or flyers.

Other printed matter: posters, banners, press releases, programs

Creating posters that can be placed at different commercial establishments is another way to create a marketing presence. Posters can be particularly useful in a small community or township. My project in Northfield, Minnesota, (population 22,000) benefited from posters placed in several popular businesses in the downtown area, which was not difficult to saturate given its size. For more populated communities, large cities, and regions, identify and target strategic locations (dance or theater studios, art centers, colleges, commercial establishments near the site) for carefully placed banners or large posters. I used these strategies for the *TaskForce* UK project in Plymouth (Photo 16.8).

Press releases

Getting commercial newspapers and magazines to devote space to art projects, especially projects that have a short performance life or are not presented by large cultural institutions, has become increasingly difficult. Much depends on where your project is located. Local newspapers in smaller communities can be more amenable to writing about the work. In contrast, big city newspapers have more material

Photo 16.8 Large *TaskForce* poster at a Plymouth, UK, bus stop, and banner printed for placement strategically around Plymouth and during performances, produced by Dartington Arts.
Photo courtesy Stephan Koplowitz.

competing for feature stories and reviews. No matter what media market you are in, it is worth the effort (however minimal) to get publicity from these sources. Regardless of size, most publications will include your event as part of their weekly or monthly listings either in print or online. A carefully crafted press release is still an important document to create. It is often the primary content for some print and/or online publications. Smaller newspapers (with a small staff) will sometimes take your press release language and turn it into an article with little editing. The same is true of online-only publications that want to give the impression that they cover all legitimate events. If a press release is disseminated without your approval or contains inaccurate language, those words could potentially appear in places that you don't want them to.

Disseminating your press release early enough to meet publication deadlines is essential. Placing a copy on your website (for downloading) is another way to ensure your release and project receive maximum exposure.

It is an unwritten rule that print and online media outlets (especially newspapers, magazines, and even specialty blogs) will be more open to writing about your project if you have purchased some level of advertising on their platform. This is not always the case, but it happens far more than people realize.

Performance/event programs

Your performance program is one of the last of the marketing materials created prior to performance. The program serves as a marketing tool in that many of the printed programs will be taken home, shared with other people, and used as a reference by audience members after the performance is over. You may not want a printed program for budgetary, ecological, or aesthetic reasons. One way to share information without a printed program is to place a large poster with program information at a central audience gathering point, perhaps with a QR code or a website address that will provide more information. The other option is to have no program information in any form.

Information to include in marketing materials

Much of the information to include in any of your marketing materials is obvious (title, place, dates, etc.), but the following are some areas that may get overlooked.

Whenever you provide information about the site's location and address, you should consider whether you need to mention transportation options (public transit, car, walking) and parking availability. The latter is always appreciated in large cities.

To allow your audience to prepare appropriately, you should provide information about accessibility to the site and any requirements for them to walk (promenade) any distance. You should also state how weather will affect your event. Is there a rain date, or does the performance continue regardless of weather? In some areas, extreme heat could be a reason to cancel an outdoor event.

When the dates of the performances are included, it is best to include the day(s) of the week and the year. The former lets people connect the date to the day of the week. The latter is for historical/archival purposes; marketing materials that omit the year become annoyingly incomplete historical documents.

Special program notes

Aside from crediting all involved, including the funders and other significant supporters, the program might include information particularly pertinent to site projects.

Notes on viewing the production

If you have designed an audience experience that includes walking, multiple simultaneous sites, several viewing areas for the same performance, etc., you can use the program to prepare and instruct your audience. Should the audience follow individual ushers? How do they identify those ushers? How is the work structured? Is it to be seen in two sections or more? It is common for proscenium productions to include the length of the work in the program and indicate if there is an intermission. For a site-specific production, your audiences will appreciate any information to help them orient themselves to the experience. Here is an example from *Open Book/Open House:*

> Notes on Viewing the Performance
> *For the safety of the dancers and comfort of the audience, we ask that there be NO PHOTOGRAPHY (flash or otherwise) taken during the performance. Refer to this program for the locations and titles of each of the performances, and feel free to ask any of our ushers located throughout the building for any further information.*
>
> Open Book/Open House *consists of two sections:*
> Section One
> *The audience is invited to walk inside and outside the building and experience different performances. Some performances are continuous, much like installations, and others are programmatic and will be repeated during the course of the first 45 to 60 minutes of the event. There is no prescribed order to viewing the performances; you may start on any floor. However, if a work in one of the classrooms has begun, please do not enter, but wait for the next performance. Please be sure to see the offices located down the halls on the second and third floors. Selected professors have designed their office spaces to be seen with special lighting.*
> Section Two
> *The audience is asked to exit the building and position themselves in front of the building on College Way/Loop Road to view the second section of the performance, a work involving 37 performers.*

Notes on the site and creation of the work

Your program is an opportunity to cite in print indigenous land acknowledgment and perhaps make note of any contemporary connections the site has to Native people in the community.

Additionally, you may want to give the audience some historical background or information about the site's unique characteristics: perhaps a short explanation of why you chose the site and a description of your creative process in relation to the site. I have included this information for many of my projects. For *Occupy*, I decided to share some of my motivations for the work. For other projects, I have simply explained what is meant by the term site-specific and its relation to this specific creation. There are no right or wrong decisions for what to include; your choice will be unique and personal. Here is an example from *Occupy:*

> *Occupy* is a site-specific work where the creative content of the work originates from the very site it is performed: Yerba Buena Gardens. The history, the design, and current use of the Gardens all contribute to this creation as does the unique make-up of the cast of dancers with and without disabilities. *Occupy* looks at how these specific bodies are affected by and affect the spaces they inhabit. The work mines the notion of space and its connection to our personal, domestic, physical, and spiritual bodies. The six sections of *Occupy* are knit together by collective bodies embodying and activating these chosen specific environments.

Lectures, Presentations

I often offer to give lectures and presentations to a community while I am in the rehearsal process. I have given such talks at local public libraries or arts centers. Topics touch on site-specific art in general and then segue to a preview presentation of the upcoming work. If time permits, offering to conduct workshops at local schools is another way to generate interest. Each of these activities creates its own publicity for the upcoming project. Even if the activity attracts only a few people, the few tend to mention it to others.

Leveraging Partnerships to Expand Reach

Whatever marketing strategies you decide to employ, it is advantageous to include as many partners in your marketing campaign as possible. Your producer (if you have one) is your first obvious choice, but there are others: the institution connected to the host site, your creative and production teams, funders, and your own ever-expanding list of contacts. These people, as well as their friends and partners, can take part in spreading the word.

Make a Plan

First, you need to assess all of the marketing options available to you based on need, budget, and labor:

1. One-to-one marketing: e.g., print mailings, emails, social media, rehearsal encounters, lectures/presentations, programs.
2. Media/broadcast outlets: newspapers (local and national), radio (local and national), television (local and national), website.
3. Paid advertising: newspapers, social media, billboards, and banners.

Next, create your message. Decide what will be the unifying words and images to tell your story across the different marketing options. Ensure that your words and images reinforce each other. And decide who will partner with you to help craft the necessary materials and direct the outreach. Will you hire a professional or go with someone who understands marketing mechanics (especially social media)? Do you need to hire someone to create a website? Who will handle daily and weekly updates of the website and social media?

Hiring a Publicist

A publicist is generally someone who manages and solicits press coverage for a client. The definition of what constitutes press has expanded in the internet age. Still, if you are working with a marketing person within your commissioning organization, the demands of the project may require marketing and publicity experience that goes beyond the scope of the institution's past practices. Hiring an outside person who has that extra layer of experience could expand your campaign's reach and garner new avenues of press coverage and publicity. If you hope to use not only local press (print, television, radio, internet, etc.) but national publications and outlets, an experienced publicist often has working relationships with these entities. Additionally, a publicist can coordinate all of the press outreach efforts and, during tech week and performances, manage the presence of any members of the press/media who arrive on site to either review or feature the work.

Do not expect any publicist or marketing director to wave a magic wand and manifest the publicity of your dreams. The pressures on today's media/print institutions are many; resources are strained; and little time and space are available in print and broadcast. People have tended to blame a publicist (or marketer) for lack of exposure, but unless lack of effort and follow-through are evident, the fault is probably not your publicist's. Attracting media attention is always an inexact science, affected by forces that are constantly in flux. Therefore, before budgeting to hire a publicist, try to get an objective opinion from someone in the field to ascertain if your project has the potential to gain traction with journalists and media outlets. Some projects are not newsworthy beyond their immediate community. Try to make your decisions with as much understanding of the intended market as possible.

Other Personnel

You should also consider hiring a professional photographer to take any publicity photos, a specific person to update the central website, and someone to manage the key social media platforms (who also usually shoots the necessary photos and writes the posts). Your budget will determine what is feasible, but it is possible to engage people who have great talent with young resumes (college students, recent graduates) who will work as interns or accept a smaller fee.

Marketing a Rogue Project (aka Guerrilla Style)

Although I do not recommend staging a rogue site-specific project, circumstances may compel you to take this direction. I outlined these in Chapter 2 (Permissions, Permits and Insurance). Marketing such an event is problematic given that staging a performance without official permission risks the possibility that the appearance of a large audience might result in a site administrator shutting down the event. If you feel you have to go rogue, I recommend you limit your marketing.

Some options:

1. Do no marketing; keep the performance a secret known only to the production participants. Your audience will then consist of a random group of people who regularly frequent the location and who suddenly discover the performance. Some public performances, like flash mobs, are predicated on the element of surprise, although some of these events often have permits and permissions.
2. Market/publicize to a closed group of people. Using your private mailing list, send out an alert (via email, text, or regular mail) sharing a time and a place. Communicating too far in advance could result in word leaking out and attracting too large an audience. Sending an email or text just before or on the event day reduces the chance of information spreading beyond your selected circle.
3. Perform the event primarily for the camera. Later, you can broadcast it to a wider audience; you can use the event's serendipitous nature as one of its selling points. Some artists create rogue events with live streaming on social media to expand the audience in real time; then they archive the recording for future viewing.

Last Thoughts

As mentioned in previous chapters, some presenters/producers are drawn to site-specific projects primarily for a project's potential to attract public attention and publicity. You can use this motivation and the marketing-specific ideas your project will generate as selling points when approaching potential partners. Site-specific work engages the real world in a manner that is natural and specific to the location, community, and environment. Spreading that message benefits all producing partners and is the ultimate goal of any marketing strategy.

17
Documentation

Preserving your work in the ephemeral world of the performing arts depends on an effective method of documentation. However, the answers to how or why artists document a work can vary wildly. Some people might be content to shoot a few photographs or a video with a single camera. Others may want to save only the marketing materials and the written program. Some treat documentation as an unessential afterthought. And others make documentation a high priority, recording and preserving their process and performances to expand their archival collection.

I belong to the last group. I believe that ignoring the preservation of your work affects your ability to communicate a clear history of your creative output to future audiences, producers, and funders. Creating an archive that represents your artistic vision and preserves your work's creative energy allows you to revisit and learn from your past projects. Maintaining a useful archival record of your work requires planning and consistent effort, but the diligence can contribute significantly to your career.

> I want to get to the point where the artists feel like the documentation is just as important as putting on their show.
>
> Nel Shelby

Why Document?

Documenting site-specific work has many benefits and uses.

Documentation as art

In general, the performing arts are evanescent, and site-specific works may be the most fleeting. While successful Broadway-style theater productions and some popular concert works in music and dance have an option for further touring, site work, unless created as site-adaptive, is inextricably connected to the location that inspired it. This connection is part of what makes the work unique. As a result, careful and thorough documentation offers the only means for preserving the work and allowing future audiences to experience it.

Recreating the full experience requires not just filming the performance but capturing significant parts of the conceptual and rehearsal process. Producing a compelling video that replicates the audience's experience and communicates

On Site. Stephan Koplowitz, Oxford University Press. © Oxford University Press 2022. DOI: 10.1093/oso/9780197515235.003.0018

the energy of the original relies on video and editing techniques that suggest the need to plan early. What sort of equipment will you need? How many cameras and microphones? Who will operate these? What's the best shooting schedule? What can you afford? Your answers to questions like these will determine the quality of the video you create. Ultimately, it is possible to produce a stand-alone documentary that is a work of art in its own right—a formal, meaningful creation with emotional power.

Although video recordings are critical, complete documentation also depends on collecting archival artifacts: posters, postcards, photographs, sound scores, production notes, correspondence, technical and costume sketches—anything that will contribute to conveying a holistic view to future audiences. From the start, you must develop a documentary mindset and create a plan that prioritizes specific steps to take during the creation of the work itself.

Documentation as a reference

A comprehensive archive provides information for reflection and inspiration and allows you to replicate past successful methods. A study of your archives is a form of continuing education that can help you develop a conscious approach to your present and future creative work.

Although revivals of site-specific work, especially Category 1, are rare, they do happen. If the opportunity arises, you will quickly discover the value of having complete and reliable documentation. Meredith Monk's historic work *Juice* (1967) at the Guggenheim Museum was remounted in 2014; Joanna Haigood's *Invisible Wings* (1998) returned in 2007; my work *Fenestrations* (1987) returned in 1999 to Grand Central Terminal. Later that same year, a section of my site-specific work *Big Thirst* (1989) from the American Museum of Natural History (New York City) was adapted for the proscenium stage at Dance Theater Workshop (now New York Live Arts). For all these works, video or film documentation was a significant factor in the reconstruction and remounting.

Documentation as a historical record of the work

Preserving and documenting your work provides contemporary and future scholars access to your process and creations.

Our website aims to archive as much of our work as possible, not only the process but also the performances. We realized that no one could do this but us. It's important for us to create some kind of wholeness of who we are and what we represent.

José Ome Navarrete Mazatl

Documentation as a strategy for future fundraising and marketing

As previously mentioned in Chapter 8 (Fundraising for Your Artistic Plan) and Chapter 16 (Promoting and Marketing the Work), your past work can support future campaigns. Documentation is part of your digital (visual) resume, which can be a useful tool for fundraising in the form of crowdsourcing or individual appeals. Additionally, when you apply for grants, government agencies, foundations, and corporations require documentation of recent work, usually within the past three to five years. The better the photographic and video quality of your documentation, the more polished your application will appear. Documentation is central for marketing yourself and building your career: creating new commissions and landing teaching positions, artist residencies, lecturing and consulting gigs, etc.

Video, a Primary Gateway

> The three A's to guide documentation: Artist, Architecture, and Audience. Make sure you have these three elements in your documentation.
>
> Elise Bernhardt

The ubiquity of mobile technology has made the recording of our daily life, both public and private, commonplace. Using their smartphones and tablets, people increasingly record every moment of their everyday life. Documenting your artwork with the high-resolution quality of these devices is also possible. Still, regardless of the technology you select, you should have at least one camera record one performance from the perspective of an unobstructed audience member. One-camera, one-performance documentation is the bare minimum required for an archival video. However, this chapter presupposes a level of documentation that goes beyond the basics and captures many more layers of your work.

Two Approaches to Video Documentation

1. *Live audience perspective*: You can recreate the totality of your audience's experience by placing multiple cameras at key sightline locations. These cameras can shoot close-ups, full-frontal, and side perspectives that, with proper editing, will create a fluid experience of seeing the work from these different perspectives—like a collage of a full-audience experience.
2. *Filmic*: Creating a filmic experience relies on multiple cameras from multiple angles, including some not available to the live audience. Techniques and technologies (Steadicam, gimbal, crane, drones, multi-frame editing, etc.) that

allow fluid camera movements and shifts in perspective will also enable you to harness the language of film. The goal is to create an immersive experience tailored to a *screen* audience.

> I've contested funders' demands for full versions of my work on video shot from one static angle because I believe that kind of documentation is reductive and fails to represent my work accurately. I started making standalone dance films as documentations of my work very early in my process. They were art films that were much shorter than the original site piece; they were heavily edited and sometimes even followed a different narrative. I made dance films from almost every site work I've created, and many of them have been shown at dance film festivals.   Noémie Lafrance

Capturing Footage

This section presents a video shooting schedule from preproduction to performance that supports a filmic approach, maximizing the number of days, camera angles, and footage while working with an experienced videographer.

Planning

> We were very protective of our production time because you never have enough time when getting ready for a premiere, and so we were always opting for another day of rehearsal rather than spending a day to document. It takes time and attention to do proper photo and video shoots. We had to learn to be willing to give up a rehearsal in order to document the production.
>
>   Sara Pearson and Patrik Widrig

Timing—Soon after project approval:
Identify possible videographers and engage someone as soon as possible, negotiating fees and shooting schedule.
Timing—Two weeks before premiere:

Schedule the videographer(s) to attend a run-through of the work on-site. Allow time after the run-through for discussions with the videographer and confirm the shooting schedule, camera angles, and documentation priorities.

Timing—One week before premiere:
Meet with the videographer to confirm the shot list, schedule, and equipment and personnel needed. If possible, have the videographer attend another rehearsal to get more acquainted with the work and the overall flow of events.

> Many artists will assume that we videographers are going to make the exact choices they would make to capture the action. It's always good to go to a run through, but often there's only money to just see a dress rehearsal. Artists then make the assumption we can memorize a work in one dress and be able to make all the right choices.
>
> Nel Shelby

Execution

The most efficient way to capture footage required for a filmic video is to have more than one, preferably two or three cameras scheduled for each shoot and give the videographer as much access to the performance as possible. Each shooting opportunity requires careful planning and could incur additional fees; so take care to cover all foreseeable eventualities in your fee negotiations and plan for contingencies.

Tech rehearsal

The complexity of your production's technical requirements will affect your ability to schedule productive videography opportunities during technical rehearsals. Have all the light, sound, or projection cues already been set, or will the tech rehearsal have to be a time-consuming cue-to-cue rehearsal to work them out? Will there be time during the technical rehearsal to run the performance or to run a section of the work under performance conditions? Some projects only require sound and need no artificial lights. For these tech rehearsals, you can work simultaneously on setting sound levels and shooting video.

Because video documentation is a priority, I ask collaborators and technical staff to have as many elements as possible set for technical rehearsals before performers arrive—cues for music, costumes, lights, and projections. This strategy effectively transforms a technical rehearsal into a first dress rehearsal. But at minimum, the documentation goal for a technical rehearsal should include a full or partial run-through before rehearsal is over. A videographer can also capture extreme close-ups and other shots during any remaining cue-setting.

During technical rehearsals, I position video cameras so as not to endanger performers or the technical crew. Camera operators can capture footage from many angles by walking through performance areas, a practice usually forbidden during actual performances. This level of camera mobility is essential for the collection of sufficiently varied footage needed for a final filmic edit. Technical rehearsals or rehearsals scheduled solely for video are the best strategy for capturing this unique material.

Dress Rehearsal

A dress rehearsal is a full performance that includes all production elements with or without an audience. Site-specific rehearsals taking place in very public locations will, depending on the time of day, still attract viewers, many of whom are not aware that a performance has been scheduled. Limiting audience access to a site during a technical or dress rehearsal is sometimes an option, but you will need to negotiate these limits at the beginning of your site-selection process.

If the dress rehearsal has no audience, you can follow the same procedure for placing cameras as suggested for tech rehearsals: Keep the cameras out of performance spaces, and put them in audience viewing areas. If dress rehearsals need an invited audience to give performers the experience of a live audience, or if producers want to convert a dress rehearsal into a fundraising VIP event, you won't be able to follow this protocol. In either of these scenarios, you have options: Schedule two dress rehearsals, one without an audience, or an extra technical rehearsal, or make it clear to the dress rehearsal audience they are part of a live recording and need to accommodate the cameras.

Performances

If the budget allows, ask for, at minimum, permission to record two performances with two or more cameras. This plan will provide more angles and perspectives and inevitably include shots of audience members, which will help communicate the excitement and feel of the event. Instruct video crews to position themselves so as not to take up prime audience space. Remember to plan a specific shot list in advance. The type of site, the extent of your technical requirements, and your budget will all affect the shooting schedule and level of complexity you and the video crew will be able to achieve.

Editing Footage

Having a plan for the final edit of the video will influence and determine your shot list. A rudimentary knowledge and understanding of editing techniques and equipment is an asset when collaborating on directing a video shoot. Entry-level or consumer-level video editing software has been available since the introduction of iMovie on the Apple platform in October 1999; a year later, Microsoft introduced Moviemaker. The beginning of consumer-based digital editing ushered in a new era of filmmaking worldwide and fueled crowdsourced websites such as YouTube, Vimeo, Instagram, Facebook, etc. Make time to acquire as much video editing experience on whatever software is most suitable for your comfort level.

Additionally, to effectively communicate editing concepts to video collaborators, immerse yourself in other documented works. Watching documentation of live events, performing arts, and art films and studying the editing techniques will add to your understanding of the language of cinema and inform your own choices when collaborating on documentation. You should watch all or as much as possible of your project's raw video footage so that you know what shots are available and can speak knowledgeably with your video editor. Reviewing much of the footage by fast-forwarding through the files saves time and gives you an understanding of editing choices.

Video Documentation: A Selection of Techniques

As my experience with videography and editing techniques has grown, I have become increasingly able to think about how best to capture the performance even while I am rehearsing. Developing this parallel conceptual process illustrates just how essential documentation has become to me. What follows are some basic concepts and methods to document site work. In general, an understanding of film terms is helpful, and studying any number of film websites or books will expand your vocabulary and knowledge.

Wide shots vs. close-ups

Once you begin to edit the performance, you will find that the classic movement between wide shots and close-ups is the standard technique. How often you toggle between them is a matter of taste and comfort. Both wide and close shots can be taken from different angles, and having a good collection of both will allow for more variety in the final edit. These clips will constitute your primary footage.

B-Roll

B-roll is supplemental footage that includes anything other than the primary action of the performance. Capturing B-roll footage of the site throughout the documentary process is essential to create the establishing shots that will orient the viewer to performance locations. Wide shots of the site, without performers, and close-ups of distinctive natural or designed visual details can be captured before, during, and/or after primary videography is completed. B-roll footage of its natural state can establish the site's scale and the relationship between the performers and their surroundings, with camera angles ranging from eye-level to elevated positions. Stock footage from Google Earth or new footage from drones can also provide compelling establishing imagery. Drones can effectively capture bird's-eye views but require special run-throughs so that their noise or appearance doesn't disrupt rehearsals or performances. Programming and operating a drone are time-consuming, skills. Several takes or rehearsals are usually needed to capture the desired footage.

At Mass MoCA, we only had documentation of the work with a single camera, but we didn't have any footage of the site itself. So we went back to the site after the performance to just shoot the site so we could integrate and contextualize the piece. We used extensive B-roll to make the single-camera documentation of the performance more understandable.

Martha Bowers

Still photography is another source for B-roll content and another way to give context to a location. I have used still shots during title sequences at the beginning of a video to introduce the site as early as possible. Photo. 17.1 is made up entirely with B-roll footage taken from all the combined sites of *The Northfield Experience* project and used in the opening credits of the video.

Split-screen editing

The *Northfield Experience* video (Photo 17.1) is an example of using a split-screen to illustrate a project's simultaneous or multiple events. Dividing the frame is also useful to combine a far-shot with close-ups, as in Photos 17.2 and 17.3.

Narration (text and audio)

If a project has conceptual elements that need description, you can place text or a voice-over narration at the beginning of the video (Photo 17.4).

Photo 17.1 *The Northfield Experience* (2018), opening video sequence, video edited by Amelia Laughlin.
Photo courtesy Stephan Koplowitz.

Photo 17.2 *Natural Acts in Artificial Water* (2012), video edited by Andy Ford.
Photo courtesy Stephan Koplowitz.

Photo 17.3 *The Current Past* (2013) video edited by Jonathan Bryant.
Photo courtesy Stephan Koplowitz.

Audience design

Filming as an audience navigates space during a promenade performance is one method of presenting and documenting the work's overall structure. These promenade shots should include the audience within some frames to capture how the audience experienced the work.

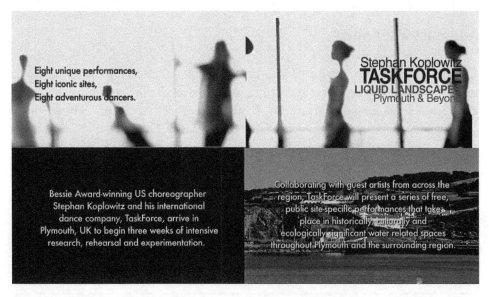

Photo 17.4 Title sequence for a short video documentary on the *TaskForce* UK (2009) creation process, video edited by Gorav Kalan.
Photo courtesy Stephan Koplowitz.

Photo 17.5 Video stills showing the camera movement that encompasses three different perspectives in one fluid motion for *The Northfield Experience* (2018) video documentation, produced by Brittany Shrimpton and edited by Amelia Laughlin.
Photo courtesy Stephan Koplowitz.

Gimbal, tracking shots

Incorporating fluid camera movements requires the equipment to achieve these types of shots and a shooting schedule that permits camera movement during the performance of the work. Gimbal style shots, which use an expensive mechanism that allows a stabilized camera to pivot or rotate, are rare, given the cost and amount of time the process takes. However, tracking shots are an excellent way to provide the viewer with a sense that they are experiencing something distinct from the live audience (Photo 17.5).

Audience interviews

If there is time post-performance, recording short interviews with audience members to ask for their reactions can capture the work's impact and provide a possible future marketing tool. Recording firsthand feedback from the public can be an effective way to illustrate the power of site-specific work.

Capturing sound

> I have now realized how important it is to get the sound for a work effectively documented. So we always have separate sound equipment to record; we don't rely on just a camera mic.
>
> Melanie Kloetzel

If your focus centers on capturing the right images and angles of a work, you might neglect the sound. Too often, artists assume that each video camera's built-in microphones will record what is necessary—resulting in poor sound quality and a distracting soundtrack.

There are two major principles for ensuring superior sound quality in your documentation:

1. Record the original sound files of the work—using either the pre-recorded score or, if live music is being amplified, a recording directly from the sound mixing board.
2. Place sound recording devices that are separate from the microphones in the cameras and capture directly the ambient sounds of the site, performers, and any unamplified music. Separate sound recording for documentation can pose a challenge for your budget and personnel, but you need high quality sound.

If separate sound-capturing is not possible, and a recorded score was part of the performance, create a soundtrack that blends the digital sound file and the live sound captured by the video microphones. The result will allow both the natural ambient sounds of the site and any recorded sounds to be heard equally well.

Video Documentation (Troubleshooting)

> When shooting live, no matter if you're the wide camera or the close camera or even the third camera, pretend like it's live television and the director could cut to you at any time. It not just about zooming in and getting the shot, but always being fluid. When you begin editing you have more options because you can go to that camera at almost any time.
>
> Nel Shelby

Scenarios

You only have access to one operator and one video camera

At a minimum, you can record the dress rehearsal and performance, and each recording can capture different types of shots. Perhaps the first pass will be an establishing, full-frame, wide shot that captures the entire production. Then, the second recording can capture close-ups and/or another angle/perspective. If there is more than one performance, you can video each one with a different shooting goal. Combining sections from all these recordings of different performances can create an effectively edited video despite variations in timing and possibly lighting (if outside). A skilled editor will find ways to smooth over problems of continuity.

You can only capture one performance with one camera

Director/videographer Nel Shelby has a succinct plan for this scenario: "If you only have one camera, it's important to have a videographer who understands the timing of dance or performance in general. They should use a remote zoom with their other hand on the exposure and the focus ring. That way they can be actively following the piece and not just capture a static wide shot." Your success in solving technical problems will depend greatly on your ability to engage the most experienced collaborators your budget allows.

You have two cameras, but only one trained videographer

Place one stationary camera where it can capture the widest shot needed, making sure it is on a tripod and will not be jostled while recording. Your videographer can then capture more intricate perspectives. In this scenario, engage a production assistant or willing volunteer to guard the fixed camera and/or move it to different locations as needed. Schedule a training session to ensure that this assistant understands how to position the wide-shot camera and can adjust the camera's exposure settings if there are changes in lighting.

The weather during the outdoor technical rehearsal and performances creates different lighting, resulting in different exposure levels

Within a limited range, it is possible to balance differences in lighting during the editing process using color correction to digitally alter the level of exposure (brightness) of a specific video file. If that method is only partially successful, another workaround may be possible. For example, instead of matching light and exposure, a well-edited compelling physical sequence that seamlessly knits together the action of the performance can overcome a viewer's awareness of any differences in light levels. The physical continuity in the video supersedes other visual variations. Capturing each performance with as many cameras as possible does mitigate the need to include footage from other performances. Still, the desire to include many different camera angles may make discomfort with different exposures palatable.

Photo 17.6 Google Earth view of Seymore House for *TaskForce* UK, and *Occupy* (2017), Yerba Buena Gardens, San Francisco, CA.
Image courtesy Stephan Koplowitz.

After reviewing the footage, you realize a critical moment is missing

This scenario occurred after we captured the performance of *Natural Acts in Artificial Water*. I was lucky. I sent an email to all performers and members of the production team describing the missing footage and asking if any of their friends or family had taken a video showing it. My appeal was successful. The addition of this new footage allowed us to avoid having to make edits to mask this omission.

Another strategy involves works that incorporate live video footage, when a camera is projecting images as part of the performance. It is often difficult for a videographer to capture both the live performance and the live video images, so it is important that you have access to the files of the projected images to ensure that no moment is missing from the final footage.

You could not afford or did not use a drone for an overhead shot and wish to create a visual perspective to orient the viewer to the geography of the site

I first used this solution when I hired filmmaker Mitchell Rose to edit documentation of the *TaskForce* UK performances. Two of the works took place over a vast space, and I asked Rose if we could show a map or other visual aid at the beginning to orient the viewer. At that time, drone technology was not readily available. Rose decided to experiment with Google Earth to see if he could incorporate its extensive photographic mapping of the world and import images into our video (Photo 17.6). Since that time, and as Google Earth's mapping of the world has improved, I've used this workaround in other projects when drone footage was not available.

Photography as Documentation

I've often found video documentation, unless you've got a great videographer and you can afford to have someone tracking the work, to be difficult. Photos are probably my main form of documentation of the actual work. A photographer often

> captures a moment that speaks more cogently of the work than the flow across time provided by video.
>
> Carol Brown

Several years ago, I prioritized video documentation over still photography, especially when video documentation became more affordable and accessible. My thinking has changed. People don't always have time to watch a video online. A still image can be an expedient way to communicate essential information and can serve as a compelling invitation to view moving images later. Thorough photographic documentation of the finished performance renders each photo an authentic and living artifact of that work—unlike mere publicity photos, which, by their nature, can only attempt to approximate the work's intentions before it is completed. The combination of artfully shot photographs and well-edited videos can create a visual landscape that is greater than the sum of its parts. Besides, while both provide valuable strategies for creating artistic documentation, photo images have the power to capture the essence of one moment that encapsulates the visual drama of a work in a way that video cannot. Photographs that you or an experienced photographer have shot with care and sensitivity can create a series of images that not only represent the work for print or online publications but stand as independent works of art themselves.

Capturing Performance Photographs

As I do with video documentation, I schedule photography as often as possible during technical and dress rehearsals. Sometimes, it is necessary to allow photo documentation during a public performance. My policy is only to allow still cameras to operate in silent mode (a feature in professional-grade cameras) and to place photographers in locations that will not obstruct or distract performers or audience members.

If you need to schedule both photographers and videographers at the same rehearsals, you must be aware of their delicate negotiations as they decide how to work together to obtain optimum sightlines and shooting angles. Documenting a site-specific work that involves simultaneous events in different locations allows for a shooting schedule that avoids having two separate camera crews in the same place. Another possibility is to schedule more than one run-through of the work during a technical or dress rehearsal and designate one for video and another for still photography. But sometimes, you will have to play diplomat and find a workable solution for both to work at the same time in the same location.

The audience's predilection for taking photographs is another sensitive area. In the age of social media, we are witnessing two approaches to audience photographers: Some producers require all audience members to place their devices in safe-keeping as they enter the event and to retrieve them as they exit. Other producers allow everyone to take photographs, hoping that the resulting images will generate social media buzz to attract larger audiences.

As a useful backup to engaging an outside photographer, I have invested in a still camera to take my own photographs. I was motivated in part by a photographer's failure to show up for a scheduled shoot during a special dress rehearsal. I had to take photos of the rehearsal using my then barely service-able consumer-grade camera. Consequently, I now take time to shoot my images with a semiprofessional camera—at times, right alongside the professional photographers I have hired. More pictures, more coverage, result in an expanded choice of visual imagery.

Documenting the Process

Documentation involves more than a filmed version of the work itself; it includes all the artifacts generated from the work's creation and production. The evolution of every production is different, and as my friend and mentor, dance artist Stuart Hodes once said, "The history of dance is not told on stage, but in the hours spent in the studio." The conversations, the trial and error, the decisions, the revisions, and the negotiations, all become part of the finished product. Preserve and collect and organize as many of the notes, texts, and audio or video records that chronicle the process as possible. The amount of documentary material you will save can vary. I'm not advocating re-cording every part of the process, from preproduction to production to performance. However, some documentation can be quite useful during the creative process.

Site Research Documentation

As outlined in Chapter 4 (The Site as Inspiration for Your Work), taking notes, photographs, and videos during your site visits is essential. Those materials also be-come instant artifacts that will document your creative process.

Creation Process Documentation
Rehearsal videos
The use of video recording as a tool for creation is commonplace in many art forms. During the production, documenting rehearsals can serve several functions:

1. If you cannot attend a rehearsal, the video documentation provides the chance to view it and give your rehearsal director feedback.
2. Videos provide a record of the staging and choreography to help you and others recall specific content from one rehearsal to another or to prepare for the next

rehearsal. Videos shot in early rehearsals can be especially helpful if you have scheduled a long gap between rehearsal periods.
3. Videos support the work of collaborators, especially the composers. Often, a collaborating composer uses videos to ensure the accuracy of timing and counts. Video footage can also help a stage manager recall cues.
4. You can use videos to keep others updated on a production's progress.

Rehearsal notes

During the creation of a work, either you or a rehearsal assistant will take notes to document newly created phrases (time signatures, lengths, movement qualities, stage directions, etc.) and keep track of sequences and order. All these notes become part of the overall documentation package. At a future date, these notes can supplement background information from videos or photographs for remounting, historical, or scholarly purposes.

> Often, I'll write about a project after the performance, so the documentation will be my journal notes, along with videography and photography. I often give the dancers a notebook, too, to document their process. I photocopy them and return them to the dancers. One time, they documented comments from every bystander who made one or shouted something out.
>
> Carol Brown

Documentation of collaborative arts

Music: Working with a composer will generate sound files consisting of early music drafts and a final soundtrack. I save all versions of the music as a record of its creative evolution. At the end of the project, make sure to collect the final sound files.

Costumes: All costume renderings, sketches, and swatches document the creative process. If future projects require a similar approach, these files become a reference.

Lighting: Preserving lighting plots and cue sheets creates a production record and a reference for future projects.

Visual Media: Visual media includes all projections, props, or sets. It may be impractical to preserve props or constructed sets, but design plans, photographs, and media files are easily stored.

Email correspondence: Keeping all correspondence connected to the work is easier when most are in email or digital form. These communications with the producer, commissioning organization, and collaborators will provide perspective on how you and your creative team discussed a host of issues: site selection, contract clauses, naming the work, the development of original material—a history of the project through time.

Marketing Materials

Some historically significant works of art have no documentation other than a poster, flyer, or postcard promoting the work. Today, artists tend to be more thorough in collecting essential documents. They recognize that all publicity materials are part of the documentation of the work and offer insights into both their and the producer's vision.

Last Thoughts

Documentation can seem like a burden superimposed on the already challenging process of creation. However, if you don't think of it as a burden, it will not be one. The approach outlined in this chapter proposes that you consider documentation as integral to your creative and production process. Sharing this mindset and strategy with your entire production team of commissioners and collaborators will support a more ambitious and seamless documentation, one that will preserve the work for future audiences.

18
Assessment

Assessment of a site-specific project, or any artistic production, is necessary to formalize self-reflection and satisfy funders who require final reports on budget expenditures, audience response, and critical response. Assessment can feel superfluous or anticlimactic after the intensity of completing a project, but it is so much more. After all your effort, all the attention and care you have devoted to the demands of creating work in the physical world, you can take the time to look inward and to gain a deeper understanding of yourself as an artist. Assessment is the final piece of the project, providing the insights that will become the launching pad for your next project. If you have been diligent in building a robust documentary archive, you can now reap the benefits: You will be able to analyze and review the many aspects of your production.

Two Distinct Functions of Assessment

Self-assessment provides a mechanism for your artistic development. It's an opportunity to take stock and reflect on your creative process, production methods, and the final work. It consists of an honest appraisal of what went well and what you could improve. Assessment can occur both immediately after a work has premiered, with the publication of reviews or feedback from audiences, collaborators, and producers, and much later, with more objectivity. Each of these periods will produce different insights that can benefit future efforts.

Assessment intended for others will result in a final report for funders, boards of directors, and any other entity or person who supported the project. Final reports are either required or appreciated as a follow-up accounting of the production. The report can include written narratives, final budget accountings, audience questionnaires, photographs, video, feature-story articles, and critical reviews.

> I've never been a person who assesses a work's impact based on formal audience surveys. But I often have discussions with dancers after the process, partly because I'm invested in what the dancers get out of a process. I typically will do a lot of writing about my own creation processes—after discussions with both dancers and audiences—because I'm interested in the larger scholarly analysis of a work.
>
> Melanie Kloetzel

On Site. Stephan Koplowitz, Oxford University Press. © Oxford University Press 2022. DOI: 10.1093/oso/9780197515235.003.0019

Self-Assessment: Who Are You?

A life of creativity is often vibrant and joyful, but also full of vulnerability and constant, very public risk-taking. What you think of yourself as an artist will be affected by your personality—how you tend to view yourself. Do you have high personal standards and find yourself rarely, if ever, satisfied with your work? Do the opinions of other people affect your perspective? Or do outside views have no bearing on how you think of your art? Are you naturally confident or tormented by self-doubt? Perhaps by acknowledging your own biases or habits of thought, you can design an assessment process that improves and expands your ability to respond to your own work.

I have high expectations for myself. When a production falls short of my goals, I am bothered and tend to look for excuses. I used to allow the failures of parts of a production to dominate my sense of the work as a whole and then, like many artists grappling with tight deadlines, to blame external factors—if only we had one more rehearsal or just a little more funding. While these clichés have a certain truth, I now realize that this mindset distorted my assessment of the work. As I've gained more experience, I am less inclined to dwell on what-ifs, preferring to accept the things I cannot change—an attitude that has allowed me to see the relative strengths and weaknesses of my productions more clearly.

For example, *Phantom Fenestrations* at the Wexner Center for the Arts was designed to harness choreographed shadows against the broad expanse of glass at the front of the building. The night before the premiere, a lengthy thunderstorm interrupted the only cue-setting technical rehearsal scheduled (which was to serve also as a dress rehearsal). The performers memorized a sequence of movements designed to be captured by the lighting in a prescribed manner that would cast shadows on the glass. The truncated rehearsal resulted in a performance that consisted of several improvised light cues that shifted the intended narrative. Although the central concept remained undamaged, along with a clear visual and kinetic quality, many of the moment-to-moment narrative details that I had worked out with lighting designer Tony Giovannetti were severely compromised.

The immediate response of the audience to the work was overwhelmingly positive. The architect of the Wexner Center, Peter Eisenman, spoke to me afterward with glowing praise, but I was mute with disappointment, only able to nod my head in appreciation for his positive words. It took me several years to re-evaluate the work and both acknowledge the artistic achievements and learn something that is fundamental to art-making and site work: You can't control everything, so best not to dwell on those factors. Weather conditions for many site-specific works are at the top of this list. I also learned to accept emotionally a truth that I had always known intellectually: Audiences will always experience art differently, regardless of existing conditions, regardless even of an artist's intentions. Artists need to recognize this inevitability and accept audience responses, whether positive or negative, as one of many elements in their self-assessment.

I had a different assessment experience reflecting on my work *Kokerei Projekt. Kohler Körper* in Essen. When the work premiered, I felt very good about it; I considered it a personal best. I was not only proud of the finished product but pleased with how I had met the challenges of working in such a large and undeveloped performance space. Several years later, I watched the video documentation of the entire work and was struck by how many sections of the work I would now revise or re-imagine. Specifically, I noticed that many sequences relied on similar structures and many movements lacked variety and detail. This new perspective came as a surprise, but that moment of self-reflection influenced subsequent work. That process of looking back critically, as uncomfortable as it was in the moment, brought energy to new projects and made me a better artist.

These moments of review that happen at different times offer the chance to discover the similarities in the arc of your work, as well as what distinguishes one work from another. This exploration and reflection provide insights into your creative decisions. The more archival material you have, the more specific and reality-based your self-assessment will be. And the more frequently you conduct these reviews, the better you will become at overcoming any tendencies to avoid self-assessment.

Other sources of useful information are the perspectives of your artistic collaborators and production personnel. Although evaluative conversations can be difficult, particularly following physically and emotionally exhausting projects, eliciting honest, candid feedback that you trust can help you gain perspective on the production itself and the whole creative process. The best way to build mutual trust is to create, from the start, a culture that promotes respectful, honest discussions: In all your interactions, you should model your ability to give the sort of feedback that you are also open to receiving. The goals are for everyone to gain a more objective view of the work and the process and for you to develop insight into your growth as an artist.

Assessment for Others

With one project, my dramaturg recorded responses immediately after the performance. She would go and ask people just to say a few things, so we got people's statements and reflections. We've also used audience questionnaires, which I tend not to like, but funders love that you've documented audience feedback. There are creative ways, like inviting people to write something on a wall or pavement with chalk to capture something about audience response. Gathering responses is important for your next funding round but also just for you to know what is the impact of the work, how is it resonating.

Carol Brown

The process of creating a final report for funders or other supporters is usually quite different from a self-assessment. All donors want to believe that their monetary support was put to good use. If your project was artistically compromised or did not receive audience or critical acclaim, you may feel a bit guilty or even defensive when drafting final reports. However, it's essential to understand that the goals and expectations of funders may be different from your artistic goals. While success for you is based on aesthetic criteria, success for most government institutions and foundations tends to be more pragmatic: Did your work achieve the promised goals in terms of audience numbers and demographics? Did you collaborate with the community artist(s) as stated in the application? Did your spending remain within budget parameters? Some foundations only support audience outreach or want to generate publicity or achieve a specific goal, like expand public access to live music, or are interested in a particular social issue. Demonstrating how the money achieved donor benchmarks may be all that is needed.

A final report's goal, no matter who the intended reader, is to project a truthful but positive narrative. If a funder requires a written assessment and a final expenditure report, make sure you understand the level of detail required. Within that context, what you include will be as important as what you decide to omit. For example, if the funder is not especially interested in critical reviews, you might mention the existence of several reviews but use excerpts only from those that were positive. Overall, these final reports written for outside funders are a more straightforward, tightly focused proposition and have clear deadlines for completion—unlike a self-assessment, which has a very different purpose and might continue, periodically, for years.

Keep in mind that your final report to funders needs to reflect the reality of what actually transpired. Many funders will send representatives to attend your performance or will be present in person. Your final report will help communicate your narrative assessment of the work and its public performance, but the in-person experience of your funders will have the most impact. Projects that seem unsuccessful (poor attendance, negative reviews, etc.) could still be viewed favorably enough for funders to continue their support of your future projects. Do not make assumptions; if you feel a new project might appeal to particular funders, make the proposal.

Possible Assessment Questions

The following are merely suggested questions that you might ask yourself as you think about your self-assessment or use in questionnaires to generate information as you prepare reports for outside funders. There will be many more questions you could ask, depending on your needs and goals.

Your self-assessment

Overall, how did you handle the pressure of creating this work with your artistic and production teams?

How organized were you during the process of creation?
Would you change your funding priorities in the future?
How close to your original vision was the final creation?
Did this project inspire ideas for a new project?

Assessment of site selection

How efficient was the process of selecting the site?
What did you learn from getting permissions and permits?

Assessment of the site

What were the significant challenges of working on-site?
Were there safety issues, and how were they resolved?
How did the audience design affect the audience experience? Positive? Negative?

Assessment of the production team

Which members of the production team (including producers) excelled at their job, and why?
Were there any challenges that could have been foreseen?

Assessment questions for the collaborative team

What were some positive/negative aspects of your collaborative relationship with the artistic director?
What could have been improved, or what would you have done differently?
What aspects of the site were the most challenging/inspiring?

Questionnaires for the audience

Was this your first site-specific performance?

Were you familiar with the site before the performance?

What new knowledge or perspective did you gain about the site because of this performance?

What aspects of the performance were the most memorable?

What aspects of the performance seemed out of place?

Did you have any emotional response to the performance?

Last Thoughts

Assessment is ultimately about seeking objectivity in a very subjective world. For funders and your own personal journey, clarity and honesty are useful guides for discovery. Depending on their personality, some artists are always engaged in thinking about and assessing their work and their career. They wake up at 4 a.m. to drag their souls before a jury of their critics. Others only occasionally set aside time for a more formal, dispassionate analysis. Finding a middle ground is probably best and will result in a more helpful and emotionally balanced approach to starting a new artistic project—and getting more sleep.

19
Last, Last Thoughts

This entire book has one overriding aim: to encourage and guide those with a nascent interest in site performance. My hope is that the ideas, techniques, and illustrations you read excited you and stimulated your imagination, suggesting possibilities rather than imposing restrictive rules or formulaic methods. Over the years, you will develop your own approach and unique voice. Experience will be your teacher. That's the joy of making art. Still, I want to leave you with some parting advice from a few of the artists whose voices I have included in this book:

> Number one: Be aware that many artists have gone before you making this kind of work and that they have a lot of insights. I say that because I've learned a ton from site artists over the years. Number two: Be super respectful of the people or community connected to a place because their relationship to place is often very emotional.
>
> Melanie Kloetzel

> I was going to say study the body of work that exists, but sometimes I don't think that's a good idea. Sometimes, I think you just want to go out there and experiment. It doesn't hurt to know what other people have done, especially in terms of all the practical and logistical issues of making site works. Study how people have gone about realizing their vision and the challenges and obstacles they've overcome. But in terms of the artistic inspiration, sometimes I think it's better to just go without the influence of anybody else's approach.
>
> Laura Faure

> You need a very positive attitude because there are so many obstacles and unconventional questions that have to be answered. Don't have a narrow perspective on what is and isn't acceptable as art because your site-specific piece may evolve as it's happening. One artist I worked with had a very specific vision and believed that it could only happen in one way and wouldn't budge. Things started to fall apart. Once you start the process, let the site speak to you almost as another collaborator. Don't fixate on one result; keep your eyes open; be aware of different possibilities.
>
> Tony Giovannetti

> Start with a solo, start with yourself. Perhaps start with a film. Get an experience of a moving body in the built environment. Think about all the many moving parts, like the trees really have a presence, maybe I don't need to do so much? Think of the site in layers.
>
> Nancy Wozny

On Site. Stephan Koplowitz, Oxford University Press. © Oxford University Press 2022. DOI: 10.1093/oso/9780197515235.003.0020

Start small, definitely start small. Pick a small space, pick a small cast, work your way up. It's grueling work. There are always limitations and barriers that you need to overcome. Research, research, research.

Mark Dendy

What Lies Ahead?

While experienced artists can offer advice to a new generation of artists, we cannot know what the future will bring or what forces will shape your art. During the past couple of years, our world has been grappling with the consequences of the coronavirus pandemic, with social, political, and environmental issues taking center stage. Social justice, global warming, and new economic and political challenges are all issues that are influencing our art and will likely have even more profound effects on your creations in the decades ahead. Although we can't predict the future, humans tend to enjoy envisioning various possibilities—some optimistic, some pessimistic. That mixture characterized my discussions with site artists:

This idea of making work based on what the post-pandemic will be is not wise because we're in it and we don't know when or if it's ever going to be over. It's not that we can't be hopeful and we can't dream another, better world. There's always been this emphasis on looking to the future. Part of the problem is that we're not addressing the now. We have to focus on the present, deal with what we have now instead of waiting for something that's not here and don't know if it's coming.

Amara Tabor-Smith

There is the nature of surveillance, distancing, space, and personal behavior. They all have real implications for our work. I feel the body is going to get policed more and more in public space. With what we're witnessing right now, I think this is a critical time for us to maintain embodied acts in public space. The whole Black Lives Matter moment is part of this critical time—people realize how important it is for the body to be in public space, and they're getting empowered by it. I feel there's a lot of possibility there, but it's also because of the other force that's coming in against them, a force to control their movement. It is a moment in time for sure.

Melanie Kloetzel

I think all of our work is moving in a direction towards site, maybe because of our emergency situation but actually not just because of Covid but because of the environment and racial tensions. It feels like all work is moving in the direction of being more political, and I love this quote from Gloria Steinem that says, "Sometimes you have to put your body where your politics are." Any site work, even the work that's not overtly polemical or political or socially conscious, is already an intervention.

Sara Hook

We could be flying. We could be dancing with holograms or interacting with technology that we can't imagine. The sky's the limit. Or we could be back in caves, dancing for each other around a fire with a closed metal door so we can't let in nuclear dust. We might be on other planets with no gravity or underground; the world could be decimated and uninhabitable. We might be relegated to only northern regions because of global warming. Who knows? We could be under total authoritarian corporate control relegated to indoor cubicles communicating virtually. Or we could rise up and break free and have a glorious tomorrow. One hesitates to project. There are dark moments and hopeful moments.

Mark Dendy

The burning desire for experiences in commerce, as in experiential marketing, and art as an immersive work will probably continue to grow interest in site work. However, the pandemic has exponentially amplified the ease with which we engage in technology which will continue to compete with live exchanges.

Noémie Lafrance

Technology has played such an important role in site-specific performance. New technologies, recorded GPS activated soundwalks for example, have opened up how artists conceive of site projects. One can be in multiple places at once. Interactive streaming technologies, VR, and AI are going to impact the field. If site work takes place in urban centers, what will our urban centers even look like in 20 years? There will be a lot of adaptations due to our changing climate. Artists will always adapt and respond to whatever the changing context is. It is what we do.

Martha Bowers

Like Martha Bowers, I tend to lean toward the light and place my hope in the artists themselves. Creativity and innovation are the hallmarks of the arts community. Given that our post-pandemic society may continue to require some physical distancing for the foreseeable future, it is likely that many arts institutions will increasingly turn to artists whose work can be easily adapted to outdoor or spacious performance venues. After all, site artists are experienced problem-solvers and experts in adjusting to constantly changing circumstances. In general, artists are always moving forward—inventing new ways to use mediums, challenging tradition, revolutionizing aesthetics and techniques. Artists see the world with fresh eyes: They "de-familiarize the familiar," as Carol Brown puts it. There is ample cause for optimism regardless of the challenges of the future.

However, I want also to sound a note of caution. Artist and scholar Melanie Kloetzel describes a concern shared by many site artists: "I worry about a dwindling comprehension of the premises of site work. I see a lot of outdoor work being done right now, which makes sense during a pandemic. But there is often little understanding that site work is a genre with a genealogy and a purpose, which is to dialogue with a site and be sensitive to its past, present, and even future." My purpose in writing this book has been to provide the next generation of site artists an understanding of the premises on which site work is based, ways of thinking about site work, and practical tools for ensuring that their work will be both site-sensitive and site-specific.

PART VII

APPENDICES

Prompts and Exercises for Project Conception

The following three exercises will enable you to put into practice some of the methodologies covered in this book. Creating a site inventory and generating initial artistic and production concepts will prepare you to share ideas with potential collaborators, funders, and producing partners.

Exercise for site selection and initial inspiration

Start by exploring your neighborhood, city, or region (whatever makes sense in terms of time and travel). Look for sites and spaces that inspire you. Find *two different sites (locations)* that could inspire you to create a site-specific work. Walk around each site, and look at it from different perspectives. Think about how an audience might view the site. Take at least 20 photographs at each site.

For each of these two selected sites, create five pieces of information:

1. A description of the design/architecture and its current use: Why does the site interest you? Is it the physical design, history, community, or personal history?
2. A summary of your audience design: Describe how a potential audience would experience the work, and make an estimate of how many could attend.
3. Select eight photographs from each set of 20: four that document the site, two that document the location of the audience, and two taken from the perspective of the audience.
4. Would your production in each site need to be seen at night or during the day? What would be the difference between seeing it at night or during the day?
5. Are there any other artistic elements (media, sound, props, etc.) that you are inspired to include?

Once completed, allow a week or more to pass before starting the next assignment.

Exercise in site inventory and research

After some time has elapsed from the completion of the first exercise, you are ready to begin the process of devising an artistic plan for one of your two selected sites. Choose one site, and then return to that site with a notebook and camera to conduct a formal site inventory as described in Chapter 4.

Look at the space from different angles and perspectives. It may be useful to measure the distance between parts of the site (e.g., interesting natural or architectural features with which you may want performers to interact).

Use these questions as prompts for information gathering and note-taking:

- What is the size of the location? Small and intimate or large and open? What are its estimated dimensions?
- Is the site mostly public or private? Is it busy (with cars, people, businesses) or quiet?
- Are there any significant design elements found on the site that could be highlighted by a performance?
- Are there any particular angles or perspectives within the site that interest you?
- What are the varieties of geometric shapes within the site? Count and describe them.
- What are the site's textures (grass, cement, sand, glass, etc.)?
- What areas or locations within the site could contain a performance?
- Are there existing lights or only natural lighting?
- What sounds do you hear?

Discovering Site History and Current Use

Using internet search engines, explore the history and current use of the site. Interview a stakeholder, an employee, and/or some members of the public who frequent. With these resources, try to answer the following questions.

History

- Has a notable event happened at the site in the past? What was it?
- Who used or occupied the site in the past?
- When was the site constructed? Who designed it? For what purpose?
- How has the site evolved?

Current use and the community perspective

- How is the site currently used, and what draws people to the site?
- How many people generally occupy the site?
- Is the site the focus of any current controversies or issues?
- Does this site "belong" to a particular community? If so, what relationship do they have with the site?
- Is the site essential to one particular group of people in the surrounding community?
- Would a performance or intervention engage them or annoy them? How likely are they to want to participate?

Writing a Project Description and Proposal

Building on your previous research and site inventory, this final exercise aims to generate a proposal for a site-specific work. This proposal could serve as a first step toward gaining the interest of collaborators, permission from stakeholders, and donations from funders and potential producing partners.

Base your proposal on the following:

Part 1: Description of the work

Write a description of the proposed work. Include a title (or working title), and summarize the project and its location. Include your conceptual ideas for the work.

Answer the following questions to prompt your description:

- Is your work site-specific, site-adaptive, etc.?
- Through what filter(s) are you examining this work? Are you focusing on the design of the space, its history, current use, community, or a combination of these elements?
- What are some of your conceptual ideas behind the work? How does the work align with your existing practice or ideas about performance/installation/etc.?
- What do you hope to accomplish with this proposed work? Why is it important to make this work for this site?

Part 2: Production/technical proposal

Thinking back to some of the guidelines and suggestions outlined in the book, what are some of the production and technical decisions you need to make to bring your work to fruition? Write an outline of the key technical decisions and reasons for making them. Include answers to the following questions:

- What is the audience design?
- What is the structure of the performance?
- What time of day is your performance?
- How many performers do you see in the space?
- Will you be using lights, sound, costumes, or other media?
- Will you need production personnel?

If you do not have many technical requirements, explain why. Is the site already equipped with the production elements needed? Is your work a guerilla-style or spontaneous performance? Or do you choose not to use external lighting, sound, etc. for aesthetic reasons?

Part 3: Planning budget

To start creating a planning budget, write down the line items needed for your project. You do not have to include the cost of these line items. Write an itemized list that describes all the elements you may need. Dollar projections can be included later.

Refer to the budget information provided in Chapter 7 on creating a planning budget, which provides guidelines about what to include. Select the budget lines most relevant to your site project.

Final Form of Your Project Description and Proposal

Your project description and proposal can take many forms depending on the intended audience. If a potential producer asks you for a budget, that would be the time to make monetary projections. Don't hesitate to populate your documents with as many photographs as possible to illustrate your descriptions and concepts. Share your final documents with a friend, colleague, anyone who can give you feedback on how well you have communicated your ideas and vision for your selected site.

Additional Resources

Some Artists Working in this Field

This is a thoroughly incomplete list of those who have been active in on-site work either as primary artists or collaborators for at least five years or have made site-inspired work a particular focus of their practice. Please use this as a starting point in your own research into the field.

D. Chase Angier: https://angierperformanceworks.com/
Zsófia Bérczi, Living Picture Theater: http://livingpicture.org/
Elise Bernhardt: www.fleurelisebkln.com
Olive Bieringa, Otto Ramstad: The BodyCartography Project: https://bodycartography.org/
Tatiana Bittar, Larissa Mauro, Kamala Ramers: Andaime Companhia de Teatro: www.andaimeciadeteatro.com.br
Martha Bowers: https://hookarts.org/
David Brick (current director), Andrew Simonet, Amy Smith: www.headlong.org
Carol Brown: www.carolbrowndances.com
Trisha Brown Dance Company: https://trishabrowncompany.org/
Simon Byford: www.simonbyfordpms.com
Yanira Castro: https://acanarytorsi.org/
Merce Cunningham Trust: www.mercecunningham.orgindex.cfm
Ann Carlson: https://anncarlsondance.com/
Quentin Chiappetta: www.medianoise.com
Jean Claude Christo: https://christojeanneclaude.net/
Simon Corder: www.simoncorder.com
Hygin Delimat, Body Architects: https://hygindelimat.com/
Mark Dendy: https://dendydonovanprojects.com/
Willi Dorner: www.willidorner.com
Heidi Duckler: https://heididuckler.org/
Sara Elgart: https://sarahelgart.com/
Kim Epiphano: http://epiphanydance.org/
Katie Etheridge, Simon Persighetti: Small Acts: small-acts.co.uk
Philippe Freslon: http:www.compagnieoff.org
Tony Giovannetti: https://agiovannettielectric.com/
Tom Greder: www.kinopan.com
Andrea Haenggi: http:www.amdat.orgindex.html
Nina Haft: www.ninahaftandcompany.com
Joanna Haigood: http:www.zaccho.org
Anna Halprin: www.annahalprin.org
Snow Huang: Against-Again Troupe: http://against-again.blogspot.com/
Anne Hamburger: www.engardearts.org
Marylee Hardenbergh: www.globalsiteperformance.org
Stephen Hodge, Simon Persighetti, Phil Smith, Cathy Turner: Wrights & Sites: http:www.mis-guide.com
Sara Hook: www.sarahookdances.com
Shannon Hummel: https://coradance.org/
Tanya Kane-Parry: https://operadelespacio.org/
Debby Kajiyama, José Ome Navarrete Mazatl: NAKA Dance Theater: http://nakadancetheater.com/
Daijiro Kawakami: Scale Laboratory: https://scalelabo.jp/
John King: www.johnkingmusic.com
Melanie Kloetzel: www.kloetzelandco.com
Eiko & Koma: http://eikoandkoma.org/home (archived website)

Silva Laukkanen-Body Shift: www.bodyshift.org
Lara Lloyd: www.coombefarmstudios.com
Sally Jacques: www.bluelapislight.org
Emily Johnson: http:www.catalystdance.com
matthae & konsorten: https://matthaei-und-konsorten.de/
Jo Kreiter: https://flyawayproductions.com/
Noémie Lafrance: http://sensproduction.org/
Tori Lawrence: www.torilawrence.org
Lenora Lee: http:www.lenoraleedance.com
Rosemary Lee: www.artsadmin.co.uk/profiles/rosemary-lee/
Liz Lerman: https://lizlerman.com/
Abigail Levine: www.abigaillevine.com
Debra Loewen: www.wildspacedance.org
Ana Mendieta: https://en.wikipedia.org/wiki/Ana_Mendieta
Meredith Monk: www.meredithmonk.org
Jennifer Monson: www.ilandart.org
Zach Morris, Tom Pearson, Jennine Willett: https://thirdrailprojects.com
Anne Marie Mulgrew: http://annemariemulgrewdancersco.org/
Allison Orr: https://www.forkliftdanceworks.org/
Eiko Otake: www.eikootake.org
Taisha Paggett: http://taishapaggett.net/
Kurt Perschke: www.redballproject.com
Sara Pearson, Patrik Widrig: www.pearsonwidrig.org
Emma Porteus: www.stompin.net
Ernesto Pujol: https://lmcc.net/artist/ernesto-pujol/
Tamar Rogoff: tamarrogoffpp.blogspot.com
Mitchell Rose: www.mitchellrose.com
Aaron Rosenblum: www.aaronrosenblum.com
nibia pastrana santiago: www.nibiapastrana.com
Svea Schneider: www.sveaschneider.com
JoAnna Mendl Shaw: www.equus-onsite.org
Nel Shelby: www.nelshelby.com
Lucy Simic, Stephen O'Connell, Ciara Adams, Lisa Humber: www.bluemouthinc.live
Judith Smith: www.axisdance.orgadvocacy
Leah Stein: www.leahsteindanceco.org
Karen Stokes: https://www.karenstokesdance.org/
Jonathan Stone: www.jonathanstone.co.uk
Amara Tabor-Smith: http:www.deepwatersdance.com
Susanne Thomas: www.sevensistersgroup.com
Sam Trubridge: https://www.samtrubridge.com/
Muna Tseng: www.munatseng.org
Gregg Whelan, Gary Winters: Lone Twin: http:lonetwin.com
Nancy Wozny: artsandculturetx.com/tag/nancy-wozny/
Pamela Z: http://pamelaz.com/

Readers can find further information about works mentioned in this book by Stephan Koplowitz at these two links: www.stephankoplowitz.com/site and www.youtube.com/stephankoplowitz.

Additional Chapter Resources

Introduction: Inspirations and Definitions

Flash Mobs and Immersive Theater:

Please refer to the Additional Reading Resources pages for two scholarly works on immersive theater and flash mobs.

Improv Everywhere: https://improveverywhere.com/
Punchdrunk Productions: www.punchdrunk.com
A first-person audience member text and photo description of the Angel Project: https://gothamist.
    com/arts-entertainment/gothamist-goes-on-the-angel-project

Chapter 2. Permissions, Permits, and Insurance

Numerous insurance companies can provide short-term event liability insurance. Here are links to two
such companies: www.theeventhelper.com and www.eventsured.com.

Chapter 4. The Site as Inspiration for Your Work

https://earth.google.com/web/

Chapter 6. Negotiating Fee and Contract

Creating New Futures, Working Guidelines for Ethics & Equity in Presenting Dance and
    Performance: https://creatingnewfutures.tumblr.com/
National Performance Network: https://npnweb.org/field/resources/
Association of Performing Arts Professionals is the premiere performing arts service organization that has re-
    sources for self-representing artists: https://apap365.org/membership/membership-types/artist-access/
The International Association of Blacks in Dance: https://www.iabdassociation.org/page/resourcesoverview
Dance/USA: https://www.danceusa.org/resources
One Dance UK: https://www.onedanceuk.org/
How to write a rider in a legal contract: https://legalbeagle.com/7233933-insert-legal-rider-document.html
    and www.catalystdance.comdecolonization-rider.

Chapter 8. Fundraising for Your Artistic Plan

https://fconline.foundationcenter.org/
www.nefa.orggrantsgrant-programspublic-art
https://foundationsource.com/
Council on Foundations: www.cof.org
Information on whether to create a non-profit corporation: https://dance-teacher.com/ start-your-own-
    dance-company-part-2/
www.gyst-ink.comstarting-a-nonprofit-arts-organization

Chapter 13. Rehearsal Safety

Event Safety Alliance: https://www.eventsafetyalliance.org/

Chapter 14. Creating for Physically Integrated Casts and Accessibility

www.axisdance.orgresources
www.dance.nycequitydisabilityworksartists
www.dance.nycequitydisabilityresources
www.disabilityartsinternational.org

www.candoco.co.uk/
Kuppers, Petra. *Disability and Contemporary Performance*. Routledge, 2003.

Chapter 16. On Line Publications, Blogs and Bloggers

Feedspot is a huge database (250,000) of bloggers, podcasters, etc.: https://blog.feedspot.com/
Writer/editor/founder, Debra Levine- https://artsmeme.com/
Writer/editor, NancyWozny- http://artsandculturetx.com/
Writer, Deborah Jowitt (as part of ArtsJournal): www.artsjournal.com/dancebeat/
Editor/Founder, Tracey Paleo, Gia On The Move: https://giaonthemove.com/
New York Theater Review: http://newyorktheatrereview.blogspot.com/
HowRound: https://howlround.com/
Dancing Times (blog): www.dancing-times.co.uk/category/blog/
Dance Magazine (newsletter): www.dancemagazine.com/news/
Writer/editor, Wendy Perron: https://wendyperron.com/

Chapter 17. Documentation

Rosenberg, Douglas. *Screendance, Inscribing the Ephemeral Image*. Oxford University Press, 2012.
Sant, Toni. *Documenting Performance: The Context and Processes of Digital Curation and Archiving*. Methuen Drama, 2017.

Additional Reading Resources

The number of books about site-specific performance and art has increased in the past ten years. Listed here is a select group of books to help start the reader on a path toward further research and understanding.

Barbour, Karen, Vicky Hunter, Melanie Kloetzel (eds.). *(Re)Positioning Site Dance: Local Acts, Global Perspectives*. Intellect Books, 2019.
Birch, A., and J. Tompkins (eds.). *Performing Site-Specific Theatre: Politics, Place, Practice. Performance Interventions*. Palgrave Macmillan, 2012.
Butterworth, Jo, and Liesbeth Wildschut (eds.). *Contemporary Choreography: A Critical Reader*. Routledge, 2017.
Carter Sanderson, Christopher. *Gorilla Theater: A Practical Guide to Performing the New Outdoor Theater Anytime, Anywhere*. Routledge, 2013.
Ferdman, Bertie. *Off Sites: Contemporary Performance beyond Site-Specific. Theater in the Americas*. Southern Illinois University Press, 2018.
Gailey, Benjamin Joseph. The performance and reception of flash mobs: authenticity, YouTube, and the fantastic. University of Illinois at Urbana-Champaign. Ph.D Dissertation, http://hdl.handle.net/2142/88276, 2015.
Hunter, Victoria (ed.). *Moving Sites: Investigating Site-Specific Dance Performance*. Routledge, 2015.
Hunter, Victoria. *Site, Dance and Body: Movement, Materials and Corporeal Engagement*. Palgrave Macmillan, 2021.
Kaye, Nick. *Site-Specific Art: Performance, Place and Documentation*. Routledge, 2000.
Kloetzel, Melanie, and Carolyn Pavlik (eds.). *Site Dance: Choreographers and the Lure of Alternative Spaces*. University Press of Florida, 2011.
Pearson, Mike. *Site-Specific Performance*. Red Globe Press, 2010.
Ritter, Julia. Tandem Dances. Oxford University Press, 2020.
Smith, Phil. *Making Site-Specific Theatre and Performance: A Handbook*. Red Globe Press, 2019.
Wilkie, Fiona. *Performance, Transport and Mobility: Making Passage*. Palgrave MacMillan, 2014.

Index

Note: In their main section listings, performance works that are not followed by a choreographer's name were created by the book's author.